A
Mor
Counterstories of Critical Asian American+ Studies in Education

In naming our community Asian American+ to signify 'diverse inclusion,' this brave book adopts a resolute stance that is unapologetic in resisting the manufactured identities historically assigned (to us). Through powerful counterstories, this ensemble of authors speak into visibility the multi-truths of AA/NHPI/AMEA lives, laying a pathway towards critical Asian American+ studies needed to honor and do justice to the rich complexity of narratives and voices we embody.

—A. Lin Goodwin
Thomas More Brennan Professor of Education, Boston College

A heartfelt collection of counterstories rooted in resistance, advocacy, and joy, this book explores identity and historical erasures while envisioning liberatory futures across Asian diasporic experiences. With a deliberate emphasis on Native Hawaiian voices, Moments and Movements features culturally sustaining pedagogies and youth-led activism, inspiring transformative change through reclaimed narratives and inclusive spaces.

—Estella Owoimaha-Church
Educator, Organizer
Liberated Ethnic Studies Model Curriculum Consortium

This collection from educators at all levels of schooling, young people, and organizers breathes life into the legacies and possibilities of Asian American studies. The way to engage Asian America, as detailed in these chapters, is not through anti-Asian hate but in how Asian America has always found ways to build, create, hope, and build solidarity of shared struggles for freedom and collective self-determination. We've needed this collection, and it is an indispensable resource for forging forward.

—Leigh Patel
Professor, University of Pittsburgh
Author of *No Study Without Struggle:*
Confronting Settler Colonialism in Higher Education (2021)

A necessary read for all educators interested in learning how to cultivate justice-focused futures and possibilities. This anthology is a warm and encouraging, yet provocative, invitation to readers to join a vibrant, collective conversation in continuing the dynamic movement for Asian American Studies and culturally sustaining education. The collective and conversational approach reminds readers that they are not alone in doing the hard but necessary work to build more humanizing futures through a solidarity ethic.

—OiYan Poon
Author, *Asian American is Not a Color:*
Conversations on Race, Affirmative Action, and Family (2024)
Co-Director, College Admissions Futures Co-Lab

Moments & Movements

CRITICAL ASIAN AMERICAN AND PASIFIKA STUDIES IN EDUCATION

Series Editors: Betina Hsieh and Roland Sintos Coloma

Asian American, Native Hawaiian, and other Pasifika (Pacific Islander) (AANHPI) perspectives remain invisible and muted in education. Despite Asian Americans being the fastest growing racial-ethnic population in the United States and the continued effects of colonization and climate change impacting Native Hawaiian and Pasifika peoples, there is strikingly little attention to the ways that formal and informal educational spaces can be used to uplift, support, and sustain AANHPI peoples within institutional systems not designed to recognize them.

This new book series will feature innovative, imaginative, and even irreverent works that challenge dominant narratives of AANHPI students, educators, families, and communities and that center their educational wellbeing. Given the rich and complex diversities within the socio-politically constructed AANHPI category, books within the series will tackle educational problems, solutions, and possibilities that address AANHPI communities or that concern a particular ethnic or regional group (e.g., Filipinx or Southeast Asian Americans). While race, racism, and white supremacy persistently shape AANHPI educational conditions, experiences, and outcomes, they are also intertwined with other vectors of power and difference, such as class, gender, sexuality, indigeneity, empire, settler colonialism, migration, citizenship, dis/ability, language, religion, and environment. Hence, books within the series will embrace critical perspectives that reckon with the dynamics of power, knowledge, and subjectivity in the discursive, affective, and structural/material foundations of education. The series will document and scrutinize how oppression, complicities, contradictions, resistance, and liberation shape individual and collective educational logics, enactments, and trajectories.

With these series goals in mind, we invite researchers, educators, and community knowledge workers to propose a book in this groundbreaking series. We aim to support both fresh and seasoned voices speaking to persistent and/or pressing contemporary issues related to AANHPI education that may be of interest to practitioner, community, and/or scholarly audiences. We are interested in works that may use, examine, or develop new frameworks or lenses towards AANHPI educational experiences, pose creative solutions to old problems, propose nonnormative epistemologies, enact dissident pedagogies, and take risky positions to imagine and build possible futures. In this series, we aim to deconstruct and construct, learn and unlearn what we have come to know and do in AANHPI education.

Upcoming Titles in the Series

Moments & Movements: Counterstories of Critical Asian American+ Studies in Education
Edited by Betina Hsieh and Roland Sintos Coloma (2025)
The Third Wave of the Asian American Studies Movement:
Advocating for & Advancing Asian American Studies in K-12 Classrooms
Edited by Sohyun An, Noreen Naseem Rodriguez and Esther Kim (2027)

If you have a proposal that you wish to have considered for inclusion in the series, please contact the series editors: Betina Hsieh (bychsieh@uw.edu) or Roland Coloma (rscoloma@wayne.edu). Prospectus guidelines can be found online at the Myers Education Press website: https://myersedpress.presswarehouse.com/pages/author-resources.

Moments & Movements

Counterstories of Critical Asian American+
Studies in Education

EDITED BY *Betina Hsieh and*
Roland Sintos Coloma

Myers
Education
Press

Gorham, Maine

Published by Myers Education Press, LLC
P.O. Box 424, Gorham, ME 04038

Myers Education Press is an academic publisher specializing in books, e-books, and digital content in the field of education. All of our books are subjected to a rigorous peer review process and produced in compliance with the standards of the Council on Library and Information Resources.

Library of Congress Cataloging-in-Publication Data available from Library of Congress.

13-digit ISBN 978-1-9755-0728-2 (paperback)
13-digit ISBN 978-1-9755-0729-9 (library networkable e-edition)
13-digit ISBN 978-1-9755-0730-5 (consumer e-edition)

Printed in the United States of America.

All first editions printed on acid-free paper that meets the American National Standards Institute Z39-48 standard.

Books published by Myers Education Press may be purchased at special quantity discount rates for groups, workshops, training organizations, and classroom usage. Please call our customer service department at 1-800-232-0223 for details.

Cover design by Katherine Bizzoco of Green Frog Publishing.
Cover Image by Charlene Hsu-Rodriguez.

Visit us on the web at **www.myersedpress.com** to browse our complete list of titles.

DEDICATION

FOR MY A-MÁ (阿嬤) maternal grandmother 陳朱綿 (Chu-Mien Chen) and my mother (媽媽), Lois (Ming-Mei) Chen Hsieh (陳敏美), whose transnational movements and courage serve as my constant inspiration, and for Nate and Johana, my children, with whom every moment is an opportunity for movement forward and through whom my commitment to possible futures endures. —BH

TO MY NIECE Helena and my nephew Aidan, our present and future are in your hands. —RSC

Contents

Contents xi

ACKNOWLEDGMENTS

THE ROAD THAT we walk on has been paved by countless Asian American, Pasifika, and Middle Eastern educators, students, and activists—many unknown and unheralded—who have labored tirelessly and made tremendous sacrifices to enable our current journey. We are deeply indebted and grateful to those who have come before us and to others walking alongside us as we continuously struggle for recognition, representation, and redistribution in K-12 and higher education curriculum that is inclusive of Critical Asian American+ Studies.

This edited book would not have been possible without the generous support of the Spencer Foundation. We are honored and privileged to receive a Spencer Conference Grant in 2022 that facilitated our in-person convening in Detroit in July 2023 and the online workshops prior to and after that convening (as detailed in this book's Introduction). We especially want to thank OiYan Poon for her encouragement and guidance in our pursuit of external funding to bring together researchers, educators, and activists from across the country. We also want to acknowledge Leigh Patel and Kevin Kumashiro who wrote letters of support for our initial Spencer grant application.

The yearlong discussions from October 2022 to October 2023 cultivated a strong community bond among conference participants through courageous, vulnerable, and loving conversations. As we learned with and from each other, we invited all participants to contribute to this edited book, and many accepted and joined this effort as chapter authors and section discussants. We truly appreciate those who contributed by submitting their written work (Richard Mui, Noreen Naseem Rodriguez, Sohyun An, Jung Kim, Monica Eraqi, Bic Ngo, Cathery Yeh, Mohit Mehta, Edwin Mayorga, Eunice Ho, and Allyson Tintiangco-Cubales) and those who were not able to write for this book yet whose insights are embedded throughout the chapters. We are fortunate to have traveled with fellow participants Lisa Chu, Katie Li, Estella Owoimaha-Church, and Jean Wu, whose intellectual, political, and pedagogical wisdom has inspired our praxis.

Kathryn Ocomen has been a true blessing with her creativity, enthusiasm, organization, and impeccable professionalism. As our project assistant extraordinaire, she made sure that our administrative logistics and operations ran smoothly. As an undergraduate education major, she is clear proof that our teaching profession is in good hands. We could not have completed our Spencer conference grant and this book project without Kathryn!

Lastly, we honor and walk alongside other educators, researchers, students, activists, and community members who work towards an inclusive and comprehensive school curriculum so that the histories, cultures, and contributions of Asian American, Pasifika, and Middle Eastern communities in the United States are documented, taught, learned, and widely shared, some of whom came alongside us in this collection, even though they were not part of our initial collective, and others whose work is not included here. Through Critical Asian American+ Studies in education, it is our fervent hope that we can address the complexities of racial and intersectional justice in this country and beyond.

Betina would also like to acknowledge my "at home" family (Hans, Nate, and Johana Protzel), who are always gracious, encouraging and generous; my "not at home" family (James Hsieh, Pan Hsieh, Asha and Aisha Blackwell), who all have contributed and continue to contribute so much to my life in so many ways; and my community of sibling-supporters, including Sherry Deckman, Tasha Austin, Sakeena Everett, Anna Kim, Cathy Imai, Tami Kailola, Alejandra Priede, Christian Bracho, Carmen Vladila, and Yafa Luria. Thanks to Jung Kim, who has been an enduring co-conspirator in this work, and to Cathery Yeh, Ruchi Rangnath, and Judy Yu, whose support as Asian American MotherScholars has been invaluable. Most of all, thanks to Roland, my co-editor, thought partner in this project, and dear friend. I am so grateful for and inspired by your enduring calm and belief in our work. I know I owe thanks to many additional colleagues and friends who have supported this journey. You are deeply loved even if you're not specifically named. Charge it to my head, not my heart.

Roland would like to thank Grace J. Yoo, Joyce Higashida, and the late Steffi San Buenaventura for their mentorship and guidance when he was an undergraduate student at the University of California, Riverside. His formative understanding of racial and intersectional justice was honed not in the classroom, but through peer consciousness raising activities when he joined fellow student activists in organizing for Ethnic Studies and supporting the advancement of racial minority and LGBTQ+ student resource centers on campus. The Asian Pacific Student Programs Office at UC Riverside—with its staff, fellow students, and high school participants—was a significant critical space for his intellectual and political formation. After 30+ years, Roland continues to cherish his initial development as an educator and activist in his alma mater. Moreover, this project (and many others in the works) would not have been possible without his co-editor, co-conspirator, and cherished friend Betina whose brilliance and dedication demonstrate that critical academic and community work is nourished and sustained by care, joy, and solidarity.

Kevin K. Kumashiro

MY DEAR AUNT Wilma passed away recently, and in tribute to her lifelong reveling in art, I put together a timeline with as many photos of her exhibits and projects that I could find. I found many, including of handmade clothing that were as fashionable as they were a political statement (in this case, about how reducing trash is necessary to protect the health of the planet). Some of the exhibits that stand out the most to me—ones from long ago that she would describe to me, often as a way to show a common thread with whatever research or curriculum or activism I was involved in at that moment—are ones I have no photos of. Instead, I must rely on her and my recountings, such as those about a phonebooth-sized black box project, filled with artifacts from an individual's life, illuminated with just one flash of a strobe light as the viewer stands inside what otherwise feels like an upright dark coffin, giving the viewer merely a quick glimpse, as if to impress upon us that all we can ever know about someone is merely a slice of who they are, a drop, a flash.

Aunt Wilma was also a historian, and I imagine that informing her art was her delving into our family history over 50 years ago, a different type of project, but a form of artistic creation nonetheless. Before she passed away, she gave to me what she gathered and wrote for this project, including interview data, handwritten notes from ancestors, immigration artifacts, photos, and archival research alongside her own memories that all seemed to come together into several competing and incomplete versions of our history, which she invited me to continue developing. I have since picked up this project, trying to tell a story even while refusing to claim to have "the" story, and trying to grasp what was happening historically in the years of our immigration even while imagining that our story(ies) may trouble what counts as that history—that is, I have been diving into the dialectic of inquiring about how historical contexts affected our experiences even while exploring how our family histories offer helpful lenses for making sense of (or, reimagining) those historical tellings. Not surprisingly, when I came to *Moments and Movements*, I eagerly dived in and relished the stories and lenses in these chapters that, similarly, help us to engage and to trouble "Asian America"—and, for that matter, "America"—through *Counterstories for Critical Asian American+ Studies in Education* that offer an interventionist framework for anti-oppressive education and movement building for justice.

I am humbled to write this foreword. Recognizing that no foreword can fully capture the significance of such a brilliant and heartfelt collection of original and wide-ranging analyses as is here, I thought I'd aim to invite readers to engage with three sets of guiding questions or provocations that emerged for me as themes woven throughout the book that build on an expansive array of existing scholarship, curriculum, and activism of at least the past few decades in our fields and that offer potential and resources for new forms of knowledge production and justice work.

First, what does it mean to *(re)frame Asian American+*? A Critical Asian American+ Studies project frames and re-frames the notion of "Asian American," such as by asking: What is Asian American; or, What does it mean to self-identify and be identified as Asian American; or, How is Asian American as a category both productive and counterproductive? As I read the book's chapters, I see explorations of at least three framings: (a) the identities and communities that *emerge* as political and socio-cultural entities, as when racialized narratives of the "model minority" or the "yellow peril" catalyze identity and community formation, as well as when such formations evolve far beyond such initial constructions; (b) the identities and communities that *expand* at geographical (and related political and cultural) borders and crossings with Pasifika and with the Middle East (especially West and Southwest Asia), as when "Asian American" both includes and erases Native Hawaiian, Pacific Islander, and Middle Eastern identities and groups; and (c) the identities and communities that *excavate* the intersectedness and implicatedness of racialization with other dimensions of diversity, including ethnicity, language, social class, gender, sexuality, religion, ability, and so on that make the "normal" or "center" ever more narrow and unattainable. Such complexities and tensions make Asian American+ a concept that is always in-the-making, and the chapters show how such contestation and situatedness are precisely what make it useful for movement building.

Second, what does it mean to *(re)story Asia+America*? A Critical Asian American+ Studies project is one that both stories the relationship between Asia and America as well as troubles those and other stories and how they bear on race relations and nation relations. I see, for example, the book chapters variously grappling with the enduring impacts of at least three ways of relating: (a) the legacies of *imperial ambitions and anxieties*, including how U.S. imperialism, like millennia of Western empires before, has long developed its identity and its imperial logic in response to Orientalist narratives of the East, reflected even today in foreign policy and in cultural production; (b) the legacies of *denationalization (erasure) and settler colonialism (occupation)*, including Asian settler colonialism in Hawai'i and other Pacific Island territories and nations that both exceed and are entangled with such dualistic framings as Black–white narratives of race and U.S.–Other narratives of nation; and (c) the legacies of *Red Scare tactics* that frame American democracy as inseparable from globalized racial capitalism, most notable in what some today call the United States' "new cold war" (with China) but which has long used anti-communism rhetoric (particularly in the form of anti-Asian rhetoric when Asia is meant to symbolize communism or anything supposedly antithetical to U.S. democracy) to mask what are ultimately goals at the intersections of neoconservatism, neoliberalism, white supremacy, and American exceptionalism. Not unlike what I described regarding the intersectionality of race and other dimensions of diversity, the book's chapters reveal how U.S. constructions of Asia have long constituted the Other ("them") in an ideological project to construct a narrow story of America ("us") that could only ever benefit a few.

Third, what does it mean to *(re)read Asian America+*? A Critical Asian American+ Studies project asks readers (of research, of curriculum, of the media, and of this book as well) to read and to then trouble our readings with a range of lenses and practices for learning about Asian America+ and learning with Asian Americans+. I find myself intrigued by at least three types of reading strategies embodied by the book's chapters: (a) reading *behind* texts, as when recognizing that every text has a hidden curriculum that not only exceeds our intended lessons or messages, and not only can be the more powerful teacher than the formal curriculum, but also, when surfaced, can be precisely what enables anti-oppressive education (such as when we grapple with the multiple lenses we use for reading and the contradictory messages in any curriculum);

(b) reading *beside* texts, as when juxtaposing a curricular text with something not normally associated with it, not normally seen together, something a bit jarring or unsettling or queer that, when read alongside the texts, can invite or provoke readers to make connections or interpretations that we would not otherwise have made; and (c) reading *beyond* texts, as when treating texts less as transparent modes of communication and more as creative works of art, or less as complete and final and more as partial and ongoing, or less as authoritative knowledge in its content and more as pedagogical experience in its structure— not unlike my aunt's photobooth exhibit that, by allowing us (only) one flash to see all artifacts, insisted that we grapple with the limits of our knowledge. Critical Asian American+ Studies is a radical scholarly intervention, yes, but it is also a profoundly pedagogical one, with implications broadly political and, as I hope that I was able to share in these few pages and as you'll see in these chapters, profoundly personal as well.

   Congratulations and thank you to the editors of and contributors to this book and to the participants of the series of convenings that generated its conceptual framework and the resulting invitation for many more of us to join in justice work. Now, as readers, let's read, discuss, inquire, imagine, act, and build!

INTRODUCTION

Moments and Movements: An Invitation to Build With Us

Betina Hsieh and Roland Sintos Coloma

WELCOME. WE ARE so glad you've found your way to our introduction for *Moments and Movements: Counterstories for Critical Asian American+ Studies in Education*. Much like the similarly titled *Asian Americans: The Movement and the Moment* (Louie & Omatsu, 2001), a foundational book in Asian American Studies reflecting on experiences within the Asian (Pacific) American movement of the late 1960s to 1980s, this book was born from community and shared commitments to challenge the ways diverse diasporas and experiences of people from the Asian continent and the Pacific Ocean are largely invisibilized, silenced, and erased. Like the editors of that volume, we chose to defy reductionist narratives by telling our own stories, stories built upon generations of struggle, resistance, advocacy, and joy, stories that hold wisdom for the current moment and for Asian American+ movements in the future. We do so particularly with a focus on Asian Americans+ in education. In this chapter, we tell the story of this collection, why we've chosen the term Critical Asian American+ Studies as an overarching framework, which stories are featured, and why they (and many others that we hope this collection will inspire) matter in broader educational discussions. We hope that you'll engage this book with an open heart, open mind, and open eyes and that wherever you're coming from, you will be ready to build with us as we push towards Critical Asian American+ Studies in education and beyond.

What Led Us Here? Reflecting on Our Trajectory

Many moments lead to movements. This book began in 2021 with an online gathering of Asian American scholars from various education fields, initiated by Cathery Yeh (co-author of "Mapping Consequential Geographies" in this book). From this initial conversation, different participants of the gathering explored potential projects and grant funding opportunities. We (Betina and Roland) decided to apply for and successfully received a Spencer Foundation conference grant to bring together scholars from Asian American Studies and education in order to develop a framework for Asian American Studies that could be adapted and used in P-20 contexts. In the midst of organizing the conference, our focus shifted as Sohyun An and Noreen Naseem Rodríguez (co-authors of "I think that we're definitely doing something wrong" in this book) led a collaborative effort to formulate an Asian American Studies Curriculum Framework (An & Rodriguez, 2022) that involved several contributors in this collection.

Consequently, we pivoted the goals of the conference. We aimed to reconsider how we could expand a pedagogical movement for Asian American Studies in P-12 and teacher education, how the conference could cultivate a space for collective sharing and growth, and how diverse voices and persistent tensions in Asian American Studies could push our collective work forward. Working within grant requirements, budget, and timeline, we wanted to create moments together that could be deeply meaningful, purposeful, and impactful beyond a single meeting.

To that end, we invited 18 Asian American, Middle Eastern, and Pacific Islander scholar-educators to spend the 2022-2023 academic year with us, participating in two virtual meetings and culminating in an in-person gathering in Detroit, Michigan. We were intentional in bringing together a group that represented diverse Asian/Pacific Islander (API) and Middle Eastern ethnic backgrounds, various regions in the United States, and education/work contexts (e.g., P-12 schools, universities, and community-based organizations). While nearly everyone in the conference group had connections with one or both of us (Betina and/or Roland), many of them didn't know one another personally. We knew that, if we were to build something together, we had to trust one another and be willing to share and open our full selves to fellow educators from across the country.

We began our collective work with two virtual meetings. The first meeting in October 2022 focused on who we were, what we brought to Asian American Studies, and what our community agreements were. We asked participants to put together an introduction slide that visually responded to the following prompts: Who are you? What has been your racialized/ethnic journey? How does that intersect/interact/engage with/problematize the notion of being "Asian American"? As you read this introduction, we encourage you to also take a moment to reflect on these questions in relation to your own racial/ethnic background and experiences.

We shared our aligned or tense relationship to "Asian American" as a social construct, centering relationality while also unpacking the possibilities, liminality, and limits of "Asian American" as a racial category. Unpacking "Asian American" meant grappling with our own sociopolitical blind spots. For instance, we wrestled with the tensions of holding space for expansiveness without erasure and working as co-conspirators and allies in solidarity without speaking for other marginalized groups. In particular, how might we engage with or include our West Asian American/Arab American colleagues, who make up a large part of the "Middle Eastern" diaspora, without erasing other communities in "the Middle East," a region that extends beyond the Arabian Peninsula geographically to include North Africa? How could we walk alongside our Pasifika colleagues without subsuming the very real issues they face, including ones that Asian Americans have been complicit in sustaining?

We were and have been mindful of the long-standing struggle for the governmental recognition of the MENA (Middle Eastern and North African) category in the U.S. Census and of the larger scholarly and political discussions regarding Asian American and Arab American communities that wrestle with shared and distinct oppressions related to orientalism and colonialism (e.g., Maira & Shihade, 2006). Moreover, we recognize that the combined "Asian American and Pacific Islander" category has not benefited Native Hawaiian and other Pasifika communities. In fact, it has erased their histories, cultures, and concerns, including Asian settler colonialism in Hawaiʻi and other Pacific Islands (Fujikane & Okamura, 2008). The start to these conversations brought forth tensions that we continue to wrestle with even in the process of writing this introduction; however, we know they are vital to our ongoing journeys.

Our second virtual meeting in February 2023 happened less than 3 weeks after two mass shootings impacting the Asian American community—one at a dance hall during Lunar New Year weekend in Monterey Park in southern California and the other in a farming community in Half Moon Bay in northern California. The session was meant to focus on the Asian American Studies Curriculum Framework's essential concepts of reclamation and joy (An & Rodriguez, 2022), and we had asked participants to create personal slides on the themes of reclaiming histories and creative expression. However, in light of the tragic incidents, we addressed our community and individual grief, which had persisted following the highly visible anti-Asian attacks during the COVID-19 pandemic. Through this process, we felt and learned about the limits of virtual spaces when dealing with deep personal and recent trauma, especially for people who hadn't met in person. It was a reminder that, even as we sought to build moments together, we had to "move at the speed of trust" (brown, 2017).

During this second meeting, we grappled with two questions: (1) How do you honor history, community, and belonging in your work? and (2) What brings you joy as you work with our communities and advocate for Asian American, Middle Eastern, Pasifika, and/or other forms of racial and intersectional justice? (As you read these questions, we again invite you to take a moment to reflect on and answer these questions for yourself.) Collectively, in our session, sharing our personal slides and discussing our responses to the questions continued to deepen our community and brought much needed light as we connected with those who inspire us, bring us joy, and ground our work.

In July 2023, 41 years after the violent killing of Vincent Chin galvanized the Asian American movement in the 1980s, 14 of us gathered in person in Detroit, Michigan. We chose Detroit to honor Chin, the rise of the Asian American movement, and several other ancestors and communities. Our gathering was held near the city's historic Chinatown, which now exists in historical artifacts, memoirs, and plaques, with a pagoda at the Cass and Peterboro intersection as a haunting remnant of the previously thriving ethnic enclave. Detroit was also where Chinese American racial and economic justice activist Grace Lee Boggs and her political activist husband, Jimmy Boggs, founded Detroit Summer and convened revolutionary thinkers and organizers to create sustainable community-based actions. Roland, who works at Wayne State University in Detroit, additionally reminded us of various communities around Detroit, including in Dearborn, the largest Arab-majority city in the United States, and in Hamtramck, the only Muslim-majority city in the country and home to immigrant communities from Yemen, Bangladesh, and Pakistan.

Our moment together in Detroit helped us to think about place, context, and coalition. We shared how the histories we held and spaces we occupied shaped our work. Soh Suzuki, a board member at the James & Grace Lee Boggs School, gave a guided tour of the city, which included Vincent Chin's grave, the James and Grace Lee Boggs Center, and the Boggs School. Mohit Mehta (co-author of "The Fight for Asian American Studies in a 'Red State'" in this book) led morning yoga sessions to foster community-centered wellness. We shared meals, ideas, projects, hopes, and fears. We built and deepened relationships. We considered how we could support one another and what liberatory futures might look like that built from and honored moments and movements from the past and present. We closed our time together around a community table with gratitudes and acknowledgments, as some of our participants' children played outside the meeting room, reminding us of the next generation whose futures are at stake now.

After the conference, we (Betina and Roland) planned our next steps, inspired by our moment together in Detroit. A major suggestion that emerged from the gathering was to put together a collection of critical counterstories. Counterstories in education can be used to center the perspectives of people of color and other marginalized groups that challenge hegemonic dominant narratives (Solórzano & Yosso, 2002). We became more deeply familiar with participants' work and journeys and wanted the world to hear about them, too.

In October 2023, a year after our first collective meeting, we facilitated a final virtual gathering to bring closure to this phase of our work. We introduced the idea of an edited book and invited participants to submit chapter proposals for the planned four sections on beginning the work, sustaining and deepening classroom-focused efforts, extending work beyond classroom walls, and envisioning collective futures. While not all conference participants ultimately chose to contribute to this book as chapter authors or section discussants, they are all represented in these pages and as part of our collective journey. After reviewing the submitted chapter proposals, we reached out to our networks of educators and academics to address key thematic gaps. For the remainder of this introduction chapter, we explain the central framework of this book, who our authors are and the counterstories they're telling, and why we believe this collection is so important in highlighting moments and continuing movements for Critical Asian American+ Studies in education.

Why Critical Asian American+ Studies? Setting a Course for Our Collective Work

A significant part of our discussions in Detroit was how to describe and scrutinize the work that we do. We had in-depth conversations making distinctions among multiple concepts, disciplines, and frameworks, such as multicultural education, Ethnic Studies, Asian American history, Asian American Studies, Pasifika and Oceania Studies, Middle Eastern Studies, and the terms "Asian American," "Asian American, Native Hawaiian, and Pacific Islander," and "Middle Eastern and North African." We talked about our desire to be inclusive without subsuming or essentializing distinct experiences and struggles. We also discussed applications of strategic (anti-)essentialism (Iftikar & Museus, 2018) and when they were appropriate. When was it important to come together as racialized communities, using numerical strength and presence to make a greater impact? When was it necessary to advocate in coalition with other racial/ethnic groups or to highlight distinct challenges, accomplishments, and opportunities?

Ultimately, these discussions led to explicitly foregrounding the importance of solidarity and ongoing reflection of our collective work. We intended to capture this dynamic by choosing the term Critical Asian American+ Studies in naming our book. We chose the term Critical Asian American Studies to emphasize criticality as central to the work of Ethnic Studies, recognizing that it is not enough to teach Asian American histories without recognizing power in relation to historical dynamics that led to systemic exclusion and oppression of Asian diasporic people in the United States and in relation to contemporary systems that position Asian Americans as "model minorities" or "perpetual foreigners" (Choy, 2022). These historical and contemporary conditions erase the racialized experiences of Asian Americans, use Asian Americans as tools to uphold white supremacy, and wedge Asian Americans from other people of color. As scholars, we (Betina and Roland) ground ourselves in Asian American Studies to epistemologically understand criticality, community, and coalition within our subfield specifically, and Ethnic Studies generally, and to acknowledge our focus on diasporic peoples from Asia in the Americas.

The addition of the plus (+) symbol in "Asian American+" was a source of extended discussion between us. While Roland wasn't sure that the symbol was legible and self-explanatory, Betina advocated for the plus as indicative of tensions in our own conversations and in the field of Asian American Studies around naming, inclusivity, and speaking with, for, or alongside other communities. The plus symbol is most widely associated with the LGBTQ+ communities and movements (Smith & Yost, 2023) and can be argued to be a symbol that allows people outside of traditionally defined paradigms (but associated with or part of a larger group) to identify themselves. The plus symbol highlights diverse inclusion and openness to various groups under a broad umbrella category. For us, the plus seeks to be inclusive of the various Pasifika, Arab, and Middle Eastern communities touched upon in this collection without eliding their distinct histories, cultures, politics, and experiences, without erasing the tensions within and across the broader category of Asian American Studies, and without claiming expertise and focus beyond the scope or larger intention of this project.

Recognizing that one collection of counterstories cannot do all things, we as editors made intentional efforts to be inclusive both within and beyond the Asian American category by seeking chapter authors from South, East, Southeast, and West Asian roots and by having multiple chapters focused on Native Hawaiian Pacific Islander (NHPI) and Arab and Middle Eastern American (AMEA) perspectives and experiences in education; however, we acknowledge that the larger overall focus, framing, and section responses still draw from Critical Asian American+ Studies perspective. We are committed to honor Pasifika and AMEA authors, friends, and colleagues who have roots or connections with the Asian diaspora and to the continent of Asia and recognize their adjacency to Critical Asian American+ Studies as well as their authority to name and claim their identities, positionalities, and work. We invite readers, especially Asian American readers, to consider how working alongside NHPI and AMEA collaborators and colleagues looks in practice. Beyond this volume, as book series editors for Myers Education Press, we intend to feature the educational theorizing, perspectives, and experiences of NHPI and AMEA scholars and educators that recognize the ways our struggles are both distinct and interconnected.

With Whom Do We Journey?
The Stories and Spaces Held in This Collection

Before we talk about the organization of the book and briefly about each chapter, we address the somewhat less traditional voice and tone in this introduction and throughout the book. As scholar-educator editors who write for various audiences, we considered and discussed who this book was for. The book's topics, located at the nexus of multiple and interconnected fields, such as education, race/Ethnic Studies, policy and community studies, have broad appeal to a cross-section of university academics, P-12 teachers and leaders, and community educators and activists. Most of the authors in this book are academics, educators, and students at various levels. (You can read about all the authors in their biographical statements at the end of this book.) It was important for us that this book honor various identities, knowledges, experiences, and perspectives in the best ways we could. Through storytelling, we wanted the chapters to be accessible to different audiences. In a sense, we hoped this book recreates what it might be like to have conversations with chapter authors about their journeys towards Critical Asian American+ Studies that feature moments, ideas, or practices that are meaningful for them. We wanted you to hear the authors' voices and learn alongside them, just as we've been privileged to do. We intended for the chapters to feel "up close" rather than at a distance and to feel more personal rather than objective. In this way, we invite you to journey alongside each of the authors in this collection.

We organized the book thematically into four sections that reflected key moments in an ongoing movement to acknowledge that each of us may be at different points in our journeys towards developing more critical perspectives or knowledge of Asian American, Arab/Middle Eastern American, and Pasifika peoples' experiences in education. As editors, we recognized that some chapters could have fit in several sections. Hence, the order of the chapters does not reflect further progression in a journey, but rather demonstrates editorial choices to bring cohesion to each section. Having section discussants was another way for us to integrate conversation in the structure of this volume. At the end of each section, an Asian American scholar offers a brief synthesis and response to the section chapters, delineates how the chapters come into conversation with one another, and connects with the overall theme of the section.

The first section, "The Moment We Begin," focuses on how we become the change we wish to see. The section starts, appropriately, with "what every person needs to know" about integrating Asian American histories into U.S. history curriculum, highlighting a conceptual framework developed by Richard Mui based on his teaching experiences in high school. In Chapter 2, Noreen Naseem Rodríguez, Esther June Kim, and Sohyun An consider how we learn from Asian American youth as to what changes need to be made in curriculum and schools, supporting their leadership development and centering their voices as we advocate for educational change. In Chapter 3, we learn from 'Alohilani Okamura and Kirsten Mawyer's work in teacher education to cultivate a Native Hawaiian Place of Learning, using culturally sustaining and revitalizing pedagogies and principles to ground their work with diverse teacher candidates in Hawai'i. Finally, in Chapter 4, Jung Kim draws from her own journey to demonstrate how we can promote educational communities needed for our own sense of belonging and professional growth rather than waiting for their emergence.

The second section, "Building an Inclusive Movement," examines how educators sustain and deepen their work within and outside of classrooms. In Chapter 5, Edward Curammeng, Giselle Cunanan, and Cheralyn Valdez employ a framework of multiple consciousness to examine how we approach Asian American K-12 praxis with recognition of the choices we make and the positionalities from which we speak. Chapters 6 to 8 bring diverse voices that are often in the margins to the center of Asian American Studies in education. In Chapter 6, Ruchi Agarwal-Rangnath affirms and honors hidden South Asian American stories; in Chapter 7, Monica Eraqi shares her journey in establishing and teaching Middle Eastern Studies in high school and how her teaching and course have evolved over time; and in Chapter 8, Norman Sales returns to a Hawai'ian context and demonstrates how educators can draw from their students' community cultural wealth (Yosso, 2005) to amplify and cultivate inclusive spaces for culturally and linguistically diverse Asian American and Pacific Islander students.

The third section, "Extending the Movement," looks at Critical Asian American+ Studies outside of classrooms and schools by attending to educational leadership, families and teacher identities, policy arenas, and educational, cultural, and community activism. In Chapter 9, Paul Koh draws from three prominent Asian American civil rights activists to offer a culturally sustaining model for justice-oriented leadership to counter stereotypical portrayals of Asian American administrators. In Chapter 10, Lawrence Teng, Cathery Yeh, and William Bae mobilize an Education Journey Mapping methodology to bring spatial analysis to racialization and, in particular, to draw attention to the ways Asianization informs teacher and student identities. Chapters 11 and 12 speak to state-level and local forms of activism and their impact. In Chapter 11, Roland Sintos Coloma explores how Asian American legislators, educators, creatives, and community leaders promote political, pedagogical, and cultural avenues to advocate for teaching AAPI histories in Michigan. In Chapter 12, Indira Moparthi, Annie Nguyen, and Mohit Mehta describe different school- and community-based organizing initiatives that led to the development of the first high school course in Asian American Studies in Texas and the importance of persistence and coalition building within this movement.

In the fourth section, "Envisioning New Worlds," we attend to what justice-focused, future-oriented movements might look like for Critical Asian American+ Studies. In Chapter 13, Wayne Au offers critical reflections on the evolution of the model minority stereotype, Asian American-ness, and his own experiences navigating and ultimately divesting from the insidious model minority myth. In Chapter 14, Sawsan Jaber poignantly narrates what it means and has meant to be Palestinian American in education and how she can imagine and create an educational homeplace for diasporic Palestinians in the United States and beyond in the face of shattered realities. Finally, in Chapter 15, One Heartbeat Collective, composed of school teachers and students, invite us into conversation, as they share their individual and combined counterstories of intergenerational fugitivity.

Why Come Along?
Building Possible Futures in Solidarity

All too often, we feel alone in doing critical community-grounded work. This is particularly true within, among, and beyond AA, NHPI, and AMEA communities in education. Yet, when we build together, we develop new insights about ourselves, our stories, and our futures, often finding affinity, renewing solidarities, and experiencing joy with one another. In this collection, we seek to push beyond prescribed borders that separate our communities and separate us into our own educational spheres (e.g., P-12, higher education, teacher education) and roles (professor, teacher, principal, student). As one of the few edited collections with such diverse perspectives, we hope that this collection provides multiple paths forward in Asian American, Arab/Middle Eastern American, and Pasifika Studies; inspires with its counterstories of struggle and success; and challenges us to consider our own next steps.

There are many more demographic, historical, and sociopolitical arguments we could make about why these chapters are important, but what is most important for us is the humanity and contribution in the spirit throughout this collection. We hope this spirit connects with yours. Whatever brought you to this book, we hope you'll make yourself a pot (or thermos) of tea, chai, coffee, or kava, grab a snack, and consider movement building with us. We are grateful that you're here.

References

An, S., & Rodriguez, N. N. (2022). *Asian American studies K-12 framework*. SF State Asian American Research Initiative. https://asianamericanresearchinitiative.org/wp-content/uploads/2022/06/aari-resources-asian-american-studies-k-12-framework-v2.pdf

brown, a. m. (2017). *Emergent strategy: Shaping change, changing worlds*. AK Press.

Choy, C. C. (2022). *Asian American histories of the United States*. Beacon Press.

Fujikane, C., & Okamura, J. Y. (2008). *Asian settler colonialism: From local governance to the habits of everyday life in Hawai'i*. University of Hawaii Press.

Iftikar, J. S., & Museus, S. D. (2018). On the utility of Asian critical (AsianCrit) theory in the field of education. *International Journal of Qualitative Studies in Education, 31*(10), 935–949. https://doi.org/10.1080/09518398.2018.1522008

Louie, S., & Omatsu, G. (Eds.). (2001). *Asian Americans: The movement and the moment.* UCLA Asian American Studies Center Press.

Maira, S., & Shihade, M. (2006). Meeting Asian/Arab American studies: Thinking race, empire, and Zionism in the US. *Journal of Asian American Studies, 9*(2), 117–140.

Smith, T. E., & Yost, M. R. (2023). The power of self-identification: Naming the "plus" in LGBT+. In E. L. Zurbriggen & R. Capdevila (Eds.), *The Palgrave handbook of power, gender, and psychology* (pp. 233–253). Palgrave Macmillan. https://doi.org/10.1007/978-3-031-41531-9_14

Solórzano, D. G., & Yosso, T. J. (2002). Critical race methodology: Counter-storytelling as an analytical framework for education research. *Qualitative Inquiry, 8*(1), 23–44.

Yosso, T. J. (2005). Whose culture has capital? A critical race theory discussion of community cultural wealth. *Race Ethnicity and Education, 8*(1), 69–91.

Part I

The Moment We Begin

CHAPTER 1

Asian American History 101: What Every Person Needs to Know

Richard Mui

ASIAN AMERICAN PACIFIC Islanders (AAPI) have been a part of the American story since our nation's colonial past. This chapter will explore the immigration history of Asian Americans. Through a closer investigation, the chapter will address how America shaped these newcomers as well as how the nation was in turn shaped by these immigrants from Asia. As immigration from Asia continues to expand, the associated themes of culture, identity, and pertinent issues and what it means to be an American will be raised for investigation. Asian Americans have been an important part of America's growth and development since the mid-1800s. While many students are familiar with the Chinese railroad workers and Japanese American incarceration during WWII, the story of Asians in America offers a deeper introspective into America's social, political, and economic development. Since the 1965 Immigration Act, immigration from Asia has seen tremendous growth. This increase in immigration has raised new opportunities as well as new challenges for the Asian American community as well as American society. This significant number necessitates a deeper understanding of Asian American stories for both Asian and non-Asian students alike. This chapter will include key curricular starting points to support educators interested in foundational AAPI histories at the secondary level.

Coming from my working-class background, I was convinced that one factor that oppressed poor people was the lack of knowledge about how the political and economic systems really worked in this country. From my lived experience in high school and college, I saw great disparities in wealth and opportunity. Of course, there was no better way to uncover these nefarious forces than to take a deeper look into U.S. history. I was further convinced of this approach when I first read Howard Zinn's (2015) *A People's History of the United States.* The alternative perspective and the evidence offered were exactly what all students needed. As an aspiring social studies teacher, I believed that students were bored by history because they did not know the "truth." So, if I could bring the truth to these students, they could come to see reality as it was. I was eager to help my students uncover these alternate views for themselves as we studied throughout the school year. To my disappointment, the untold and sordid history of the United States was of minimal interest for the students. Most displayed the same general apathy towards the subject matter as in their previous social studies courses. For others, a deeper look into history confirmed that everything was a scam and that the political and economic systems only served those in power. Instead of making them more curious, it only made the students more cynical. At this point, it would have been easy to blame the usual suspects for the disinterest. This ranges from the widespread use of cell phones and social media to the decline of American culture and education. The answer to my predicament came from the team of teachers I collaborated with. They have worked on the problem of students' boredom and interest throughout their teaching career. Their answer to the question was to develop conceptual frameworks. A conceptual framework in the classroom includes the basic information needed to begin to understand the topic. If students develop an accurate conceptual framework around a concept, they can quickly incorporate new knowledge into that framework and begin making connections to other ideas. In this chapter, I offer the conceptual framework I use for a high school Asian American history course.

1849–1924 The Early Years: Inclusion Then Exclusion

The most important lessons regarding Asian immigration consider how and why immigration occurs and who immigrants are. Because of the ways mainstream history curriculum and standards are constructed, many students will have a basic understanding of immigration from a European perspective. The push factors—political instability, famine, limited social mobility, and persecution—and the pull factors—economic opportunity, political freedom, and better living conditions—are well documented. Furthermore, there were waves of European immigration: first, the Irish and Germans who were later replaced by southern and eastern Europeans. This framework can be connected to immigration from Asia as well. The first major wave of Asian immigrants to the present-day United States were Chinese sojourners that sought wealth from Gold Mountain, as America was referred to after the discovery of gold in California. While actual wealth from gold mining was limited, due in part to the difficulty in finding gold but also to discrimination by other miners and through the law, the Chinese found other ways to prosper in America. The Chinese sought opportunities in the laundry and the restaurant businesses that catered to the miners. Other opportunities included building the Transcontinental Railroad. While Irish laborers built from the East, Chinese labor crews built from the West. In fact, the 1868 Burlingame Treaty eased restrictions and made it easier for the railroad companies to recruit Chinese labor. Resentment against Chinese work began to build on the West Coast. White working men resented the competition for jobs and the subsequent lower wages. The economic concerns soon gave way to racist cultural stereotypes about the character of the Chinese people and their ability to assimilate into American culture. Ultimately, these fears culminated in the 1882 Chinese Exclusion Act that restricted Chinese labor from immigrating to America. Using the early Chinese immigration story as an example, students can explore themes of migration for economic opportunity, how many immigrant communities were pitted against one another, and racism and xenophobia targeted towards Asian migrant communities.

The Chinese were not the only workers coming to America in search of opportunity and a better life. Japanese immigrants began immigrating in large numbers to America in the late 1800s. Like the Chinese, Japanese immigrants were chasing economic opportunity in America. However, their stories diverge from the Chinese in a couple of notable points. First, the early Japanese immigrants were escaping economic hardships under the Meiji Restoration. Taxes were high and economic opportunity was low. Secondly, the Japanese journey to America included a stop in Hawaii to work on the sugar plantations. Ironically, the ban on Chinese labor caused companies to look elsewhere for their labor supply. This need is what increased Japanese immigration to America. Whereas Chinese immigrants were victimized by cultural stereotypes that dehumanized their existence, the Japanese sought to avoid that fate. Through the picture bride system, Japanese immigrants sought to create families and settle permanently in America. Despite their efforts to navigate cultural stereotypes differently, the Japanese could not escape the same fate as the Chinese. In 1908, the Gentlemen's Agreement between Theodore Roosevelt and the Japanese government was put into place. In exchange for ending the segregation of Japanese schoolchildren in San Francisco schools, the Japanese government voluntarily limited immigration to the United States. The Japanese immigration story allows for students to see distinctions between the (immigration) stories of various Asian diasporic communities in America, challenging a tendency for there to be a single narrative applied towards Asian Americans while also illustrating that in spite of their best efforts, often distinct Asian ethnic communities face similar racialized consequences.

While the Gentlemen's Agreement benefited Japanese Americans, it did not lessen the need for labor, especially on the Hawaiian plantations. Companies turned towards other countries, including other Asian countries, for labor. Korea, which was a Japanese protectorate at that time, proved to be a suitable candidate. Fleeing political and economic instability, Koreans began arriving in Hawaii after 1903 to work on the sugar and pineapple plantations. The recruitment of Korean labor was aided by Christian missionaries who helped bring Koreans to America and established churches to help provide a cultural hub for the immigrants. Although Korean immigrants in the early 20th century never reached the numbers of Chinese or Japanese immigrants, Korean immigrants were still subject to the push and pull factors that brought Asian immigrants to America's shores. Filipino immigration also has ties to labor exploitation, this time through colonialism. The Philippines came under colonial control of the United States after the 1898 Spanish American War and the subsequent Philippine American War. Because of immigration restrictions, Hawaiian plantations again had difficulty finding workers to sustain their business. This is when Filipino migrants were brought in to work. Filipinos were not subject to the immigration policies because they resided in American territory. Although their legal and political status were unclear, the ambiguity allowed for Filipino labor to come to American shores.

The one Asian diasporic group that came in this early period but does not neatly fit a similar pattern is that of Indian (South Asian) immigration. Their story is similar in that they were fleeing British control in India as well as economic hardship, coming to the Americas for economic opportunity. However, Indian immigrants took a more circuitous route. Indian immigrants, mostly from the Punjab region at that time, had difficulty emigrating directly to the United States. However, because they resided in British-controlled territory, Indians could more easily get passage and admittance into Canada. From there, the immigrants would travel to the Pacific Northwest where they often found employment in the lumber mills.

There are many similarities in the factors that brought Asian immigrants to America. Unfortunately, there are also many similarities in the treatment here in America. The historical record shows many riots around the country—Bellingham, Washington towards the Japanese; Stockton, California against the Filipinos; Rock Springs, Wyoming against the Chinese—which all served the common purpose of driving out Asian immigrants from the United States. The xenophobic attitude was fueled by popular contemporary authors like Lothrop Stoddard who stoked fears of the white race being replaced by the growing number of people of color, including those from Asia. Those fears played on the racist beliefs that immigrants were unassimilable and sought to dominate the world. The culmination of these fears was the 1924 National Origins Act. The 1924 National Origins Act severely limited immigration from southern and eastern Europe. It completely banned all immigration from Asia. The pattern of Asian immigration, resentment of economic competition, fears of cultural pollution, and corresponding backlash has been present throughout American history. Ideally, students will be able to recognize that theme and identify ways to disrupt the cycle.

1924–1965 Time of Resistance

The time period between the prohibition on Asian immigration in the 1924 and the 1965 Immigration Act posits a challenge for Asian Americans. How should Asian Americans react to the overt racist immigration laws and the discriminatory domestic atmosphere that are by-products of the laws. Ultimately, it is a question of what it means to be an American.

The first responses to be considered are the two Supreme Court cases *Takao Ozawa v. U.S.* (1921) and *United States v. Bhagat Singh Thind* (1923). Although both cases just predate the beginning of this time period, both cases address the question of what it means to be an American. Ozawa argued that by practice, he is an American. He spoke fluent English, attended church, was educated in the American schools, and many other traits that are associated with Americans. Ozawa even argued that his skin complexion was fairer than many other Americans. Ultimately, justices ruled that Ozawa was not Caucasian and therefore ineligible to be considered "white" and then, consequently, an American. Thind's case rested on the argument that he was from the Caucus region and a member of the highest caste in India. Furthermore, Thind fought for the United States in WWI and should be eligible for citizenship. Despite satisfying the criteria set forth in the Ozawa case, Thind was deemed ineligible for citizenship. According to the Supreme Court majority, Thind was not "what the average man on the street considers to be white" (US v. Thind, 1923). Both the Ozawa and Thind cases reveal the shifting definition of whiteness and the desire for proximity to whiteness that sought to exclude others.

Another approach to claim the privileges of American citizenship came from figures in entertainment like Anna May Wong and Sessue Hayakawa. Both movie stars rose to prominence in their movie careers during the 1920s and 1930s. Despite their acting prowess, both stars soon hit the "bamboo ceiling" in Hollywood. The roles available to them were relegated to seductress in Wong's case or the villain plotting to take over the world for Hayakawa. Both stereotypes played into society's existing views of Asians as unassimilable and always with ulterior motives. Wong and Hayakawa's careers include the importance of representation in Hollywood and elsewhere, but also raise important questions: To what extent are stereotypes a reflection of societal beliefs? Are stereotypes resulting from the limited images offered to the American public? Should (these) Asian American actors continue in their limited movie roles and perpetuate the stereotypes? Or should Wong and Hayakawa have found some other form of resistance, potentially at risk of their movie careers? Their choice is the same choice that confronts many contemporary Asian Americans. Where Asian Americans work and live, they are confronted by stereotypes. While all people have stereotypes to address, the pernicious beliefs tied to Asian Americans' race and ethnicity pose ongoing navigation and self-questioning.

The last scenario during this period in which Americanness was called into contention for Asian Americans was during World War II. When Japan bombed Pearl Harbor and America entered the war, it set the stage for how society viewed Asian Americans and how Asian Americans viewed themselves. First, the incarceration of 120,000 Japanese and Japanese Americans, of which two-thirds were American citizens, laid bare the racist views in society and the government. Many of the arguments provided included assimilability and questions of loyalty that harkened back to xenophobic views of the early 1900s. The fact that only Japanese and Japanese Americans from the West Coast, and not Hawaii or the rest of the country, were forcibly moved shows the incongruent and shallow argument made for incarceration. The dilemma faced by the incarcerated is similar to one faced by Asian Americans daily. Should you cooperate and risk your life to show loyalty to the country that has incarcerated you and your family? This was the option that was chosen by the 442nd regiment, an all-Japanese American fighting force. Or do you resist the constitutionality of incarceration and sue for freedom like Fred Korematsu and Mitsuye Endo? Or resist cooperation in all ways like the No-No Boys? When asked if they would give up their loyalty to the Japanese government and be willing to fight for the United States military, the No-No Boys responded in the negative, in part because they believed these questions to be misleading, based upon assumptions of loyalty to the Japanese government, not assumed of other immigrants.

For non-Japanese Asian American groups, WWII provided opportunities to demonstrate their loyalty and their "worthiness" of inclusion in American society. Chinese Americans took advantage of this opportunity and worked hard to fundraise for the war effort on behalf of America and China. For Filipinos, the fierce fighting on the Pacific front demonstrated that Filipinos were deserving of American respect for their courage and determination. While many of these efforts came with an attempt to distance oneself from Japanese-ness (or Japanese Americans), racial scapegoating still occurred for even groups of Asian Americans seeking to prove their loyalty to the United States.

1965–1990 The Old and New Americans

The 1965 Immigration Act was a watershed moment for the Asian American community. Building off the success of the Civil Rights Movement to create a more equitable society, the new immigration law repealed the restrictive provisions in the 1924 National Origins Act. The national origins quota system was removed and replaced by an emphasis on family reunification. Additionally, special considerations were given to individuals that possessed skills that were high in demand, including science and medical fields. This act has transformed the face of America. Since 1965, immigrants from Asia have been the fastest growing segment in society. It is expected that by 2060, Asian Americans will overtake the Latinx population and become the largest minority group in America.

This rapid growth came with unexpected effects. One such effect was a reshaping of the predominant stereotype shaping the contemporary Asian American experience from one of unassimilable immigrant (or forever foreigner) to the model minority myth. The model minority myth posits that Asian Americans through a combination of natural talent and cultural work ethic are more likely to be academically successful, particularly in math and science. This myth is created in part because of provisions in revised immigration laws that privileged scientists and medical professionals being awarded visas to the United States, particularly from East and South Asia. What is unspoken is the harm to the many Asian American students who don't fit this myth and struggle against societal expectations. Additionally, the model minority myth is perpetuated in part as a slight to other minority communities to suggest they can, would, and should succeed in America, if they only did the right thing, like Asian Americans. The model minority myth emphasizes the importance of individual meritocracy over structural racism.

This period also includes the Vietnam War. While the American war in Vietnam is discussed in high school classrooms, most standard textbooks and curriculum rarely look at the impact of the war on the Vietnamese people and other Southeast Asians. Authors such as Viet Thanh Nguyen have worked hard to change that narrative with his Pulitzer Prize winning novel, *The Sympathizer* (2015). History textbooks further fail to address the fates of thousands of war refugees from Vietnam, Laos, and Cambodia, including the Hmong who helped the CIA during the war. The influx of immigrants from Southeast Asia literally changed the meaning of what it meant to be Asian American. The demographics of the Asian American community changed to include refugee community members who had lower access to education, rates of educational attainment, and economic capital. More importantly, Southeast Asian Americans' stories of immigrating to America and adjusting to a new culture and new surroundings differed from the traditional narrative from an East Asian perspective. Their story is further complicated by settling down in a country where emotions were still raw and the population still divided over the meaning of the Vietnam War.

Concurrent with the influx of Southeast Asian immigrants, more established Asian American communities also experienced critical events that showed their continued "othering." Vincent Chin was a young engineer in the Detroit metro area. He and his friends were celebrating Vincent's upcoming marriage. While out at the club, Vincent got into a fight with two unemployed auto workers, Ronald Ebens and Michael Nitz. The night ended with Nitz and Ebens brutally beating Vincent Chin with a baseball bat; Chin died 3 days later. Nitz and Ebens subsequently being sentenced to 3 years of probation and a $3000 fine drew the ire of the Asian American community. Vincent Chin's death and the lenient sentencing for his killers raised questions about justice and how much American society has really changed since the days of the Chinese Exclusion Act and the race massacres that took place at that time, setting off large protests for justice. During the 1980s, there was a wave of anti-Japanese hysteria over the increasing market share of Japanese automakers at the expense of GM, Ford, and Chrysler, creating the conditions for the injustice surrounding Vincent Chin to take place.

Another incident that showed the state of race relations in America was the 1992 LA uprising (riots). The uprising took place after the acquittal of four police officers in the recorded beating of a Black motorist, Rodney King. One target of looting and destruction was the Koreatown section of Los Angeles, uncovering simmering tensions between the Black community and the Korean store owners. Since the 1960s and the Third World Liberation Front, there had been hopes of collaboration between communities of color to bring about a more just society. The LA riots and their aftermath revealed the continuing struggle to build meaningful coalitions that acknowledge the historical injustices while working through present-day challenges. While much attention is paid to incidents like the killing of Vincent Chin and the LA uprisings, the impact of cross-racial and pan-ethnic Asian American solidarity (in relation to the Chin case) and to cross-racial community rebuilding (following the 1992 uprisings) as counternarratives that highlight the ebb, flow, and complexities of racial relations are rarely discussed.

2001–Present Modern Day Asian America

In the conceptual framework I use, the exploration of modern day begins with a tragedy. The 9/11 attack on multiple targets inside the United States stands as one of the most shocking and horrific events in American history. That tragedy would engulf Asian Americans, particularly those of Muslim or Sikh faith, as the nation looked for a scapegoat for the violence. Twenty years later, there would be another resurgence of anti-Asian violence surrounding the COVID-19 pandemic. As deaths due to the virus surged, the president explicitly tied the virus to a country and its people contrary to the World Health Organization's naming conventions. Hate incidents against Asian Americans across the country surged, including many attacks against the elderly. Finally, 2021 saw the murder of spa workers in Atlanta. Six of the eight people killed were Asian women. The convicted killer claimed sex addiction, and not race, motivated him to commit the crime. The fact that it was Asian American women working at the spa, skeptics would claim, was merely coincidental to the crime itself.

All three situations raise the question of how much progress this nation has made regarding equality and justice for Asian Americans. Asian Americans have become part of the economic, political, and social tapestry of this nation. Those of Asian heritage can easily be found in all corners of society. However, many Asian Americans continue to face a similarly tenuous "acceptance" with an underlying belief in unassimilable difference. Like the 1800s when Asian immigrants were targeted with discriminatory laws and violence in response to seeming economic and cultural threats, Asian Americans are still not fully perceived as American by many.

Despite all the challenges they have faced, a powerful part of the Asian American experience is joy. Asian Americans have had an impact on the political, economic, and cultural life in the United States. Political leaders such as Vice President Kamala Harris, Representative Judy Chu and APIA Vote executive director Christine Chen all lend their voice to raise issues that are pertinent to the Asian Americans. Similarly, in the economic arena, Asian Americans are leading the way. There are 42 CEOs of Asian heritage leading Fortune 500 corporations, including Google/Alphabet, Microsoft, and NVIDIA. There are also over 3 million businesses owned by Asian Americans across the nation. Food such as boba tea, sushi, and ramen are ubiquitous and have become part of the American diet. Similarly, entertainment such as K-pop music and BTS or the Academy Award Winner for Best Picture, *Everything, Everywhere, All at Once* (Kwan & Scheinert, 2022), reflect the mass appeal of entertainment with Asian themes or elements.

One question raised by the cultural spreading is, "What does it mean to be Asian American?" Particularly, when it comes to food, music, or clothing, categories are constantly being fused and altered. One question that is brought to the forefront is the question of authenticity. Is there a threshold where something ceases to be Asian and it is now part of American culture? Is Asian American culture distinct or part of larger American culture? Or does it depend on the producer and/or the consumer? When does cultural appreciation become cultural appropriation, or are these lines purely subjective? Whereas discussions of food or music may seem trivial, they take on a greater importance when discussing one's identity. Who gets to call themselves Asian American? Multi-racial Asian Americans are one of the fastest growing segments of the Asian American community. Alongside that growth has been a steady trans-racial adoptee population; all the while there is still a steady flow of immigrants from Asia still arriving in America. The difficulties in identifying who is Asian American can be seen in titling the category. To be more accurate and inclusive, the name has been labeled as Asian American, Asian Pacific American, Asian Pacific Islander American, Asian American Pacific Islander and, more recently, Asian Pacific Islander Desi American. More important than a label is the question of what binds people of Asian heritage together. The question might have been answered one way back in the 1960s when the term Asian Americans was coined. Today, it requires constant revisitation and reflection.

Conclusion

This framework is not intended to be an exhaustive list of meaningful Asian American people, places, and events. Rather, it is structured to give learners a foundation to understand how immigrants from different regions in Asia arrived in America. Hopefully, by creating a framework, learners will understand different circumstances for emigration and subsequent challenges when settling in America. Exploring the similarities across Asian American experiences can establish connections that bind the Asian American community together. From there, Asian American narratives can be seen as an integral part of the American story. Asian American histories are critical to understanding the American story and, as such, they can engage all of us as learners.

References

Kwan, D., & Scheinert, D. (Directors). (2022). *Everything, everywhere, all at once* [Film]. A24.
Nguyen, V. T. (2015) *The Sympathizer*. Grove Press.
Ozawa v. United States, 260 U.S. 178. (1921). https://www.loc.gov/item/usrep260178/
United States v. Thind, 261 U.S. 204. (1923). https://www.loc.gov/item/usrep261204/
Zinn, H. (2015). *A people's history of the United States*. Harper Perennial Modern Classics.

CHAPTER 2

"I think that we're definitely doing something wrong": Learning From Asian American Youth About Identity, Advocacy, and Educational Change

Noreen Naseem Rodríguez, Esther June Kim, and Sohyun An

EDUCATION RESEARCHERS FREQUENTLY dismiss efforts to diversify curriculum and to implement Ethnic Studies in conservative states, focusing instead on places like California and Illinois where efforts have already been successful. In this chapter, we highlight youth perspectives from two Republican-led states to examine efforts to create affinity and educational spaces for Asian Americans. In Texas, Asian Americans are the fastest growing population in the state, expected to grow to 6 million by 2050 (Diaz, 2020). Similarly, the Asian American population in Georgia is nearly double the national rate of increase (Skinner, 2022). Despite what outsiders might assume, communities in these states *are* engaged in grassroots movements for curricular inclusion at various levels, and studying these nuanced approaches offers important insights for others in politically conservative contexts, particularly in the American South.

A deeper understanding of the youth and their stories requires some knowledge of the specific contexts in which they live and seek to transform. Therefore we offer brief backgrounds of Asian American growth and political advocacy in Texas and Georgia.

Texas

Texas is a state often associated with conservative politics, cowboys, and country music, but these associations with whiteness belie the state's history and ethnoracial diversity, as Texas is the second most diverse state after California. Asian American demographics increased exponentially after the 1965 Immigration and Nationality Act, now composing the fastest growing group at 5% of the state population. In recognition of the lack of political engagement and coalitions among Asian American and Pacific Islander (AAPI) constituents, organizers and activists in Central Texas created Asian Texans for Justice (ATJ) in 2021 to support AAPI policy advocacy and voters.

In 2020, as the COVID-19 pandemic spread and protests against racial violence emerged across the nation and the world, legislators in Texas were hopeful that the time was right to propose standards for an Asian American Studies (AAS) elective after the recent passage of state standards for Mexican American Studies and African American Studies. While the passage of these standards was contentious, the moment of racial reckoning seemed ideally suited for further expansion of curricular diversity. Yet 2021 witnessed a fierce backlash among white conservatives in the state and beyond, as ideologues like Christopher Rufo orchestrated an assault on purported "critical race theory" and diversity, equity, and inclusion efforts, resulting in book bans and districts backpedaling on anti-racist curriculum and instruction. But communities remained undeterred, and one Central Texas school offered an AAS elective[1] during the 2023–2024 academic year. Elsewhere in the state, youth organized within and outside of school spaces, creating affinity spaces for Asian American students and their allies.

Georgia

Only after the passage of the 1965 Immigration Act did Georgia's Asian American population begin to grow, nearly doubling in size over the last two decades. Today, Asian Americans make up 4% of Georgia's total population (Skinner, 2022). Georgia's history and legacy of enslavement and anti-Black oppression has often overlooked Asian Americans in the public imagination and policy making. This invisibility is reflected in the state's curriculum, in which Asian American histories and narratives are almost nonexistent (An, 2022). Making matters worse, the conservative state legislature passed an anti-CRT bill. The Atlanta Spa shootings occurred against this backdrop when a white man killed six Asian immigrant women in 2021.

To collectively reckon with the mass murder of Asian migrant women in their local community, more than 100 Asian American parents, students, educators, activists, and allies in Georgia attended a virtual town hall meeting. The consensus from the gathering was a critical need for the teaching and learning of Asian American histories at school to interrupt racism and violence against Asian American communities. Largely composed of Asian American parents and educators, Asian American Voices for Education (AAVEd) was established with the mission to advance Asian American Studies and Ethnic Studies in Georgia's K-12 schools. Meanwhile, Asian American teachers in metro Atlanta formed the Asian American Students Committee (AASC) as a safe space for Asian American students and educators. AASC is now youth run and seeks to empower Asian American youth to enact change in their world.

Who We Are

We are three Asian American social studies teacher educators and researchers who have long been committed to supporting the teaching of Asian America in K-12 classrooms. In 2023, thanks to the generous support of the Spencer Foundation,[2] we organized three convenings for advocates of K-12 AAS in Texas, Georgia, and Virginia. As educators who live/have lived and taught in these conservative states, we are acutely aware of the past and present tensions between white supremacist legislators and community members and communities of color that demand more inclusive and accurate curriculum. In each of these states, we conducted site visits prior to organizing the convenings. At these site visits, we met with several young people who were actively working to change the systems and structures of their schools to better recognize and reflect the diverse students who attended them. After our convenings, we invited the youth to participate in individual and small group interviews so we could learn more about their advocacy work.

In relaying their stories, Asian American Critical Race Theory (AsianCrit) was a guiding conceptual framework. As an extension of Critical Race Theory, AsianCrit centers Asian American experiences and voices to disrupt white supremacy and intersectional oppressions (Chang, 1993; Iftikar & Museus, 2018). Three AsianCrit tenets were particularly relevant for our study: Asianization; (re)constructive history; and story, theory, and praxis. Asianization refers to the racialization of Asian Americans as a monolith, ignoring the diversity and complexity of Asian American experiences. (Re)constructive history underscores how Asian Americans have been largely excluded from American history and highlights the need to construct a collective Asian American historical narrative and reanalyze existing histories to incorporate the experiences of Asian Americans (Lee, 2016). Story, theory, and praxis emphasizes important connections and intersections across experiences. Together, these tenets center how Asian American youth identify and challenge the racism and intersectional oppression they face in and outside school and highlight their agency and resistance against power and oppression.

The Youth

This chapter uplifts the experiences of a dozen young people from Texas and Georgia—six from each state. As mentioned previously, we met these youth at convenings we hosted in both states and wanted to learn more about their individual paths toward advocacy and politicization. Table 2.1 lists pseudonyms for each of our participants as well as their grade level, ethnicity, and state identifiers that only capture a thin slice of who they are but illustrate their ethnic diversity and the heavy representation of high school seniors in the group. Several of the young people were familiar with each other prior to the covenings; in Texas, Crespin, Tyler, Savitri, and Mán Mán were close friends who were active in the Asian American student organization founded by Mán Mán at their urban high school. Sai and Lily, who attended a nearby Texas suburban high school, were classmates taking their school's first AAS elective course. All of these youth except for Tyler attended the Austin AAS convening.

Khi, a university sophomore, was unable to attend the Georgia AAS convening but met with the authors beforehand. While in high school, Khi was active in AASC, the group that Soo-young was leading at the time of our interviews, and Sana was also a member. April, Mishu, and Sunny[3] were well-acquainted through their work with AAVEd, which Soo-young and Sana later joined. Therefore, compared to the two groups of Texas high schoolers, the Georgia youth had more well-established interpersonal relationships and agreed to do their interviews in small groups: Soo-young and Sana interviewed together while April, Mishu, and Sunny did a separate group interview.

Table 2.1 *Study Participants*

Pseudonym*	Grade	Ethnicity	State
Crespin	12th	Mexican/Indian	Texas
Lily	12th	Korean	Texas
Mán Mán	12th	Chinese adoptee	Texas
Sai	12th	Indian	Texas
Savitri	12th	Indian	Texas
Tyler	12th	Korean/White	Texas
Sana	12th	Vietnamese	Georgia
Soo-young	12th	Vietnamese	Georgia
April	12th	Korean	Georgia
Mishu	7th	Pakistani	Georgia
Sunny	10th	Korean	Georgia
Khi	University sophomore	Vietnamese	Georgia

What the Youth Told Us

Four themes emerged from the interviews with Asian American youth: identity, curricular representation, advocacy, and articulation of educational change. We first highlight mentions of identity specific to the participants' contexts and recent sociopolitical experiences, including their observations related to curricular inclusion of Asian Americans. Next, we uplift how the youth built community spaces and engaged in a range of advocacy work and how that advocacy work shifted as the world attempted to return to "normal" after the COVID-19 pandemic. Lastly, we share their views on the changes necessary for a more just and equitable society.

Being Asian American

The youth clearly noted tensions between their own understandings of their Asian American identities and how they are perceived by their peers. Mishu, who is Pakistani American, described being met with confusion when sharing where her family is from. Peers would not even know what Pakistan was, or they would respond, "Oh, so you're basically Indian." Mishu stated, "That's kind of how I figured out that the education system wasn't really doing Asian Americans justice, because if (students) can't, if they don't even recognize the country I'm saying, then I think that we're definitely doing something wrong." While the lack of awareness suggests a general ignorance of world geography among young learners, Mishu's example also indicates that her teachers did not feel compelled to discuss the ethnoracial identities of their students in any meaningful way. Her and other students' experiences revealed how pervasive Eurocentrism remains in early childhood and elementary classrooms despite increased calls for culturally relevant pedagogies.

Lily spoke in detail about her experiences with racism at school, particularly in a charter middle school in rural Texas. "I got slurs a lot, very often," she recalled, often related to her physical appearance or the extracurricular activities she participated in. When she reported these racist incidents to her teacher, her peers would call her a snitch or tattletale. "As I get older," Lily reflected, "I look back on the situations I face(d), and I have to tell myself, that wasn't just a joke. That wasn't even just a microaggression, that was flat out racist." Hearing racial comments—both positive and negative—was a common occurrence during the COVID-19 pandemic, even from people that the youth perceived to be their friends. Also typical in their experiences was the lack of intervention by teachers who neither responded to (or perhaps themselves engaged) in outright racism, nor with meaningful curricular choices.

Examining Curricular Representation

Beyond the Asian American Studies course offered at Sai and Lily's school, youth recognized other (albeit limited) opportunities to see their and other Asian ethnicities and cultures highlighted in schools. While social studies courses would be ideally positioned to integrate Asian American content into U.S. history, none of the 12 youth recalled meaningful examples of Asian American inclusion in social studies instruction. Instead, Soo-young and Khi noted the absence of Vietnamese voices in high school textbook coverage of the Vietnam War.

Students in Texas described opportunities to read about Asian diasporas and Asian American experiences in English Language Arts courses, where Asian and Asian American books were included as options in class reading lists, such as *The Newlyweds* by Mansi Choksi, *The Ramayana*, and *Pachinko* by Min Jin Lee. Tyler and Mán Mán had *A Tale for the Time Being* by Ruth Ozeki as required summer reading for their AP Literature and Composition course, but Mán Mán noted that many students didn't read it or forgot about it since it was not read during the academic year.

While the youth stressed the importance of learning about *all* marginalized groups' experiences, they also expressed a need to learn about the histories and cultures of their ancestral homelands—a notion affirmed by Mishu's memories of discussing ethnicity as a child. Lily expanded on this need, emphasizing the ignored aspects of Asian history:

> I would have appreciated a more holistic review of the countries . . . as representative of your homeland. Because I feel, especially when we're taught about Asia, there's either ancient Asian history or just modern success. They don't teach about the gap in the middle, where there was a lot of poverty and a lot of suffering.

The periods of "poverty" and "suffering" Lily describes are significant in the Asian American experience, because if taught critically, they could help students better understand one catalyst of the Asian diaspora: Western intervention and its consequences. Educators cannot assume that second generation immigrant children have in-depth knowledge about their homelands.

Moreover, educators should certainly not expect children to serve as class experts on their homelands, as Mán Mán's teacher did by asking her to comment on China's one-child policy or as Savitri's peers did when learning about the Dutch East India Company.

Taking Action and Becoming Advocates

A clear distinction between the youth interviewed in Texas versus the youth in Georgia was the starting point for their activism. Several of the Texas youth described a range of ways that their advocacy for greater inclusion—specifically for Asian Americans but not exclusively—began prior to the COVID-19 pandemic. For Crespin, Boy Scouts was an early space where he advocated for more ethnoracial diversity; similarly, as a member of Campfire Girls, Mán Mán and her mother taught her white peers about Lunar New Year and how to use chopsticks. For Lily, her Korean church played a central role in developing her strategies for caring for others.

Savitri's advocacy journey began in 2020 in anticipation of Donald Trump running for Presidential reelection, which she described as "the most consequential election of our lives":

> I was like, I can't sit and just watch this happen! I felt like I have to do *something* . . . I learned how to text bank and we would send texts specifically to South Asian elders, and you know, just South Asians in general, to encourage them . . . to go and vote and to check their voter registration and all that kind of stuff.

Although Savitri was too young to vote in the 2020 election, she was adamant that she would find a way to make an impact. Similarly, Sai and Lily also became more politically aware through ATJ. Lily also volunteered with an Asian American media outlet and an organization centered on Asian American health initiatives. When the possibility of having an AAS course offered in their high school arose, Lily and Sai both worked diligently to support the course and later enrolled in it themselves.

In contrast, nearly every youth in Georgia identified the 2021 Atlanta spa shootings as a pivotal moment in sparking their advocacy work. For example,

Sunny described the shootings as "the most impactful (event)" as "it was 10 minutes from where I lived," but none of her teachers said a word about the murders. She realized she could not wait for change to happen. Indeed, feelings of shock, grief, anger, and frustration from the spa shootings were shared by all the youth participants in Georgia, propelling them to "do something." Khi, Soo-young, and Sana joined the student group AASC, whereas Mishu, April, and Sunny became involved in grassroots organizing for K-12 Asian American Studies through AAVEd, the parent-led advocacy group. These organizations taught them about Asian American histories and issues and engaged in various initiatives for educational justice.

As COVID-19 vaccines became widely available and the world returned to some semblance of normalcy, Khi, Soo-young, and Sana noticed declining interest and engagement from their peers. Soo-young described the first years of AASC as very popular. "But now there are literally just a few students," he lamented. "I am also an officer for a school club, and sometimes I feel like I am talking to a wall." Sana added, "It's probably the hardest part to get people to care. TikTok and social media, we look at things superficially. Desensitized." Khi, however, remained optimistic about the need to continue these efforts: "It would take a longer time, but (it is) still possible." For her, building awareness and coalitions are key to sustaining advocacy work, but she also realizes that these efforts take time and patience.

As Khi pointed out, when anti-Asian sentiment and violence were normalized, it took a tremendous act of violence for some students to see outside the school and social curriculum that taught them to passively accept whatever they and their *"forever foreigner"* families were graciously granted by the United States. When oppression, resistance, and activism were erased in classrooms, students had to find or create their own communities to learn and collaborate.

Articulating the Changes They Want to See in Education

While affinity groups and coursework were the primary areas in which youth found space to feel fully understood and learn about Asian American experiences and histories, they clearly identified the lack of support they observed from educators and school administrators. Many of the participants noted the lack of teachers of color and how teachers' lack of knowledge about race and non-European histories and cultures negatively impacted their pedagogical and interpersonal decisions. Lily and Sai specifically named administrators as part of the problem regarding course offerings and overall racist school environments.

Sai recounted student efforts to have a school-sanctioned celebration for the Hindu holiday Holi: "(The principal) labeled (Holi) a satanic activity on campus. And with that, it's very hard to be in a system that's just so discouraging for students of color." As religion is an important part of many people's identities (and is increasingly forefronted in Southern states through the centering of conservative Christian beliefs), decisions to dismiss Asian religions were viewed as deeply offensive and harmful.

Soo-young critiqued systemic issues, suggesting that we "restructure the purpose of education in such a way that it's not about training workers, but actually educating for a better society, making a more whole society where we all come together," an idea that echoed previous student suggestions about more inclusive histories and learning about cultural differences.

Relatedly, Sai came to a somber conclusion about the education system's impact on her own attitude towards learning:

> I'm not learning. I'm not curious anymore. . . . We become like machines that only care about college, and after that, finding a job and after that, building a family. . . . Even if we have all these opportunities (like Asian American Studies courses), a lot of students might not be interested in taking (them), which I think needs to happen, like it needs to change in a way that only I think advocacy and activism could do it to bring light to these problems.

For many of the youth we spoke with, their advocacy efforts for affinity spaces and Asian American curricular inclusion were grounded in their dissatisfaction with the current status quo. Yet, as Sai and Soo-young noted, larger systemic issues exist that result in schooling conditions grounded in capitalism and individual achievement rather than the democratic purposes of developing an informed citizenry working toward an equitable society.

What We Learned as Educators

The fight for educational justice and equity is a long and arduous one. Sustained commitment, as participants related, is a real concern. As memories of the pandemic and the Atlanta spa shootings fade, the passion and awareness around anti-Asian American discrimination and violence have waned. The Ethnic Studies movement of the late 1960s was marked by solidarity, but current efforts are not necessarily focused on cross-racial and ethnic alliances. Rather than students of color across communities advocating together for more faculty representation and Ethnic Studies for all, the current context seems more fragmented along racial and even ethnic lines (e.g., Korean American Studies courses in California).

Yet, participants in this study remained committed to transforming their world into one that is better for everyone. They took the time to learn from elders—both historical and present—in their own ways, (re)constructing the narratives they know are missing from school curriculum. These youth have a practical knowledge of the world, how it works, and how to creatively claim their own spaces to do advocacy work and show solidarity with others. The stories and praxis of the youth we interviewed made clear that they aren't waiting for adults to save them. Today's movement for educational transformation may not be exactly the same as what took place in the past, but what is significant is that students remain at the vanguard.

As educators, we were struck by how obvious solidarity was to these youth in Georgia and Texas. Amongst adult colleagues and co-conspirators, we often struggle to explain distinctions in racialization histories and contemporary experiences. The young people we spoke with, however, easily recognized the need to uplift our shared humanity—this was not a controversial issue for them to wrestle with, but a simple fact. While adults may be quick to write off such thinking as naive or inexperienced, we found it deeply assuring and inspiring. Much of the extant research on teaching and learning focuses on educators and quantitative measures of learning, leaving little room for students to describe their schooling experiences holistically or to articulate how their experiences beyond the classroom impact how they make meaning of what is formally taught to them and what is omitted. Our study suggests that young people hold tremendous insight into ways that curricular change might be possible if the adults in their lives take the time to listen and learn from them.

Endnotes

1. Establishing a pilot course for approval as an Innovative Course is one way to circumvent the passage of state standards for an elective in Texas. After the pilot course is completed, the course is evaluated by the Texas State Board of Education, which votes on whether the course merits Innovative Course designation. More information at https://tea.texas.gov/academics/learning-support-and-programs/innovative-courses.
2. The research reported here was made possible by grants from the Spencer Foundation (Reference #202300289) and the Youth Equity Project at Michigan State University. The views expressed are those of the authors and do not necessarily reflect the views of the Spencer Foundation or Michigan State University.
3. Sunny is the daughter of one of the authors. She agreed to participate in the post-convening group interview but her mother was not present while it was conducted.

References

An, S. (2022). Re/presentation of Asian Americans in 50 states US history standards. *The Social Studies, 113*(4), 171–184.

Chang, R. S. (1993). Toward an Asian American legal scholarship: Critical race theory, post-structuralism, and narrative space. *California Law Review, 19*, 1243–1323.

Diaz, J. (2020, September 7). *Overlooked no more: How Asian Texans shape the state* [Radio broadcast]. The Texas Standard. https://www.texasstandard.org/overlooked/.

Iftikar, J., & Museus, S. (2018). On the utility of Asian critical (AsianCrit) theory in the field of education. *International Journal of Qualitative Studies in Education, 31*(10), 935–949.

Lee, E. (2016). *The making of Asian America*. Simon & Schuster.

Skinner, J. (2022, May 31). *Asian/Pacific Islander populations in Atlanta*. The Atlanta Regional Commission. https://33n.atlantaregional.com/data-diversions/asian-pacific-islander-populations-in-atlanta

He Moʻolelo No Kupa: Cultivating Culturally Sustaining and Revitalizing Pedagogy Through Kanaka ʻŌiwi Epistemology

ʻAlohilani Okamura and Kirsten Mawyer

THE HAWAIIAN TERM moʻolelo comes from the word moʻo, which means succession or lineage, and the word ʻōlelo, which means language, speech, or to talk, and combined can mean story, history, tradition, or legend (Pukui & Elbert, 1986). In Hawaiian thought, moʻolelo calls to mind the potency of discourse and the role or stories in social and cultural life. Moʻolelo has also emerged as a significant decolonial and Indigenous methodology (Smith, 2021) for critical scholarship in Hawaiʻi (Kaliko Baker & Hailiʻōpua Baker, 2023; Lipe, 2015). In this chapter we share the moʻolelo of Kahalewaihoʻonaʻauao, a secondary teacher education program at the University of Hawaiʻi Mānoa (UHM). In so doing, we highlight how our program was designed to respond to the contemporary challenge of advancing a critical equity perspective, social justice, and cultural revitalization in teacher preparation (McCarty & Lee, 2014; Teaching Tolerance, 2018) in a Kanaka ʻŌiwi (KʻŌ), Indigenous Native Hawaiian, community-serving context.

As a writing team, we are multiracial, Kanaka ʻŌiwi and kamaʻāina (native born) to Hawaiʻi. This book chapter represents our ongoing kuleana as kumu and kupa Hawaiʻi to challenge the lingering impacts of settler colonialism in Hawaiʻi and promote KʻŌ ways of knowing in teacher education. This chapter is organized in two parts. We begin by sharing the Kahalewaihoʻonaʻauao curriculum that centers KʻŌ ways of knowing, being, and doing. Then, we use the Kupa Framework to tell 'He Moʻolelo No Kupa, the story of Indigenous epistemology and pedagogy, transformation, and teaching practice.

Papahana: Curriculum

Kahalewaihoʻonaʻauao's papahana, curriculum, centers 'O Hawaiʻi ke kahua o ka hoʻonaʻauao, 'Hawaiʻi is the foundation of learning' (Lupenui et al., 2015). On the first day of our three-semester program, teacher candidates (TCs) and faculty come together to create a lei piko, utilizing lau nahele, native flora. As we weave together the lau nahele, each person tells their moʻolelo of becoming a teacher. Together we create a lei that is a physical embodiment of our pilina kaiāulu, community connections, which are the foundation for Kahalewaihoʻonaʻauao.

Later in the first semester, we enact two projects that challenge TCs to think critically about aloha 'āina, aʻo and ea, loosely corresponding to care for place, reciprocal relationships, and sovereignty (see later for extended discussions of these terms). These projects are termed the Wai and Hau projects. The Wai project asks candidates to explore stories, historical sites, and culture to better understand K'Ō epistemology. The Hau project challenges candidates to incorporate K'Ō ways of knowing, being, and doing as they collaboratively design an interdisciplinary culture and place-based lesson.

In the second semester, TCs engage in the Hoʻokupa Hawaiʻi to become a citizen of Hawaiʻi Project. They create a community asset map and inventory of their classroom, school, and ahupuaʻa, land division extending from the mountains to the sea, in which their school is situated. Also, they engage in an inquiry into place by identifying wahi pana, places of geographic significance, moʻolelo, and history of the school. This project specifically addresses the TC's ability to: (a) know and value where their students come from; (b) identify the assets of learning environments; (c) understand the communities their students belong to; (d) establish and cultivate a relationship with 'āina, culture and history of Hawaiʻi; and (e) connect these local learning environments to global concerns.

In the final semester of the program, TCs create a social justice unit. Building on the Wai, Hau, and Hoʻokupa Hawaiʻi projects, TCs identify an injustice in the community that they teach in and design a social justice unit that addresses the injustice. This assignment helps TCs draw on KʻŌ ways of knowing, doing, and being to design learning experiences that connect secondary students to the place they live and create a strong sense of piliana kaiāulu.

Throughout the three-semester program TCs are invited on huakaʻi, learning journeys, to foster pilina kaiāulu. TCs visit loʻi kalo, wetland kalo farms, and loko iʻa, manmade sustainable fishponds, connecting students with the ʻāina. TCs also engage in huakaʻi focused on kilo, sense abilities, of the natural world including winds, rains, clouds, birds, plants, etc. as they paddle a waʻa, canoe, or ʻohi pua, gather useful plants or flowers. Immersing TCs in the practice of aloha ʻāina makes visible and advances the goals of culture-based education to increase cultural identity and competency, sociocultural maturity, Hawaiian language vitality, and positive academic outcomes. So while there is overlap in these goals, they also differ in important ways (Kawaiʻaeʻa, 2012).

In a culminating activity at the end of the program, TCs create a kīhei—a traditional KʻŌ garment worn during ceremony and protocol. Each TC designs a kāpala, stamp, depicting their *pilina*— one's relationship to place and recognition of the interconnectedness of people, place, and more-than-human entities made visible through the elements of wind, rain, and water. The kāpala design is printed to create a kīhei to be worn at convocation and commencement indicating the successful completion of the program.

Kupa Framework

During the time of Queen Liliʻuokalani, last reigning monarch of the sovereign Kingdom of Hawaiʻi, citizenship was extended to KʻŌ people of the land as well as to others who migrated to Hawaiʻi. All who became citizens of Hawaiʻi were considered kupa. Today, Kahalewaihoʻonaʻauao asks TCs to work towards becoming a contemporary citizen of this place by responsibly exploring and engaging with the rich historical and ancestral knowledge of Hawaiʻi. Essential to kupa, in the context of learning to teach in Hawaiʻi, is the kuleana, right, privilege, responsibility to "educate themselves on the history of the land they stand on and the people who they've come to educate" (Adams, 2021, p. 3). Unfortunately, the history of public education in Hawaiʻi is one of dispossession of land, loss of culture, banning of language, and subjection to settler colonialism

(Fujikane 2021; Goodyear-Kaʻopua, 2013; Tuck & Yang, 2012). In Hawaiian, kumu means the source or foundation. In the Kʻō worldview teachers are kumu because they are the source of knowledge (Kanaeokana, 2024). A primary goal of our program is to grow the capacity of TCs to become kumu kupa, teacher citizens, who incorporate Kʻō epistemologies, language, and sense of place to purposefully transform legacies of colonization through language and culture revitalization, as well as community-based accountability (McCarty & Lee, 2014; Seawright, 2014).

Seeking to understand and make sense of our secondary teacher education program Kahalewaihoʻonaʻauao after its first six cohorts, the Kupa Framework (see Figure 3.1) makes visible what we now see as key dimensions of becoming a kumu kupa. The framework consists of three primary dimensions including: Indigenous Epistemology and Pedagogy (Kahua); Transformation (Lilo); and Teaching Practice (He kumu). This framework can serve as a mechanism for teacher preparation in Hawaiʻi and with relevance across the (post)colonial Pacific to consider how teachers are embedding physical place, cultural place, and historical place in their curriculum. Programmatically, Kupa is a useful tool because it provides a common language that program faculty can use to inform iterative design to more intentionally and explicitly attend to culturally sustaining and revitalizing pedagogy through Kʻō epistemology. It makes space for us to ask questions such as: How can huakaʻi, community visits and excursions, explicitly engage TCs in Aloha ʻĀina, place-based care and responsibility? In what ways does a particular assignment foster Hoʻopili ʻĀina, relationships of care to place? How can we hold TCs accountable for designing ʻāina or land-based lesson plans?

In the remainder of this chapter, we invite you to listen to He moʻolelo no kupa and consider the question: what is the kuleana of kumu kupa?

Indigenous Epistemology and Pedagogy: Kahua

Kahalewaihoʻonaʻauao was designed as a transformative experience that provides TCs intentional opportunities to explore the legacies and injustices of settler colonialism on education in Hawaiʻi, think critically about positionality, and understand their kuleana as kumu kupa to bring Kʻō ways of knowing, being and doing into their teaching. Kahalewaihoʻonaʻauao uses the *reclamation and revitalization practices* of Aloha ʻĀina, Aʻo, and Ea as our Kahua (foundation) to help TCs cultivate culturally sustaining and revitalizing pedagogies (see Figure 3.2).

Figure 3.1 *Kupa Framework*

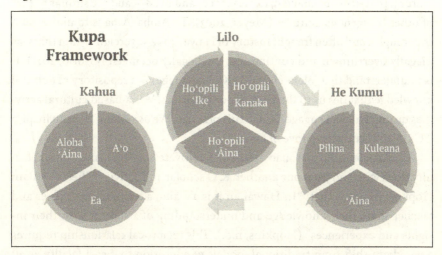

Note. The Kupa Framework tells He moʻolelo no kupa of Kahalewaihoʻonaʻauao.

Figure 3.2 *Kahua (Foundation)*

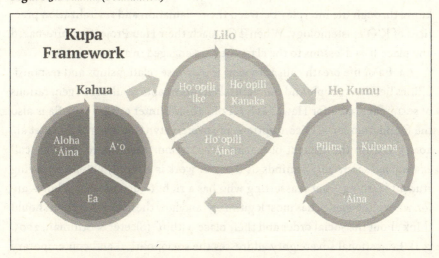

Note. Kahua is comprised of Aloha ʻĀina, Aʻo, and Ea.

Aloha ʻĀina. Aloha is a complex concept that is all at once an expression of love, empathy, kindness, compassion, and charity. ʻĀina is derived from the KʻŌ concept "that which feeds" and includes sustenance, knowledge, and inspiration. The land, sky, and ocean are considered the classroom in which cultural practices are enacted, experienced, and lived—and are similar to that of other Indigenous cultures (Meyer, 2003). To Aloha ʻĀina is to understand the complex and often fraught history of Hawaiʻi as a sovereign nation that was illegally overthrown and continues to be illegally occupied (Osorio, 2021). It is to understand that ʻōlelo Hawaiʻi (KʻŌ language) is a repository of cultural knowledge that ties us to the ways of our ancestors. ʻĀina-based cultural activities during Huakaʻi engage TCs in this practice. We use Aloha ʻĀina to inspire TCs to cultivate a deep love of Hawaiʻi.

Aʻo. Kahalewaihoʻonaʻauao uses Aʻo to cultivate how TCs and program faculty learn with and from one another. KʻŌ scholar and activist Alberta Pualani Hopkins explains that: "In Hawaiian it is aʻo aku, aʻo mai when learner and teacher share their knowledge and understanding of a subject with their insights and experiences" (Hopkins, n.d.). This reciprocal relationship requires a paradigm shift from traditional models of education that cast faculty as all knowing and TCs as receivers of information. Instead it positions all members as part of a community of inquiry working collectively to explore kuleana as kumu through the interplay between the reclamation and revitalization practices of KʻŌ epistemology. When TCs teach their Hau Project culture-based and place-based lessons to the class they are engaged in aʻo aku, aʻo mai.

Ea. Ea or life breath calls into view the diverse relationships and responsibilities between people and our natural environments resulting in generations of sustainable care for Hawaiʻi (NHPoL, 2019; Winter et al., 2018). Ea is also the foundation for KʻŌ conceptions of sovereignty (Goodyear-Kaʻopuaet al., 2024). Within the context of teacher preparation, attention to what we call *educational sovereignty* reminds us that our work is not only about improving student learning, "but reasserting who has a right to define what schools are for, whose knowledge has most legitimacy, and how the next generation should think about the social order and their place within" (Sleeter & Stillman, 2005, p. 1). Educational sovereignty addresses the sociopolitical and contemporary contexts of "asymmetrical power relations and the goal of transforming legacies of colonization" (McCarty & Lee, 2014, p. 103). Learning about moʻolelo, place names, and culturally significant sites through Hoʻokupa Hawaiʻi makes ancestral knowledge available to inform curriculum design and engage in educational sovereignty.

While Aloha ʻĀina, Aʻo, and Ea are firmly rooted in KʻŌ epistemology, TCs in our program experience these practices that extend, evolve, and transfer into contemporary forms and spaces—including classrooms. Our goal is to foster respect for and to Hawaiʻi and ensure that kuleana, service, and gratitude become part of the narrative of what it means to teach in this place. Through Aloha ʻĀina, Ea, and Kupa we ask aspiring kumu, regardless of heritage or place of origin, to center their pedagogy in *ʻO Hawaiʻi ke kahua o ka hoʻonaʻauao*, 'Hawaiʻi is the foundation of learning' (Lupenui et al., 2015).

Lilo: Transformation

Lilo is a wonderful term that summons to mind the process of transformation including senses of relinquishing, becoming, and overcoming. In ancient times, stories of gods and goddesses often spoke of their ability to transform into earthly forms. For instance, Pele the goddess of fire could turn into lava or an old or young woman. Lilo is also the act of transformation from one stage of development to another as from a caterpillar to a butterfly. Here we see Lilo as the mechanism for TCs to transform their teacher pedagogy to deepen their understanding of the relations to the people, the land, and the knowledge of a KʻŌ way of knowing.

We talked story with Kahalewaihoʻonaʻauao graduates, who we will refer to as kumu, and asked them to share their moʻolelo of how the teacher preparation program laid the foundation to cultivate culturally sustaining and revitalizing practice for their teaching journey. As we listened to what kumu said about the program, they expressed how the program challenged their own worldviews and pedagogy to incorporate KʻŌ epistemology. These conversations made visible and brought into focus three dimensions of Lilo: Hoʻopili ʻIke, Hoʻopili Kanaka, and Hoʻopili ʻĀina (see Figure 3.3).

Figure 3.3 *Lilo (Transformation)*

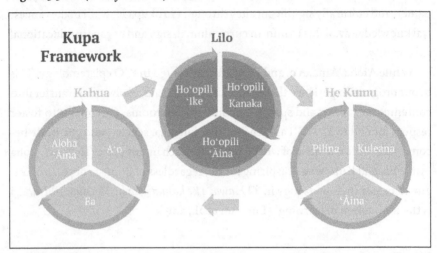

Note. Lilo is comprised of Hoʻopili ʻIke, Hoʻopili Kanaka, and Hoʻopili ʻĀina.

Hoʻopili ʻIke. Hoʻopili ʻIke is the relationship of one's positionality and ways of knowing with respect to teaching. Kumu spoke of the need to develop a KʻŌ perspective that prioritizes approaches to learning that challenge the dominant Western narrative that currently shapes public education in Hawaiʻi. One kumu noted it "should be a lens that decisions and policy is made" and that unfortunately "it feels in a lot of ways like an afterthought." Another kumu noted that our program helped them to see "having this lens that values the history of Hawaiʻi and what it could be together makes this space for others to look at their own histories." Making space for and prioritizing KʻŌ ways of knowing and doing throughout the program led to the critical insight that "you didn't have to be Hawaiian to care about this place." Through Hoʻopili ʻIke our kumu came to understand the importance of KʻŌ knowledge as foundational to teaching in Hawaiʻi.

Hoʻopili Kanaka. Hoʻopili Kanaka, building relationships and a sense of community, is another critical dimension of our kumu's Lilo. Based on our conversations, our program helped kumu view teaching as a "kākou" thing. In Hawaiian language kākou is a pronoun that is used to indicate a "we" that is inclusive of three or more people. It embodies a sense of belonging of the individual to the group. Kumu conceptualize teaching from a KʻŌ perspective as a "we" endeavor versus an "I" activity. As an example, teaching in Hawai'i means "being a part of the community, being proud of it and giving back," and should be seen as "our collective work." Developing Ho'opili Kanaka is also "taking care of our community because it's important to know where you come from and to take care of all the people and lands and everyone around you;" as a teacher, "it's such a part of our identity."

Ho'opili 'Āina. The third dimension of Lilo is Ho'opili 'Āina—developing a relationship and connection with the land and understanding one's kuleana to place. Kumu indicated that the act of mālama 'āina, caring for the land, is essential in developing the relationship between oneself and the 'āina. As teachers, their kuleana is to act as the "stewards of the land. And we are caretakers of where we live, our community. We're responsible for where we live." As teachers they believe that an essential component of their kuleana is to help students develop a relationship with 'āina because they "don't feel like they're responsible. They don't feel like they belong enough to want to be responsible." Kumu reported that intentionally creating opportunities in their curriculum for more 'āina-based learning will strengthen students' kuleana to Hawai'i.

He kumu: Teaching Practice

In the first semester of the program, TCs are introduced to the concept of kuleana as kumu (Figure 3.4). Throughout the program, students learn of the weight of the term kumu that goes beyond the English term teacher, encompassing a deep responsibility for the learning and development of one's students. In Hawaiian, we ask, "'O wai kāu kumu? Who is your kumu?" which extends to the idea: from whom did you learn from? Who has developed and nurtured your talents and shaped your K'Ō epistemology? The process to become a kumu is a complexity of responsibilities that are interwoven connections to the past, present, and future.

We talked story with Kahalewaiho'ona'auao kumu and asked them to share their mo'olelo of how the teacher preparation program laid the foundation to cultivate culturally sustaining and revitalizing pedagogy in their teaching. As we listened to their mo'olelo of implementing Aloha 'Āina, Ea, and A'o in their teaching practice they all talked about the importance of pilina, kuleana, and 'āina.

Figure 3.4 *He kumu*

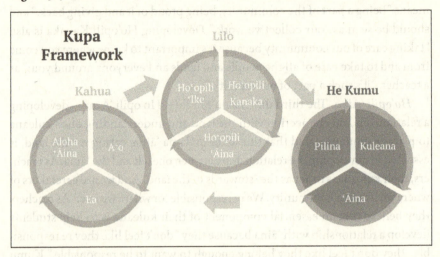

Note. He kumu is comprised of Pilina, Kuleana, and ʻĀina.

Pilina. The first dimension of He kumu is Pilina (relationships). Kumu shared that KʻŌ Epistemology and Pedagogy in practice was developed through fostering Pilina with students and between students. A mechanism for Pilina is cultivating deep cultural knowledge through teaching and sharing in small groups. KʻŌ students are "teaching their fellow classmates that maybe are not as immersed in the culture and then they are teaching each other." Pilina helps students to develop a sense of agency because when KʻŌ students share traditional ways of knowing and doing "they're bringing something valuable into the classroom" that helps them "comfortably navigate the Western and the Hawaiian." Another teacher shared that "we specifically look at traditional Hawaiian values to determine what our community is gonna look like . . . how we're gonna value each other." All the teachers we spoke to wanted to foster a sense of belonging as the foundation for successful teaching and learning. One teacher summed this up by saying, "instead of learning facts I'd rather they get a sense of community and a sense of belonging. We're all a collective. We all contribute and everybody benefits."

Kuleana. The second dimension of He kumu is Kuleana (responsibility). One teacher has her students keep Kuleana notebooks that have "a little circle that has themself, and then a bigger circle that's their ʻohana, and then a bigger circle that's community, then Hawaiʻi, and the world. They fill in with pictures and words of what their Kuleana are in those things." Their notebooks are a resource for comparing Kuleana of historical figures like King Kalākaua to their own. Similarly, another teacher has her students explore how "Kuleana is a connection of past, present, and future that can be seen in everyday practices" by examining the Kuleana of Queen Liliʻuokalani as a leader and "relating it to their histories and their lives and taking it forward." Understanding Kuleana in a historical context helps students apply KʻŌ ways of knowing and doing as they ask themselves: what is my Kuleana?

ʻĀina. The third component of He kumu is ʻāina-based learning. When teachers step outside physical classrooms, ʻāina becomes a living entity that "can rise up and teach you things that you cannot yourself as people, as Kanaka, as human beings." For example, one teacher connects to the ʻāina through traditional planting practices such as following the "traditional Hawaiian moon calendar. We would learn about varieties of kalo and what would sustain Kanaka during hurricane season, when there is drought or famine." Another teacher takes her students to "our loʻi kalo and the kids learn everything from measuring water quality to how many gallons of water comes through the loʻi each day," which helps them to understand that "water for our kūpuna, [was] that which determined everything." Another teacher has his students connect to the ʻāina through traditional planting practices by following "the traditional Hawaiian moon calendar. We would learn about varieties of kalo and what would sustain Kanaka during hurricane season, when there is drought or famine." Using ʻāina as a classroom engages students in KʻŌ ways of knowing and doing and helps students to "develop an even greater appreciation or aloha for the land."

Conclusion

In this chapter we have invited you to listen to He moʻolelo no kupa and consider the question: what is the Kuleana of kumu kupa? We began our moʻolelo by unpacking the Kahalewaihoʻonaʻauao curriculum, then we turned towards highlighting and reflecting on the relevant KʻŌ epistemologies and pedagogy through which we have come to understand how this work is advancing or doing for TCs. What we have worked to highlight here is our stance that cultivating culturally sustaining and revitalizing pedagogy for teacher preparation, and subsequent teacher practice advancing student success and achievement, is best grounded and supported through centering KʻŌ epistemologies in our program design and implementation. Importantly, as we've storied here, the transformative success of this program is evident across diverse backgrounds and positionalities in our teacher community which includes many non-Hawaiian persons. By making the conceptual and epistemological foundations of our program explicit for our TCs, we have been providing anchors for them to create, maintain, or transform their understanding of, responsibilities to, and engagements with community and place in Hawaiʻi's (post)settler, multicultural, yet Indigenous context. He moʻolelo no kupa is an epic story that, as faculty, we weave with aspiring kumu kupa to cultivate culturally sustaining and revitalizing pedagogy (McCarty & Lee, 2014) rooted in KʻŌ ways of knowing, being, and doing.

He moʻolelo no kupa
He Pipi holo kaʻao…and so the story is told.

References

Adams, K. (2021). *To teach in Hawaiʻi, educators must honor indigenous land.* EdSurge. https://www.edsurge.com/news/2021-09-20-to-teach-in-hawai-i-educators-must-honor-indigenous-land

Fujikane, C. (2021). *Mapping abundance for a planetary future: Kanaka Maoli and critical settler cartographies in Hawaiʻi.* Duke University Press.

Goodyear-Kaʻopua, N. (2013). *The seeds we planted: Portraits of a Native Hawaiian charter school.* University of Minnesota Press.

Goodyear-Kaopua, N., Hussey, I., & Wright, E. K. A. (Eds.) (2024). *A nation rising: Hawaiian movements for life, land, and sovereignty.* Duke University Press.

Hopkins, A.P. (n.d.) A o Aku A o Mai. University of Hawaii System. https://www2.hawaii.edu/~walbritt/ics212/examples/ao.htm

Kaliko Baker, C. M., & Hailiʻōpua Baker, T. (Eds.). (2023). *Moʻolelo: The foundation of Hawaiian knowledge.* University of Hawaii Press.

Kanaeokana. (2024). *Kumu Careers.* https://kanaeokana.net/wp-content/uploads/2019/11/Kumu-Careers.pdf

Kawaiʻaeʻa, K. C. (2012). *Kūkohu: Ka nānaina kaiaola o nā kaiaaʻo ʻōlelo Hawaiʻi (A Study on the cultural ecology of Hawaiian-medium and Hawaiian immersion learning environments)* [Unpublished doctoral dissertation]. Union Institute & University.

Lipe, K. (2015). Moʻolelo for transformative leadership: Lessons from engaged practice in Kanaka ʻŌiwi methodologies. In K. R. Oliveria & E. K. Wright (Eds.), *Moʻolelo and metaphor* (pp. 53–71). University of Hawaiʻi Press.

Lupenui, C. K., Sang, D. K., Seward, H., Lee, H., Walk, K., Benioini, K., Kawaiʻaeʻa, K., Albert, A., Duarte, M. P., Zeug, M., Morris, M., & Kahumoku, W. (2015). *Nā Hopena Aʻo HĀ Statements: BREATHE.* Department of Education State of Hawaii. http://www.hawaiipublicschools.org/DOE%20Forms/NaHopenaAoE3.pdf

McCarty, T., & Lee, T. (2014). Critical culturally sustaining/revitalizing pedagogy and Indigenous education sovereignty. *Harvard Educational Review, 84*(1), 101–124.

Meyer, M. A. (2003). *Hoʻoulu, Our time of becoming: Hawaiian epistemology and early writings.* ʻAi Pohaku Press.

Native Hawaiian Place of Learning Office (NHPoL). (2019). *Aloha ʻāina.* https://manoa.hawaii.edu/nhpol/aloha-aina/

Osorio, J. H. (2021). *Remembering our intimacies: Moʻolelo, Aloha ʻAina, and Ea.* University of Minnesota Press.

Pukui, M. K., & Elbert, S. H. (1986). *Hawaiian dictionary: Hawaiian-English English-Hawaiian revised and enlarged edition.* University of Hawaii Press.

Seawright, G. (2014). Settler traditions of place: Making explicit the epistemological legacy of white supremacy and settler colonialism for place-based education. *Educational Studies, 50*(6), 554–572.

Sleeter, C., & Stillman, J. (2005). Standardizing knowledge in a multicultural society. *Curriculum Inquiry, 35*(1), 27–46.

Smith, L. T. (2021). *Decolonizing methodologies: Research and Indigenous peoples.* Bloomsbury Publishing.

Teaching Tolerance. (2018). *Social justice standards: The teaching tolerance anti-bias framework.* https://www.learningforjustice.org/sites/default/files/2020-09/TT-Social-Justice-Standards-Anti-bias-framework-2020.pdf

Tuck, E., & Yang, K. W. (2012). Decolonization is not a metaphor. *Decolonization: Indigeneity, Education, & Society, 1*(1), 1–40.

Winter, K. B., Beamer, K., Vaughan, M. B., Friedlander, A. M., Kido, M. H., Whitehead, A. N., Akutagawa, M. K., Kurashima, N., Lucas, M. P., & Nyberg, B. (2018). The moku system: Managing biocultural resources for abundance within social-ecological regions in Hawaiʻi. *Sustainability, 10*(10), 3554.

CHAPTER 4

Finding and Building Community: Stop Waiting for Someone Else

Jung Kim

ASIAN AMERICANS ARE often represented as being the "model minority" (Poon et al., 2016) in schools, the hardworking, overachieving student that is "over-represented" in advanced and gifted classes. In the current debates around affirmative action, they are also used as a racial wedge to demonstrate to other marginalized groups that racism and systemic inequity are not real (Kim, 1999). Often stereotyped as unfeeling and inscrutable, hyper-competitive and robotic, these racist tropes have obfuscated the humanity of Asian Americans and the very real need they have to be acknowledged as part of America's fabric. The truth is though, that Asian Americans—like all human beings—need community and connection to their history. Drawing upon tenets of Asian Critical Race Theory (Iftikar & Museus, 2018), this personal narrative explores how I was racialized as an Asian American in schools, my struggles in navigating inequitable systems to pursue my development as a scholar, and the ways in which these experiences have shaped my desire to help further spaces of community and collaboration for the Asian American community.

Asian Critical Race Theory (AsianCrit) is an offshoot of critical race theory (CRT) (Bell, 1995). CRT is built upon the centrality and intersectionality of race and racism and commitment to social justice and prioritizes the experiential knowledge and voices of people of color (Crenshaw, 1995). AsianCrit grew out of Robert Chang's (1993) work to examine how the model minority myth and the forever foreigner trope (Tuan, 1998) shaped the ways Asian Americans were racialized in this country. Museus and Iftikar (2013) then developed a seven-tenet framework to use in education. The two tenets from Museus and Iftikar most relevant in this chapter are: *(re)constructive history*, which underscores the importance of (re)constructing authentic historical Asian American narratives, and *story, theory, and praxis*, which underscores the importance of counterstories.

So much of what this chapter is about is the erasure of Asian American stories and the importance of sharing our stories and experiences to further build and develop our communities.

PK-12 Experiences

Like thousands of other Asian American kids east of California (30% of the Asian American population lives in California; Pew Research Center, 2022), I grew up in predominantly white spaces. Although born in Korea, I migrated with my grandmother to meet my parents in the Chicago suburbs at the age of 4. We lived in suburban communities that were majority white, and I attended Catholic schools which were even whiter. My family was usually one of the only Asian American families in the school or parish. As a result, I was confronted as a kid with questions about where I was "from," confusion over whether I was Chinese or Japanese (I was offered no other option), and a fair amount of racial taunting about my non-white features. As a result, my Korean or Asian self and my school self felt relatively separate (Lee et al., 2016). Home was for Korean food, language, and customs. School was for all things "American." I never really considered what it meant for me to be Korean American, rather it felt like I was Korean in one space and sort of American in another ("off brand" my daughter might call it, as I wasn't readily identified as American despite my own claims to the label).

When my family moved from the suburbs of Philadelphia to the suburbs of Chicago, I experienced culture shock in many ways, particularly as I entered public school. While not very diverse by most measures, it was more diverse than what I was used to. The community had a significant Asian population, and I struggled to understand my place in it. One of my most vivid memories from the first day of school was a group of Korean American girls asking me which church I went to. After much confusion, we realized that we were not from the same faith background (Koreans have separate words for Catholic churches and Protestant churches). From there through high school, it felt like I picked all the "wrong" things as an Asian American student. I was in marching band instead of orchestra, debate and the literary magazine instead of math team, was Catholic instead of "Christian," and was not in the AP science or math classes. These "wrong" choices meant that I was in spaces that were mostly white, so most of my friends were also white.

This sense of being "not Asian enough" is one I wrestle with even now (Hsieh et al., 2020) and did not go unnoticed by others, as I got called a "twinkie" in the lunchroom one day my first year of high school. Embarrassingly, I had to have this person explain the term to me as I had never heard the term before. The fact it was used against me by a biracial Japanese American kid who mostly hung with Koreans confused me further. I still felt very Korean at home and wasn't trying to "act white," but I also could not determine what it meant to be Asian or "Asian enough" in others' eyes. It seemed like you could be "super Asian" and only hang out with other Asian kids and do "Asian" things like orchestra or math team, or be "whitewashed." There was no sense of what being Asian *American* meant—not in my classrooms, the curriculum, or in my community. Like the outdated hyphenated "Asian-American" label (Fine, 1994), my sense of identity was one forged in two separate selves joined together at the hyphen— not a fully realized and distinct Asian American identity.

College

Even as I left for college, I wrestled with what it meant to be Asian American. While I saw Asian American students in my Asian American literature classes, I can only think of one other English literature class in which I had another Asian American student—an upper-level class junior year. I felt a sense of incongruity as an Asian American English major. When I registered for my first Asian American literature class my second semester of college on a lark, I had no idea what to expect. It was in this class that I realized that being Asian American and a literature major did not have to be mutually exclusive, and where I encountered Asian Americans thinking and writing about race and family and culture and identity. From there, I became involved with an Asian American student activist organization and registered for another Asian American literature class.

Mostly apolitical in high school, the confluence of these choices shaped my growing political and racial awareness. It was in these spaces that I finally learned about Asian Americans—the complicated histories of im/migration, Japanese incarceration, feelings of being "Other" but also in-between, solidarity efforts with other movements, and about generations of Asian American activities. And it was here that I found other Asian Americans who believed in issues of social justice and equity, who were interested in the arts and activism, movement building and solidarity, and where being Asian wasn't just about being good at math or going to the right church or speaking your heritage language fluently. I no longer had to choose to represent as Asian in some spaces and American in others, but could encompass being fully Asian American in all spaces. Seeing this kind of full-throated Asian American representation was healing and important for me, and something I would try to do for others in the future.

The fact that I never encountered any of this in my PK-12 education is problematic. Despite Asians having been on this continent since the 1400s (Lee, 2015), I learned nothing in schools about Asian American history or accomplishments. I—and many of my peers—grew up on a steady diet of Asian Americans being newly arrived immigrants and as the model minority myth and forever foreigner trope. Being Asian American always felt like bridging two distinct worlds and not a unified identity. The fact that I did not see other ways of being until college is not right. All individuals should be able to see a spectrum of identities possible for them.

Academia

After college, I became a high school English teacher. I ended up teaching at an all-Black school where I was the only teacher who was neither Black nor white. My students who lived in one of the most highly segregated cities in the country were confused by my Asianness. I had to do a lot of teaching at school about what it meant for me to be Korean specifically and Asian broadly, get my students to engage in a lot of unlearning of stereotypes about Asians, and constantly navigate what it meant for me to not exist within the Black-white dichotomy of race in the school and city. When I started graduate school to get my doctorate in education, I briefly considered investigating what it meant to be Asian American and racialized in such a binary but I didn't think there would be interest or support for such a topic. I also chafed against what I felt was an unspoken expectation that people from marginalized backgrounds should study their "own" people. Later I would realize (1) this need to "prove" myself as a scholar by studying something that was *not* Asian American was internalized racism, but also (2) few non-Asian scholars seem particularly interested in Asian American issues or are aware of the long history of Asian American history and solidarity—if I didn't do it, then who would?

The racial dynamics of academia confused me. Being a first-generation graduate student and a woman of color, I struggled with navigating large academic conferences. I didn't feel comfortable within traditional white literacy scholarship, nor did I find ready access to the networks of scholars into which I saw my Black and Latinx friends being enfolded. The few Asian scholars I saw seemed to all be transnational. As with my high school teaching context, I struggled to understand where I stood in relation to others and how to seek out the community and support I longed for.

While I still did not find a space specific to being Asian American, I did eventually find one that supported me professionally, as a scholar of color, through participating in the National Council of Teachers of English's (NCTE) Cultivating New Voices Among Scholars of Color (CNV) mentoring program. In an organization that has over 10,000 members, the NCTE conference can be an overwhelmingly white space, and CNV was a lifeline for me. Despite the close community formed with other emergent scholars in CNV, I still longed for a space that was Asian American, particularly for other Asian Americans like me, who were in literacy and literature-related spaces.

For years, I had attended NCTE and noted the Black, Latinx, and American Indian caucuses. I wondered about the absence of an Asian American Caucus and brought it up repeatedly with others in the hopes that someone somewhere would start one. After doing this for several years, I finally accepted that if I wanted this space, I would have to start the caucus myself.

It was extremely slow going at first. My first year of the caucus (2015), I struggled to get just a handful to attend. I had made small flyers to leave in central locations at the conference to try and attract people, but they didn't seem particularly effective. Because Asians are generally (although not always) physically identifiable, I could see that there were many more Asian American educators at NCTE than were showing up at the caucus. I racked my brain and resorted to a tactic from my college days where I used handbills to promote concerts on campus. Cue the cringe. I began approaching people who looked Asian to me and asking, "Are you Asian?" (awkward) and handing them a handbill with the caucus information. I couldn't find it in me to do this to every Asian-looking person I saw, but I did the best I could.

This is how I found my collaborator, co-author, and co-conspirator, Dr. Betina Hsieh, through a handbill on an escalator. Eventually, through awkward handbilling, more people came and began to handbill (people who are probably way better and more approachable than this introvert), tell their friends and colleagues, and use social media to recruit. Now, our Asian American Caucus events regularly host around 40 or more people. We have had people burst into tears finding a room full of Asians at a primarily white event; people say they had planned on not coming back to NCTE until they found us; and people who have found whole new lines of inquiry and scholarship, developing confidence to explore Asian American–related literature and experiences in education. This space of community (Kim & Hsieh, 2022) has been one many people have longed for and not realized existed.

This space of community and connection was particularly important and needed during the COVID-19 pandemic. We hosted several virtual events that not only allowed us to connect with one another in the midst of the onslaught of anti-Asian attacks and rhetoric, but it also allowed us a space to laugh and still find joy.

This sense of community has created such a rich and productive space. In 2015, the NCTE annual convention had one session that included the word Asian American—a session I was in. In 2016, there was again just one session, and that was the Asian American open forum session (i.e., the meeting for the caucus). In 2023, there were seven presentations that included "Asian American" in the title. In the years since those initial awkward meetings, the group has become a home place for many Asian American educators at NCTE. And while there are different "official" definitions of who is considered Asian American, we have purposely worked to create a space where the self-claiming and self-definition of being Asian American lies solely within the individual. This mirrors the origin of the word Asian American, a word that came out as a result of trying to self-define and name who they were and as a counter to the age-old "Oriental" (Kim & Hsieh, 2022).

"Asian American" was created as a politically unifying term, not a racial one, and I adhere closely to that understanding. To this end, multiple multiracial Asian Americans who may not immediately present as Asian have found community and belonging with us, even collaborating to create conference sessions about their experiences. We have also tried to reach out and include Pacific Islanders, Native Hawaiians, and others who are often overlooked in their representation within Asian America. Finally, we've discussed the possibilities of intentionally including Arab Americans within our caucus or supporting them as they've sought to create a similar affinity space for themselves.

Building in and From Community

Just as I constantly questioned (and continue to question) how Asian Americans were/are so often left out of spaces that are supposedly for people of color or meant to be inclusive, I also challenge myself to be as inclusive and welcoming in the use of the Asian American umbrella term as I can. I make sure that I do not overgeneralize my experiences as standing in for those of all Asian Americans. I heartily appreciate Dr. Noreen Naseem Rodríguez, who always pushes me to consider if I'm consciously including South Asians when I talk about Asian Americans, whether it be literature or history or research. I'm particularly aware that when there is an over-representation of East Asians in an Asian American space that we do not dominate conversations or assume all experiences are similar to those of East Asians and vice versa.

I am also very aware of how my presence and representation in diverse spaces allows others to see that Asian Americans are not a monolith, that we can be many things. In a community that often talks about race but very much within a Black-white binary, I made a conscious choice to run for my local school board and to publicly run with a friend on a women of color platform. It is important for me to be a public Asian American figure and fight for racial equity, to show solidarity, and to talk about race.

I believe that as a result of this organizational work and the collaborative relationships I have developed with others along the way, I finally found the courage to pursue Asian American research in my own scholarship. I began to understand how overlooked Asian Americans are in educational research. As a result of the model minority myth, scholars generally do not think Asian Americans have "issues" to study. Even in conducting a literature review for a professional organization report (Willis et al., 2021), I realized that there was woefully limited scholarship on Asian Americans in education, particularly in the field of literacy, and I knew many of the contemporary scholars that were doing this work. In other words, "If I don't do this, who will? If *we* don't do this, who will?" So, I began the work I had considered (but dismissed) so long ago in graduate school, exploring the racialization of Asian American teachers in PK-12 education.

Before the national teacher study Dr. Betina Hsieh and I conducted (Kim & Hsieh, 2021), I had conducted a pilot study (Kim, 2022) with a dozen Asian American teachers in the Midwest, primarily in the Chicagoland area. This was my first project of the heart. I wanted to see if the experiences I'd had as an Asian American educator were unique to me or if there were similarities with others. While interviewing other Asian American educators in the study, I was both frustrated and relieved to discover that I was not alone. Others—across both studies—echoed similar experiences with not seeing themselves in the curriculum and struggling with their understandings of race. One teacher in the pilot specifically expressed her frustration in not grappling with her racial identity until well into her 20s. This false belief that Asian Americans are doing "just fine" and thus do not need culturally relevant education, access to their history, or opportunities to grapple with their race and identity formation has been a harmful one. When I was growing up, we did not even learn about Japanese incarceration despite studying WWII, or the Chinese railroad workers despite studying the transcontinental railroad. I did not see a place for myself within the fabric of America.

Yet there is hope. Asian American curriculum mandates like the TEAACH (Teaching Equitable Asian American Community History) Act in Illinois are fighting to change this. By requiring schools to teach about Asian American history and contributions, youth (of all backgrounds) today can learn about themselves, the experiences of those who came before—including their activism and solidarity work, and about each other. Initiatives like these not only allow for the intellectual and racial development of all students but also serve to further humanize and contextualize Asian Americans within the fabric of America.

Looking Forward

I think about the stereotypes that exist about Asian Americans, from the lonely nerd to the hypersexual temptress to the sneaky foreign spy, and the ways in which we have been demonized and marginalized, erased from history and school books. It is this systematic erasure and misrepresentation that allows others to see Asian Americans as less human and makes it easier for others to attack us as foreigners, but it also keeps us in the dark about our own rich history and the activism of which our communities have long been a part. Asian Americans have not been passive victims in history. They have been on the ground organizing and working in solidarity with other communities for centuries.

For much of my PK-12 career, I believed that individual hard work and motivation were what would drive me to success. However, as I've gotten older I've learned how important community and collaboration are to me—not just to my scholarship but to my ongoing development as a human being. And while I may have kickstarted the first Asian American Caucus meeting on my own, it was through the collaborative efforts of all the people who kept showing up—particularly Dr. Betina Hsieh—that the group has become so robust. Dr. Valerie Kinloch—former president of the National Council for Teachers of English—drew upon a June Jordan quote for the year she was conference chair: "We are the ones we have been waiting for." Dr. Hsieh and I have found ourselves over and over realizing that we cannot wait for someone else to create the space, take the lead, organize the event. We must do the work in front of us and "make the road while walking."

To this end, I encourage all of the readers of this chapter to think about how you can create spaces of community and belonging—where each student can learn about themselves, learn about others, and learn how to address the ways in which inequity and injustice keep us separate and apart. We need to do this for all of our students, not just those that seem the loudest or the most at risk, but pay particular attention to those whose histories have been erased and obscured. I was a quiet student through most of my K-12 education, and I probably slipped through the cracks because I was "just another quiet Asian girl." However, I was hurting in school and needed a connection all that time. This seems particularly important in our post-pandemic era where students are struggling with anxiety, disconnection, and loneliness.

References

Bell, D. (1995). Who's afraid of critical race theory? *University of Illinois Law Review, 4*, 893–910.

Chang, R. S. (1993). Toward an Asian American legal scholarship: Critical race theory, post-structuralism, and narrative space. *California Law Review, 81*, 1241.

Crenshaw, K. (1995). Mapping the margins. *Critical race theory: The key writings that formed the movement, 3*(15), 357–383.

Fine, M. (1994). Working the hyphens: Reinventing the self and other in qualitative research. In N. Denzin & Y. S. Lincoln (Eds.), *Handbook of qualitative research* (pp. 70–82). Sage. https://doi.org/1077800407309328

Hsieh, B., Kim, J., & Protzel, N. (2020). Feeling not Asian enough: Issues of heritage-language loss, development, and identity. *Journal of Adolescent & Adult Literacy, 63*(5), 573–576. https://doi.org/10.1002/jaal.1030

Iftikar, J. S., & Museus, S. D. (2018). On the utility of Asian critical (AsianCrit) theory in the field of education. *International Journal of Qualitative Studies in Education, 31*(10), 935–949. https://doi.org/10.1080/09518398.2018.1522008.

Kim, C. J. (1999). The racial triangulation of Asian Americans. *Politics & Society, 27*(1), 105–138. https://doi.org/10.1177/0032329299027001005.

Kim, J. (2022). "Never anything about the Asian experience": An AsianCrit analysis of Asian American teachers in the Midwest. *Multicultural Perspectives, 24*(2), 52–61. https://doi.org/10.1080/15210960.2022.2067857

Kim, J., & Hsieh, B. (2021). *Challenging Asian American teachers' invisibility: Understanding marginalization, persistence, and resistance in the U.S. educational system.* Routledge.

Kim, J., & Hsieh, B. (2022). "I do not have to stand alone": Finding ourselves reflected in the community of NCTE's Asian/American Caucus. *Voices in the Middle, 29*(4), 48–49. https://doi.org/10.58680/vm202231929

Lee, E. (2015). *The making of Asian America: A history.* Simon and Schuster

Lee, S. J., Park, E., & Wong, J. H. S. (2016). Racialization, schooling, and becoming American: Asian American experiences. *Educational Studies, 53*(5), 492–510. https://doi.org/10.1080/00131946.2016.1258360.

Museus, S. D., & Iftikar, J. (2013). An Asian critical theory (AsianCrit) framework. *Asian American Students in Higher Education, 31*(10), 18–29. https://doi.org/10.1080/09518 398.2018.1522008.

Pew Research Center. (2022, October 10). *Key facts about Asian Americans, a diverse and growing population.* https://www.pewresearch.org/short-reads/2021/04/29/key-facts-about-asian-americans/

Poon, O., Squire, D., Kodama, C., Byrd, A., Chan, J., Manzano, L., Furr, S., & Bishundat, D. (2016). A critical review of the model minority myth in selected literature on Asian Americans and Pacific Islanders in higher education. *Review of Educational Research, 86*(2), 469–502. https://doi.org/10.3102/0034654315612205

Tuan, M. (1998). *Forever foreigners or honorary whites? The Asian ethnic experience today.* Rutgers University Press.

Willis, A. I., Smith, P., Kim, J., & Hsieh, B. (2021). *Racial justice in literacy research.* Literacy Research Association. https://lira.memberclicks.net/assets/docs/Final%20-%20 LRA%202021%20Racial%20Justice%20in%20Literacy%20Research.pdf

The Moment We Begin

Theodore Chao

THE FIRST FOUR chapters in this collection of powerful stories, narratives, and histories center the experiences of Asian American Native Hawaiian Pacific Islander (AANHPI) students, educators, and communities. These stories invite us to challenge old narratives, break down stereotypes, and recognize new paths forward in our schools and communities. But to me, the most powerful part of these chapters is not just the knowledge being dropped, but how personal they are. While the authors write about education, pedagogy, and curriculum, these chapters really reveal the ways forging and honoring AANHPI identity is an ongoing collective effort, involving all parts of our lives, our struggles, and shared resilience. And these stories give us a glimpse of how all of us can start this journey.

The Power of Our Stories

The core of this section is the recognition of just how powerful storytelling is in changing our world. As one of the core tenets of Asian Critical Race Theory (AsianCrit), stories, theory, and praxis are not just inextricably linked, but one of the mechanisms for which we create a shared humanity and solidarity (Iftikar & Museus, 2018). We can't create change unless we begin with and recognize our stories.

And so, the stories shared in this opening section build off another AsianCrit tenet: (re)constructive history, retelling our narratives in ways that are honest, critical, and empowering. The authors here break down the one-dimensional stories imposed upon us and construct new narratives that reflect the richness of our AANHPI experiences. And as these stories unfold, they reveal how we move from understanding the problem to taking action—praxis .

I loved reading the stories in this section. Whether it's Richard Mui's "Asian American History 101: What Every Person Needs to Know," which summarizes 175 years of AANHPI history with stories from the perspective of the actual Asian Americans; Jung Kim's "Finding and Building Community: Stop Waiting for Someone Else," which recounts her struggle to find a community among literacy educators; the youth organizing and building their own community in Noreen Naseem Rodríguez, Esther June Kim, and Sohyun An's "I think that we're definitely doing something wrong": Learning From Asian American Youth About Identity, Advocacy, and Educational Change;" or 'Alohilani Okamura and Kirsten Mawyer's "He Mo'olelo No Kupa: Cultivating Culturally Sustaining and Revitalizing Pedagogy Through Kanaka 'Ōiwi Epistemology," which shows a Native Hawaiian lens on culturally sustaining and revitalizing pedagogy, these stories are what push our work forward. It's in their telling and retelling that we recognize our shared humanity and see the possibility of change.

Stereotypes and the Dangers of Misrepresentation

From the moment Asian Americans set foot in the United States, we've been battling stereotypes. Whether it's the image of the "quiet, studious Asian" or the "forever foreigner," these harmful narratives have shaped how others see us and, in turn, how we see ourselves. Mui's chapter takes us back to the beginning, showing how the exclusion and marginalization of Asians from the very start built a foundation of harmful stereotypes that persist to this day. This history, from the Chinese Exclusion Act of 1882 to the racialized violence against South Asian laborers, are not just part of a distant past, but haunting episodes that echo in today's schools. For instance, the blatant lie of Ohio newcomers eating pets has been dangerously amplified in the media, even echoed by a presidential candidate in xenophobic language that echoes the rat-eating and dog-eating accusations of Asian Americans for more than 150 years (Najarro, 2024; Takaki, 1998).

Without a critical examination of AANHPI history in schools, stereotypes dangerously become the only narrative that students ever see. Students learn that Asian Americans are "good at math," "silent workers," or even "robotic overachievers," and these ideas stick. Worse yet, students who don't see themselves represented in the curriculum are left to figure out their identity through the fog of these misrepresentations. Kim recounts growing up in predominantly white spaces where her identity was always questioned or misread. Her story reminds us that when schools fail to teach authentic AANHPI histories, they reinforce a monolithic, dehumanizing view of who we are.

This failure in the curriculum not only perpetuates stereotypes—it erases the complex and diverse stories of AANHPI communities. Stories of resistance, solidarity, and cultural richness are left out, creating a void where harmful stereotypes thrive. The invisibility of these histories, particularly in education, feeds a dangerous narrative that dehumanizes AANHPIs and leaves many students feeling like their identities do not matter. These chapters remind us of the importance of reclaiming those stories, of bringing visibility to the people and experiences that have been erased or misrepresented. Whether it's through the retelling of Chinese American contributions to building railroads or the struggles of Southeast Asian refugees, these narratives serve as essential counterstories to the dominant discourse that too often ignores or distorts AANHPI lives (Solórzano & Yosso, 2002).

Additionally, as we examine Okamura and Mawyer's chapter, "He Moʻolelo No Kupa: Cultivating Culturally Sustaining and Revitalizing Pedagogy Through Kanaka ʻŌiwi Epistemology," we see just how Native Hawaiian and Pacific Islander voices have been invisibilized within the broader AANHPI discourse. This was the first time I've ever heard of the Kahalewaihoʻonaʻauao curriculum or the Kupa Framework, powerful examples of teacher education rooted in ancestral and community knowledge. It reminded me that, too often, the stories of East and South Asians dominate our conversations, overshadowing the histories and contributions of Native Hawaiians and Pacific Islanders. This chapter's detail on the ways a teacher education program in Hawaiʻi works to bring those voices from the margin to the center by revolving around Kanaka ʻŌiwi ways of knowing, being, and doing in the preparation of future teachers. By grounding their pedagogy in aloha ʻāina, reciprocal relationships, and sovereignty, the program cultivates a deep cultural connection between teachers and the land, a connection that is essential for Native Hawaiian education. A powerful reminder that AANHPI is not a monolithic identity and that our efforts toward educational justice must uplift *all* voices within our complex, diverse, and intersecting community (Museus & Kiang, 2009).

The Model Minority Myth: Will This Be the Last Generation Dealing With This?

For me, one of the most pervasive and damaging stereotypes in my life is the model minority myth, which paints AANHPI students as academically gifted, hard working, and problem free. This myth might seem positive on the surface, but it ignores the diversity within AANHPI communities and the unique struggles many in our community face. It also pits AANHPI against other marginalized groups, suggesting that systemic racism doesn't exist—after all, if Asian Americans can "succeed," why can't everyone else?

Mui describes the ways that the model minority myth was created through "revised immigration laws that privileged scientists and medical professionals being awarded visas to the United States, particularly from East and South Asia" after the Immigration and Nationality Act of 1965. This selective immigration created a new population of Asian Americans that were only allowed to be American because of their academic success, creating a dangerous myth that not just conflated Asianness with doing well in math and science, but creating competition within Asian Americans to define themselves only in these characters.

Kim's story describes her own personal struggles with this myth, recalling the pain of not fitting into the mold of what a "real" Asian American student was supposed to be. She wasn't on the math team, didn't play violin, and didn't take advanced science courses. Instead, she found herself in spaces that were predominantly white, feeling disconnected from the stereotypical expectations placed on her. The weight of the model minority myth is suffocating, making our children feel like they are never enough—not smart enough, not "Asian" enough, and not enough to matter.

What's more, the model minority myth erases the stories of those who don't fit the narrative of success. It silences the struggles of Southeast Asian refugees,

Pacific Islanders, and others whose experiences are far from the glossy image of AANHPI "achievement." I love the way that Kim even references how Noreen Naseem Rodríguez, the author of another chapter in this section, reminds her that AANHPI is a solidarity group inclusive of South Asians too. Another reminder of how certain voices can be invisible, even within our collective AANHPI discourse.

And speaking of Rodríguez, her chapter with Esther June Kim and Sohyun An shows the power of young AANHPI activists organizing against these myths in states like Texas and Georgia. These students show how to resist the pressure to conform to the model minority ideal and are instead advocating for a curriculum that reflects their full humanity.

My heart wept when Sai, one of the Texas students in this chapter, points out the ways that the AANHPI histories are not just invisible, but viewed as non-American, when her principal labeled a school-sanctioned Holi celebration as a satanic activity. The beautiful young people in this chapter recognize that this myth dangerously removes the kindness, attention, and care that other marginalized groups receive. This new generation isn't having it. They're pushing back, organizing, and speaking out, demanding that their schools reflect the reality of who they are—rather than relying on cookie-cutter stereotypes.

In reading this section, I'm overcome with hope that the model minority myth dies with this generation, as the young people of today fight for their own nuanced, complex stories about who they are and bury these racist stereotypes once and for all.

Looking Forward

Through these stories, we see that education isn't just something that happens in classrooms. It's happening in community centers, in grassroots organizing spaces, and in everyday conversations between students and their teachers. It's happening every time a student like Mishu from Georgia speaks up about the absence of her Pakistani identity in the curriculum. It's happening when teacher candidates in Hawaii design place-based lessons that center the stories of their local communities. Each of these moments is a beginning—a step toward reclaiming what has been erased and building something better in its place.

As we look to the future, we see that the work of reshaping AANHPI education is already underway. The stories in this book are evidence that a new generation of students, educators, and activists are taking up the mantle of resistance and advocacy. They are challenging the stereotypes that have limited our potential, dismantling the model minority myth and creating spaces where all AANHPI identities thrive.

Our young people are telling our stories. They are moving beyond the binaries of "Asian" or "American," "success" or "failure." They are embracing the complexities of our identities and histories, creating a future where every student can see themselves reflected in the curriculum, not as a stereotype, but as a full, complex human being.

This is the moment we begin.

References

Iftikar, J. S., & Museus, S. D. (2018). On the utility of Asian critical (AsianCrit) theory in the field of education. *International Journal of Qualitative Studies in Education, 31*(10), 935–949.

Museus, S. D., & Kiang, P. N. (2009). Deconstructing the model minority myth and how it contributes to the invisible minority reality in higher education research. *New Directions for Institutional Research, 2009*(142), 5–15.

Najarro, I. (2024, September 11). Amid political attacks on Ohio immigrants, how schools can support newcomers. *Education Week.* https://www.edweek.org/teaching-learning/amid-political-attacks-on-ohio-immigrants-how-schools-can-support-newcomers/2024/09.

Solórzano, D. G., & Yosso, T. J. (2002). Critical race methodology: Counter-storytelling as an analytical framework for education research. *Qualitative Inquiry, 8*(1), 23–44.

Takaki, R. (1998). *Strangers from a different shore: A history of Asian Americans* (Updated and Revised). Little, Brown and Company.

Part II

Building an Inclusive Movement

CHAPTER 5

A Deliberate Choice: Multiple Consciousness and K-12 Asian American Studies Praxis

Edward R. Curammeng, Giselle Cunanan, and Cheralen A. Valdez

As SCHOOLS, SCHOOL districts, and states begin to institutionalize Ethnic Studies (ES) in policy and practice, we examine the ways Asian American Studies (AAS), a subfield of ES, has informed teachers' praxis at the K-12 level. Drawing from K-12 Asian American teachers' experiences, we weave "Radical Asian American Studies pedagogy" with legal scholar Mari Matsuda's earlier work (1992) around "multiple consciousness"—the "deliberate choice to see the world from the standpoint of the oppressed" to understand how these teachers utilize AAS in their classrooms with the students they serve. We provide pedagogical examples of how both teachers and teacher educators can tap into the affordances of AAS in ways most of the field of teacher education has yet to consider. The chapter closes by offering insights for elementary and secondary educators and teacher educators on why it is necessary to make a deliberate choice to engage K-12 Asian American Studies praxis across Asian America, ES, and beyond and how they can do this work in community.

The confluence of education and Ethnic Studies is more apparent than ever. California's historic passage of Assembly Bill 101 will require all students attending a public high school to take a course in ES. The 2021 assembly bill has spurred many teacher education programs and school districts alike to consider how they will prepare teachers to adhere to the new requirement. A sobering reality is that there are significantly few ES-trained or AAS-trained teacher ed-ucators in education, just as the field must consider how it will prepare teachers to meet the state's mandate. Scholars and community members connected to ES share apprehension about the kind of ES that will unfold. In other words, how do we ensure ES not be reduced to a sanitized telling of heroes and holidays and maintain ES' concern with power, structures, and systems and the center-ing of Black, Indigenous, communities of color? We write from the vantage of being students of ES and AAS, now professors and scholars whose work is at the nexus of ES and education. It was through AAS specifically that our critical consciousness was raised; AAS became a "protective factor" or barrier against everyday and institutional racism (Acevedo & Solórzano, 2023) as we navigate fields through interdisciplinarity. That is, we are at once Asian Americanists and ES scholars—two of whom reside in education and one whose work engages critical ES. Marginality is a part of our consciousness; it informs how we move in the academy, how we support our students and prepare future teachers, and how we push our respective fields with the activist energies and political imper-ative characteristic of ES education. In this way, we make sense of our worlds and un/learn the limits of our formal schooling, offering insights to the tensions concerning how we should prepare future ES teachers.

Our chapter highlights the experiences of K-12 Asian American teachers. All of the teachers studied and learned AAS and ES in their teacher education program. The program provided a less common experience we hope can be accessed to more future teachers not solely because of the rollout of ES-focused policies. Rather, because the value of ES in teacher education is transformative and political, reflective and trenchant. We take up legal scholar Mari Matsu-da's (1992) conceptualization of "multiple consciousness" to craft a portrait of possibilities for the field and for the future learnings of all students. Matsuda (1992) describes multiple consciousness as involving "that shifting in and out, that tapping of a consciousness from beyond and bringing it back to the place where most people stand" (p. 8). She further elaborates multiple consciousness as a "well-defined and acknowledged tool of analysis" (Matsuda, 1992, p. 8). We consider: What does a consciousness of lived experiences under supremacy and racial hierarchy bring to education? What is the potential for a K-12 Asian American Studies praxis for teachers and teacher educators?

We invite readers to sit with these questions and learn alongside the teachers' narratives with hopes that the "deliberate choice" is one that all educators make to better serve their students.

Merging "Multiple Consciousness" With Asian American and Ethnic Studies Pedagogies

Ethnic Studies exists amidst white supremacy's undoing of diversity, equity, and inclusion efforts. At the same time, the curtailing of civil rights protections and programs, delegitimization of critical race theory and other ES fields—particularly African American/Black Studies—requires a strategic response concerned with the material needs of minoritized communities, ensuring our collective futures. Two cornerstones of ES are culturally and community responsive pedagogies. Together they are responsive to students' needs, centering their knowledges and epistemologies with opportunities for students to apply what they learn in their ES classes to respond and develop solutions to challenges in their communities (Tintiangco-Cubales et al., 2014).

As important as it is that ES teachers utilize culturally and community responsive pedagogies, it is also important that they apply what Matsuda (1992) calls "multiple consciousness." Matsuda describes this as an unapologetic decision to view and understand worldviews from the standpoint of minoritized peoples. While Matsuda applies multiple consciousness in a legal context, her method helps name and describe the ways that justice-oriented teachers can prioritize seeing the world from the position of the oppressed. She takes seriously the multiple positions that those made vulnerable hold. Matsuda's work necessarily intersects with ES pedagogy. An ES teacher that can practice multiple consciousness is able to critically teach with and through an ES pedagogy. ES teachers' commitment to and study of ES deepen the ways their multiple consciousness can be utilized to better serve students and their communities.

ES pedagogy emphasizes the lived realities of our students as it challenges the belief systems about power and value hierarchies that constitute the racial order of our society today (Elia et al., 2016; Tintiangco-Cubales et al., 2014). It challenges teachers to think relationally about how all of us are differently situated to state violence and white supremacy, and how teachers can be models for building solidarity across difference. ES pedagogy also involves self-reflection because teaching ES requires much self-assessment, continuous learning, and unlearning. Today, ES teachers who exercise multiple consciousness may be able to creatively strategize protecting ES curriculum, teachers, and students from the policing, surveillance, and punishment that comes with teaching any curriculum that questions the eurocentric [1] canon regularly taught in K-12 schools (Gelman, 2024).

Radical Asian American Studies Pedagogy (RAASP) (Sacramento et al., 2023), a development and expansion of ES pedagogy, is observable in the myriad ways teachers in this chapter enact and embody their K-12 Asian American Studies praxis. Sacramento and colleagues (2023) describe RAASP as a "praxis that centers the experiences of Asian Americans in order to examine power relations, community building, resistance, and justice formations" (p. 209). They continue, "we theorize a pedagogy that amplifies the diverse and complex experiences within Asian America while valuing relational racialization as a vehicle toward developing 'deep solidarities'" (Sacramento et al., 2023, p. 209). ES educators that utilize multiple consciousness and RAASP in the classroom have a unique opportunity to make an impact on students' lives by teaching students the tools and education that can set them free. Matsuda (1992) concludes, "We know it's time, our time, and we will make it so" (p. 10). We are energized by the urgency in her assertion and use it to respond to the needs of our students in this pressing moment. The merging of multiple consciousness and RAASP demonstrates the role of reflection and relationships; a systems analysis; and a collective dreaming toward liberatory futures.

K-12 Asian American Teachers' Praxis

Highlighting the experiences of four K-12 Asian American teachers, we share how they used their multiple consciousness. Across all the teachers' narratives was a clear understanding of their positionalities. The deep and necessary work to engage positionality provided opportunities to reflect critically on where they locate themselves in the context of their social identities. Because of their racialization and unique teacher preparation through Asian American and Ethnic Studies, the teachers' experiences reveal the multiple ways their praxis was utilized. Here, primary and secondary teachers share how they make sense of their praxis, the affordances and challenges associated when they wield AAS and ES in their teaching.

ES curriculum challenges the notions of how teachers perceive learning to look across age levels and to engage in ways that reconceptualize the intellectual capacities of their students through the co-construction of thinking and learning. ES teachers must engage in their own multiple consciousness when considering each grade level curriculum while also understanding the importance of subjectivity to design a curriculum that is engaging, relevant, and revolutionary.

Primary Asian American Teacher—Grace Delgado

Grace Delgado (Pinay), for example, is a kindergarten teacher at a math, science, and aerospace magnet school located in Los Angeles that primarily serves Black youth. Grace discusses the realities of teaching from an ES lens to her young students. She writes, "Because I teach kindergarten students, I find it a little more difficult to explicitly teach ES because of the needed background knowledge to understand very complex dynamics within it." Teaching about complex concepts regardless of age is challenging. Some skeptics of ES suggest children and youth are "too young" to learn about concepts like race and racism or power. Indeed, these concepts are incredibly complex and require a lens, pedagogy, and understanding of the students and community you teach in. In Grace's classroom, students draw from personal reflections and connections from who they are and their community experiences. This demonstrates how she taps into a systems analysis appropriate for schools' youngest learners. Teaching ES at the elementary level, challenging yes, impossible, no. Grace continues:

> I try to build on this experience in the classroom. Examples in the classroom, classroom environment, language, and music are usually embedded in what is familiar to them; ways in which they can celebrate ES and who they are at school. Drawing connections to larger, much more complicated concepts like race and racism are simplified

in ways in which they can be understood. For example, when learning about Dr. Martin Luther King Jr. and segregation, students were asked how they might feel if they had to go to an unkept, under-resourced school while other children got to go to schools with nice playgrounds and lots of school supplies. This helped students draw an early understanding of segregation and helped them critically draw connections to their own lives.

What Grace describes is supporting her students' "community responsive literacies" that "include an ES lens grounded in critical consciousness, critical thinking and are authentic and responsive to local communities" (Curammeng et al., 2016, p. 415). Grace also demonstrates the possibilities for ES in elementary contexts. She reflects:

> As an Asian American educator teaching at a predominantly Black school, I do hope to engage in ES in my classroom. The students need a space where they can learn about their history through a critical lens. The students need a space to question systems of power and the "why" of oppression. Why do people get treated differently based on the color of their skin? How and why are whole systems, like education, able to strive under these pretenses? I hope that through this, at their young age, they can build their narrative so when they are old enough and thrust into the world, they can build on their strengths and defy the systems of oppression in place and hopefully dismantle it all and rebuild.

The powerful inquiry Grace teaches, the "why of oppression," gestures toward a growing body of scholarship demonstrating how ES can be engaged in elementary classrooms. Valdez (2020) writes, "elementary teachers must actively challenge the colonial standards and curriculum, beginning with taking the time to reflect and complicate curriculum" (p. 12). Grace's insistence on supporting young students to "build their narrative" captures the power and potential of AAS and ES for teachers and the students they serve.

Primary Asian American Teacher—Makenna Enomoto

Makenna (Japanese American), a 1st grade teacher working in an elementary school in LA Country's South Bay region, remarks on the importance of creating a responsive curriculum aligned to the age group of students she teaches. She shares how her classroom is a space for students to share their personal experiences and connects her student narratives to children's films. She states, "I tailor ES to the developmental and engagement levels of the students.... To assist students in comprehending history, I connect the narratives to animated children's films that touch upon these concepts." Makenna's search for age-appropriate texts reveals a challenge with access to ES resources. She explains, "The biggest challenge that arises when trying to draw from ES is the access to culturally responsive and accurate material for younger children. There's a larger library of resources for secondary schools and even the higher levels of elementary school, however it's difficult to find for the primary grades (K-1). Oftentimes the books that focus on culture and history provide a biased perspective from the dominant culture." Makenna's multiple consciousness is evident in this example, ascertaining the limited resources appropriate for teaching through an ES lens and using her own critical media literacy to support the teaching of histories outside of dominant narratives she and her students are exposed to. Her example reminds us how schooling is built upon standards reflecting eurocentric, dominant practices that fail to recognize the ways one's multiple consciousness can be a means to resist reproducing systems of oppression. This is especially salient in the field of early childhood education (ECE) that reflect white normative ideologies under the guise of standards of developmental appropriateness. From this perspective, teacher education *and* ECE will greatly benefit from Asian American and ES pedagogies in ways that would better serve all children.

Secondary Asian American Teacher—Aaron Saldaña

Centering experiences of people of color as a means to connect students to their learning does not only occur in history or English language arts classrooms. Aaron (Mexican and Japanese American), a high school ceramics teacher working in the South Bay region of LA, discusses how he uses a radical AAS pedagogy in art. He shares, "I choose to engage AAS and ES in my classroom because I feel that it promotes students to be open-minded by learning about other people's experiences and cultural/ethnic values and struggles." As leaders in districts across the country figure out ways to ensure ES is offered in their schools, much attention has been on ways history/social studies or English/language arts teachers can teach it. Yet, Aaron's study of and implementation of ES and AAS reveal the interdisciplinarity of ES, how ES pedagogies and concepts can be found in all content areas and in his case, the art classroom. Aaron states, "I use PowerPoints and ceramic projects to introduce an art style or historical aspect of ES (ex. Dia De Los Muertos). We create clay skulls in honor of a passed loved one and write something about them on a small piece of paper, and place it inside the skull. Once the clay skull rattles are fired in the kiln the paper also burns, symbolizing letting go of something or someone."

Secondary Asian American Teacher—Vincent Gutierrez

Vincent (Filipino and Mexican American) is a 9th grade ES teacher who works in South Los Angeles. His praxis can be summed up as embodying a "community responsive pedagogy" that uses "education as a vehicle for liberation through the awakening of students' critical consciousness, which leads to actions that promote wellness through racial and social justice in their personal lives, families, communities, and our world" (Tintiangco-Cubales & Duncan-Andrade, 2021, p. 6). "The objective of this class is for student[s] to grasp and feel comfortable of their identity, understand the historic and contemporary forms of oppression (ideological, institutional, interpersonal, and internalized), explore theories of liberation, resistance, and emancipation from these oppressions and phobias, and apply these theories when conducting their Youth Participation Action Research Final," Vincent shares. He continues:

> The main themes of ES in my classroom center around identity, storytelling, learning about the different types of oppression (the 4 I's of oppression) that have impacted different ethnic groups in the United States, historically and contemporary, as well as concepts such as intersectionality, theories of liberation, critical consciousness, subversive music, and Youth Participatory Action Research. My class is

> a reading and writing intensive class where we read primary and/or secondary sources, students answer text dependent questions and write a CER (cite, evidence, and reason) paragraph. We then move into a more rigorous form of writing when we start analyzing primary sources using the five levels of analysis (explicit, implicit, interpretation, theoretical analysis, and application).

Vincent's approach toward a writing-intensive course aligns with the research found in secondary ES courses. In her examination of transnational students' writing, de Los Ríos (2020) described how ES approaches "allow us to rethink how historically marginalized and racialized youth think about and use writing from their own lived vantage points" (p. 4). Vincent's ES course reflects the social and academic transformation that much of the research supports (Dee & Penner, 2017; Sleeter, 2011). Vincent's narrative is illuminating for in-service teachers and teacher educators. It speaks to the challenges that all new teachers face regarding access to ES curriculum. While researching and building his own curriculum, Vincent expressed, "I feel that a lot of ES curriculum floating around on the internet is totally 'whitewashed.' It falls heavily on the historical framework where students are presented with an investigative question and presented with both sides of an argument, rather than focusing on the critical consciousness of systemic oppression and exploring ways for social change." What we find ourselves in, then, is the curricular challenges ensuring the influx of curricula tagged as "ES" or "Asian American Studies" is multicultural at best. It was Vincent's multiple consciousness and Asian American Studies praxis that prompted him to ensure his teaching of ES remained incisive, connected to the pursuit of eradicating racism and other systems of oppression.

Choosing a K-12 Asian American Studies Praxis Deliberately

The teachers highlighted in this chapter reflect the impact that studying Asian American Studies and Ethnic Studies can have on one's positionality, thus influencing their epistemologies and ultimately informing their pedagogical practices. Matsuda's (1992) "multiple consciousness" challenges us to look beyond positionality by recognizing the significance of histories "from below." For elementary and secondary educators, the decision to teach from an AAS praxis requires learning about the students and communities they serve. For Grace, this meant understanding what it means as a Pinay and Asian American working in a predominantly Black community. Aaron and Makenna began with examining the self then towards understanding racialization, the histories of one's family, culture, and community, and connecting them to the community they serve. Vincent's knowledge and experience was the bedrock of his unwavering commitment for ES to be taught with fidelity honoring its activist and critical roots.

For teacher educators, an AAS praxis and ES lens demands not shying away from the political imperative and activist vigor that prompted the Third World Liberation Front to demand a relevant education in the first place (Curammeng, 2022). Examining the readings, theorists, and practitioners in one's teacher education program is a good start; then, ensuring continuous critical professional development of all faculty and instructors should follow. Further, AAS and ES embedded into teacher education will shift foci depending on local contexts; foregrounding issues of colonialism, empire, and anti-Blackness, and understanding legacies of resistance, survival, solidarity, and collective power are crucial to reimagining teacher education, as our understandings of local communities that teacher education programs serve. In reconsidering the role(s) and responsibilities of teacher education, we adhere to Matsuda's call to make the deliberate choice to use our multiple consciousness stoked in Asian American Studies and ES as it "encompasses as well the search for the pathway to a just world"—a world we long for and know is on the horizon.

Endnotes

1. We made the deliberate editorial choice to use a lowercase "e" challenging imperial grammars and decenter Europe. Our intention aligns with the authorial practices prominent in critical race scholarship.

References

Acevedo, N., & Solórzano, D. G. (2023). An overview of community cultural wealth: Toward a protective factor against racism. *Urban Education, 58*(7), 1470–1488.

Curammeng, E. R. (2022). Knowing ourselves and our histories. *Teacher Education Quarterly, 49*(3), 27–47.

Curammeng, E. R., Lopez, D. D., & Tintiangco-Cubales, A. (2016). Community responsive literacies: The development of the ES praxis story plot. *English Teaching: Practice & Critique, 15*(3), 411–429.

Dee, T. S., & Penner, E. K. (2017). The causal effects of cultural relevance: Evidence from an ES curriculum. *American Educational Research Journal, 54*(1), 127–166.

de los Ríos, C. V. (2020). Writing oneself into the curriculum: Photovoice journaling in a secondary Ethnic Studies course. *Written Communication, 37*(4), 487–511. https://doi.org/10.1177/0741088320938794

Elia, N., Kim, J., Redmond, S. L., Rodriguez, D., See, S. E., & Hernández, D. (2016). *Critical ethnic studies: A reader.* Duke University Press.

Gelman, E. (2024). The world upside-down: Zionist institutions, civil rights talk, and the new cold war on ethnic studies. *Critical Ethnic Studies, 8*(2). https://doi.org/10.5749/ces.0802.09

Matsuda, M. J. (1992). When the first quail calls: Multiple consciousness as jurisprudential method. *Women's Rights Law Reporter, 14*, 297.

Sacramento, J., Curammeng, E. R., & Tintiangco-Cubales, A. (2023). Toward a radical Asian American studies pedagogy. *Journal of Asian American Studies, 26*(2), 207–219.

Sleeter, C. E. (2011). *The academic and social value of ES: A research review.* National Education Association Research Department.

Tintiangco-Cubales, A., & Duncan-Andrade, J. (2021). Still fighting for ES: The origins, practices, and potential of community responsive pedagogy. *Teachers College Record, 123*(13), 1–28.

Tintiangco-Cubales, A., Kohli, R., Sacramento, J., Henning, N., Agarwal-Rangnath, R., & Sleeter, C. (2014). Toward an ES pedagogy: Implications for K-12 schools from the research. *The Urban Review, 47*(1), 104–125.

Valdez, C. (2020). Flippin' the scripted curriculum: ES inquiry in elementary education. *Race Ethnicity and Education, 23*(4), 581–597.

CHAPTER 6

Affirming and Honoring the Voices of South Asian Americans in the K-12 Classroom

Ruchi Agarwal-Rangnath

RACHNA WALKED INTO *her 4th grade classroom, feeling all the feelings most kids experience on the first day of school: excited, scared, and nervous to meet her new teacher. Her long black hair was in a French braid, with some coconut oil in it, and her clothes smelled of her mom's cooking: tamarind, chili pepper, gharam masala, coriander, and other Indian spices.*

Being the new kid in school, there were no familiar faces. Rachna sat next to the only girl in the class who had smiled at her, another girl with skin the shade of chocolate. Her stomach clenched as the teacher began roll call. "Rockna? Ratchna?" She raised her hand. "It's Ruh-ch-nah," she said quietly. "Oh Rash-na. Let's just call you Rachel," the teacher said and moved on to the next name.

Rachna's experiences on her first day of school were no different than mine, or the many other South Asian American children in K-12 schools. The mispronunciation of names is just one aspect of how the family and culture of South Asian American communities can be ignored in the classroom. When children come to school, "teachers—consciously or not—mispronounce, disregard or change the name, they are in a sense disregarding the family and culture of the students as well" (McLaughlin, 2016, para. 7). The stories of their ancestors, including their struggles and contributions to society, are too often left unheard and invisible from the K-12 curriculum (Kohli & Solorzano, 2012). In this chapter, I share ways in which we can affirm and honor the hidden stories of South Asian Americans in classrooms and schools so that we can better understand

their diverse experiences and collectively work to build solidarity and understanding across differences.

South Asian American Invisibility in the Curriculum

The stories of South Asian American people and communities are often
left invisible, especially in classrooms and schools. Although nearly 5.4 million South Asian Americans live in the United States, the experiences of South
Asians in America, their struggles, resistance, acts of solidarity, and contributions are rarely, if ever, taught in classrooms, reflected in textbooks, and seen
and heard in popular media.

The South Asian American community reflects a wide diversity of religions,
cultures, and languages, filled with complex and unique lived experiences. According to SAALT (n.d.),

> Nearly 5.4 million South Asians live in the United States, a 40 per-
> cent increase in population size from the Census count in 2010. Our
> growing and diverse communities trace their roots to Afghanistan,
> Bangladesh, Bhutan, India, Nepal, Kashmir, Pakistan, Sri Lanka, the
> Maldives, and the diaspora, including but not limited to Trinidad/
> Tobago, Guyana, Fiji, Tanzania, and Kenya.

The stories of South Asian Americans are uniquely complicated because of
their cultural, religious, and racial differences (Nadal, 2019). For example, there
are over 2000 languages spoken in South Asia, and a multitude of religions
practiced, including Hinduism, Christianity, Sikhism, Buddhism, Jainism,
and Christianity. Each region of South Asia has its own unique customs, food,
religious and cultural traditions, which families continue to practice in the
United States. Although South Asian Americans are commonly grouped under the Asian American umbrella, their stories are unique and continue to be
excluded from the larger Asian American narrative, lacking representation in
Asian American Studies and popular media.

The complexity of the South Asian American story continues to be invisible
in the K-12 curriculum as well. The starkest example of this is post-9/11 and

the depiction of South Asian Americans as terrorists. During this significant moment of history, the heightened hate violence and discrimination against those perceived as "terrorists" fundamentally altered South Asian, Arab, Muslim, and Sikh immigrant communities in the United States (Iyer, 2017). Young people continue to be taught a Eurocentric, sanitized history of post-9/11 America that neglects the experiences of targeted community members. These Eurocentric narratives fail to highlight the resistance and solidarity of South Asian American communities and their ability to stand against violence and hatred (Iyer, 2017).

The silencing and erasure of South Asian American stories are also complicated by the *model minority myth*. The term *model minority* refers to portrayal of Asian Americans as a minority group that is able to achieve socially, academically, and financially through quiet determination, hard work, submissiveness, and assimilation (Zhou, 1997), thus making them a "model" for other communities of color (Takaki, 2000). Despite its prevalence, the model minority myth continues to ignore the historical and present-day struggles of Asian Americans. The myth has been used to pit Asian Americans against other minority groups, minimizing racial discrimination and justifying policies that overlook systemic injustices (Chou & Feagin, 2008). Additionally, it complicates movements of racial solidarity and raises tensions within the Asian American community. For South Asian Americans specifically, Venugopal (2020) argues that the portrayal of South Asian Americans as model minorities neglects their history and portrayal as problem minorities, including the xenophobia and racial violence they faced, in relation to immigration laws, work, and social divides.

Ethnic Studies and Humanizing Education

An established body of research finds that a rigorous and well-designed curriculum, connected to students' identities and lives and taught in a culturally sustaining manner with high academic expectations and concern for student livelihood, has a positive academic and attitudinal impact on students (Sleeter & Zavala, 2020; Tintiangco-Cubales et al., 2015).

However, standardized classroom materials often misrepresent history, withhold knowledge about racial injustice, minimize or negate racial incidents, and fail to uplift stories of strength, resilience, and interracial and intersectional resistance. Decades of research have detailed the whitewashed nature of traditional curriculum in U.S. schools and the ways that curriculum is framed around the perspectives and experiences of white people, thereby privileging whiteness as normalized (equating Americanness with whiteness) and normative (equating whiteness with superiority) (CARE-ED, 2018; Sleeter, 2011). Although publishers have addressed some obvious biases in textbooks, researchers have found the experiences and worldviews of European Americans to remain dominant in our structured K–12 history and social studies textbooks (Sleeter, 2011).

Ethnic Studies creates a path and praxis for teachers to address inequities and build a more humanizing and just world for current and future generations. It is a movement for curricular and pedagogical projects that reclaim marginalized voices and histories, create spaces of healing, critique structures of racism, and challenge the oppressive conditions that impact teachers personally, socially, and systemically. Ethnic Studies can serve as a pedagogical approach towards education that honors student identities and agency as a vehicle towards community activism and involvement.

Cathery Yeh, Betina Hsieh, and I developed a framework of four elements of Ethnic Studies for the K–12 classroom: identity and belonging, understanding systems and power, building community and solidarity, and transformation and change (see Agarwal-Rangnath et al., 2022). Although each of these elements is integral to the work of Ethnic Studies, for the purpose and scope of this chapter, I focus on identity and belonging, as a way to affirm and honor their hidden stories of South Asian Americans in classrooms and schools.

Identity and Belonging

To more deeply understand the richness and diversity of the South Asian American experience, allowing students to grapple with their understanding of identity and belonging is essential. Identity, in this way, is seen as a state of Becoming (Prashad, 2000), a journey filled with complexity, pain, joy, and healing. Asking students questions such as: Who are you and where do you come from? What are the stories that you hold and what are the stories you can learn from? Allowing students to learn about who they are and where they are from can create a collective, humanizing space for students to develop a critical analysis of themselves and the world around them.

For South Asian Americans, their experiences may include privilege and discrimination. They may see themselves as targets of racism, especially post-9/11. Being targets of bullying may also impact their identity, being called a "terrorist" or "sand nigger" because of their religion, accent, or the color of their skin. The internalizing of white supremacist, Eurocentric narratives may also contribute to self-hate; seeing the color of their skin, features, ways of being as not good enough, not white enough. Whiteness deeply impacts South Asian American communities, as being light skinned comes with innate privileges especially in relation to beauty and self-worth. Research shows that skin color bias affects one's perceptions of themselves and others in ways that can be both subtle and profound (Bergner, 2009; Knight, 2015).

In *Karma of Brown Folk*, Vijay Prashad (2000) asks South Asian Americans, "How does it feel to be a solution?" (p. 6). In his groundbreaking book, he challenges South Asian Americans to consider the ways that they have been used as weapons in the white supremacist war against Black America. Asian Americans have been used as a convenient tool to denigrate questions raised by other people of color around fairness, equity, liberation, and freedom. Prashad's question can challenge students to go deeper with their understandings of identity, to think about ways South Asian American identity has been constructed over time in relation to whiteness and blackness. For example, after reading an excerpt from *Karma of Brown Folk*, teachers may ask questions such as:

- What does it mean to be South Asian American?
- How are your identity and feelings of self-worth connected to what you see around you?
- How might South Asian American identity be constructed in relation to whiteness and Blackness, and how does that change over time?
- How have South Asian Americans participated in and benefited from anti-Black racism?

- What are the ways South Asian identity intersects with other folks of color, and in what ways do they not?
- What must I unlearn, learn, and heal from to live my full authentic self?

To ask these questions requires a deep study of identity and the stories of South Asian Americans' experiences in the United States. These stories can be curated from students' lived experiences, if you have students who identify as South Asian in the classroom, or from books such as *Karma of Brown Folk* (Prashad), *Uncle Swami* (Prashad), and *We Too Sing America* (Iyer), and resources such as SAADA (https://www.saada.org/). The stories of South Asian Americans are unique, complicated, and deeply rooted in and impactful to U.S. and world histories (Bhandari, 2022). Examining and learning about the stories of South Asian Americans is essential for addressing inequities, building solidarity, and understanding across differences.

Seeing Representation

By lifting up the voices and experiences of South Asian Americans, students may see history in a different light. They may learn about the stories of people who look like them and their struggles to overcome discrimination and racism. They may hear about their ancestors' acts of resistance toward unfair practices and wages and also of their contributions to our country's growth and development. They may also learn from stories of everyday people whose bravery and courage impacted change in our country and the ways their stories intersect with their own. Lastly, they may hear of those who used their privilege and resources to serve as allies and support systems to those struggling to obtain freedom and rights. In each case, students may feel inspired and empowered to hear the stories of members of our society who fought against discrimination, racism, and oppression to make change in our world. Through the exploration of multiple perspectives, including the stories of South Asian Americans, students may see that our country was built by the complex contributions of many people, not just the ones listed in our textbooks. Moreover, the stories of those who contributed to our country may not just be limited to narratives of happiness and victory, but entangled with hardship, fear, anger, distrust, and worry. Our history is not a sanitized list of facts, but a complex and dynamic story that worked to give power to some and deny power to others.

When intentional steps are made to center the voices of those who have been historically silenced and marginalized in textbooks, teachers give students the opportunity to see themselves in history. In this way, students learn to identify bias in texts and understand that multiple truths can be told about any event (Agarwal-Rangnath, 2022). As students see and hear the contributions and actions of their ancestors, students may be more empowered and motivated to make changes in their communities. Students may also feel empowered by others' stories of struggle and resistance to serve as co-conspirators and help others in their fight for justice. As we integrate diverse and comprehensive histories into the curriculum, we simultaneously teach our students to analyze, read, learn, and ask questions about the world. Our classrooms embrace pluralism as we create and enact a curriculum inclusive of the needs of our diverse students. As teachers, we draw from the contributions and lived experiences of all our learners and build community solidarity in the classroom by drawing threads between our similarities and differences, past and present.

For South Asian American students to more deeply understand themselves and the world around them, they need opportunities to hear their stories in classrooms. The stories of South Asian Americans are linguistically, culturally, and religiously unique, intersecting with gender, sexuality, and ableism. There are more and more books, including picture books, that honor and affirm the South Asian American experience. I encourage reading them from a critical literacy perspective, questioning whose voices are heard or not heard, and what perspectives we get to hear. For example, with the book *My Name* by Supriya Kelkar, a teacher could ask the following questions:

- What was the author's message or intent with this book?
- How do you feel about the main character in the book? Can you relate to him or her in any way? How does he feel excluded or different?
- Who was the book written for?
- Whose perspective do we get to hear?

- Whose perspective do we not get to hear?
- Who may have been missing from the storyline?

Each of these questions could easily be adapted for any book, video, or poem shared in class. They deepen students' critical literacy, allowing students to question whose voice is heard or not heard, and connect with characters in deeper ways. The narratives of exclusion and the ways South Asian American communities have worked in solidarity with other racial groups are rarely seen in K-12 curriculum. Also missing from textbooks are the contributions of South Asian Americans and their great impact on the community across several fields of civic life (see SAADA, 2024). The affirming and lifting of South Asian American stories within a dominant Eurocentric paradigm requires unlearning what was taught in K-12 classrooms. It requires one to learn to think intentionally and critically about how and why curriculum is enacted in the classroom. Educators, alongside their students, must question what is included and what is excluded in the curriculum, who is valued and who is not valued, who has power and who does not have power, who is heard and who is silenced, and who is represented and who is not. Curriculum can never be neutral. Certain perspectives will be included while others excluded. Educators who teach South Asian American studies must learn the stories of struggle, contributions, solidarity, and intersectionality, as each of these stories is deeply woven into the complex fabric of what it means to be South Asian American in the United States. For a list of books that integrate South Asian narratives and social justice, see here: https://socialjusticebooks.org/booklists/south-asian/.

Conclusion

The silencing and erasure of the South Asian narrative from the K-12 curriculum is essential to students' sense of identity and belonging. Through Ethnic Studies and the intentional teaching of South Asian American history, students can engage in humanizing curriculum that challenges problematic Eurocentric framing of the curriculum by giving voice to communities underrepresented in education. Being exposed to the histories and viewpoints of communities of color not only benefits children of color, but also allows all children to understand diverse perspectives, create interracial and interethnic understandings, develop critical thinking, and build community solidarity across differences (Sleeter & Zavala, 2020).

Prashad (2000) argues that identity is always in the state of Becoming, layered with tensions and contradictions. As a child of South Asian immigrants, I struggled to find my racial identity within a world of whiteness. I thought if I worked hard enough I could be like everyone else, everyone else being white. I worked hard to manipulate my words and actions to be someone white people would like and accept. I hid my Indian clothes, wore lots of sunblock to avoid getting dark, and isolated myself from other Indian kids with the hope that no one would see me for who I was. However, hiding was not always an option. Like when someone said, "I can only see your eyes," when it was dark outside. Often, classmates would mock my parents' accents or ask me why Indian people wear a dot on their head.

As an adult, I can now see that these feelings of erasure and invisibility were deeply connected to not knowing my identity and the stories of my South Asian American community. In disconnecting from the distinctness, uniqueness, strength, and intersections of the South Asian American community, I only saw myself at the margins. I now have had the opportunity to learn, understand, and see what it means to be Brown and how I have internalized ways of thinking that hurt and disempower me. Studying the histories of folks of color has not only acknowledged and affirmed my own story, but allowed me to recognize and identify the many complex stories of intersectional strength, struggle, and resistance that counter the hegemonic white, male, heteronormative narrative in textbooks. Additionally, I have found role models, friends, colleagues, organizations, and mentors who have pushed me to see the pain and joy that being Brown carries. Working to heal my "fractured collective identity" (Camangian, 2010, p. 179) has been especially important, as this has allowed me to better understand myself with and alongside other folks and communities of color.

Through my journey of Becoming, I learned the stories of my great grandparents, freedom fighters who fought alongside Gandhi protesting colonial rule. Every evening at 4 pm, they would take out their charkas and spin. All of the clothes they wore were spun by them and then the mill would convert the thread into very fine or thick fabric like wool for them to wear. They walked with Gandhi, wearing khadi as a symbol of resistance. They participated in a salt march, a protest against British efforts to prevent Indians from collecting and selling their salt. Police hit and beat them, but they believed in nonviolent protest. These counterstories, stories that are far removed from dominant narratives, now frame my identity, as I have learned that my identity matters and that protest, activism, and resistance are my legacy.

It is through learning each other's stories that we can develop a deep empathy for one another and the world around us. As bell hooks (2015) reminds us,

> The journey of naming and reclaiming who we are is a space of healing and radical opening: we are transformed, individually and collectively as we make radical creative space that affirms and sustains our subjectivity, which gives us a new location from which to articulate our sense of the world. (p. 23)

References

Agarwal-Rangnath, R. (2022). *Social studies, literacy, and social justice in the elementary classroom: A guide for teachers*. Teachers College Press.

Agarwal-Rangnath, R., Yeh, C., & Hsieh, B. (2022). We need to see each other as human: Ethnic studies as a framework for humanizing K–12 education. In T. K. Chapman & N. Hobbel (Eds.), *Social justice pedagogy across the curriculum* (pp. 217–229). Routledge.

Bergner, G. (2009). Black children, white preference: *Brown v. Board*, the doll tests, and the politics of self-esteem. *American Quarterly, 61*(2), 299–332.

Bhandari, S. (2022). The history of South Asians in the United States. *South Asians in the United States: A guide for social workers and other helping professionals*, 1–16.

California Alliance of Researchers for Equity in Education (CARE-ED). (2018). *Ethnic studies and critical multicultural education: Educating for democracy in California and beyond*. http://www.careed.org.

Camangian, P. (2010). Starting with self: Teaching autoethnography to foster critically caring literacies. *Research in the Teaching of English, 45*(2), 179–204.

Chou, R. S., & Feagin, J. R. (2015). *Myth of the model minority: Asian Americans facing racism*. Routledge.

hooks, b. (2015). Choosing the margin as a space of radical openness. In A. Garry & M. Pearsall (Eds.), *Women, knowledge, and reality* (pp. 48–55). Routledge.

Iyer, D. (2017). *We too sing America: South Asian, Arab, Muslim, and Sikh immigrants shape our multiracial future*. The New Press.

Knight, D. (2015). What's colorism?. *Learning for Justice.* https://www.learningforjustice.org/magazine/fall-2015/whats-colorism

Kohli, R., & Solórzano, D. G. (2012). Teachers, please learn our names!: Racial microaggressions and the K-12 classroom. *Race Ethnicity and Education, 15*(4), 441–462.

McLaughlin, C. (2016). The lasting impact of mispronouncing students' names. *NEA Today.* https://www.nea.org/nea-today/all-news-articles/lasting-impact-mispronouncing-students-names

Nadal, K. L. (2019). The Brown Asian American movement: Advocating for South Asian, Southeast Asian, and Filipino American communities. *Asian American Policy Review, 29.*

Prashad, V. (2000). *The karma of brown folk.* University of Minnesota Press.

South Asian American Digital Archive (SAADA). (2024). *Home.* https://www.saada.org/

South Asian Americans Leading Together (SAALT). (n.d.). *About SAALT.* https://saalt.org

Sleeter, C. E. (2011). *The academic and social value of ethnic studies: A research review.* National Education Association Research Department.

Sleeter, C. E., & Zavala, M. (2020). *Transformative ethnic studies in schools: Curriculum, pedagogy, and research.* Teachers College Press.

Takaki, R. (2000). Asian Americans: The myth of the model minority. In J.H. Skolnick & E. Currie (Eds.), *Crisis in American Institutions.* Allyn and Bacon.

Tintiangco-Cubales, A., Kohli, R., Sacramento, J., Henning, N., Agarwal-Rangnath, R., & Sleeter, C. (2015). Toward an ethnic studies pedagogy: Implications for K-12 schools from the research. *The Urban Review, 47,* 104–125.

Venugopal, A. (2020). The truth behind Indian exceptionalism. *The Atlantic.* https://www.theatlantic.com/magazine/archive/2021/01/the-making-of-a-model-minority/617258/

Zhou, M. (1997). Growing up American: The challenge confronting immigrant children and children of immigrants. *Annual Review of Sociology, 23*(1), 63–95.

CHAPTER 7

What I've Learned Creating and Teaching a High School Middle Eastern Studies Elective for the Last 16 Years

Monica Eraqi

> *"We don't know any good Arabs or Arab Americans."*
>
> —10TH GRADE STUDENT

A MUCH BELOVED student made this statement during a 10th-grade social studies class think-a-loud. It was the first year of my teaching career, 18 years ago, but it has been repeated almost the same way every year since. Students completed a think-pair-share activity where they discussed a prompt about the "Middle East." There were the usual responses of sand, oil, desert, rich, and hookah, followed by some countries like Saudi Arabia and Iran. When I prodded for famous Middle Easterners or Middle Eastern contributions, the conversation stopped. After a few moments, the usual names were whispered: bin Laden, Saddam Hussein. I wrote the names on the board, and after broke the silence, "Do we have any other names we could add? Perhaps positive contributions? Maybe even Middle Eastern Americans?"

"We don't know any good Arabs or Arab Americans," one student mentioned. I noticed students nodding their heads in agreement. "I didn't ask for only Arabs or Arab Americans," I replied with a smile, "and I think you could name famous Arabs and Middle Easterners." "Well, that's who lives in the Middle East," another student remarked. "Only Arabs live in the Middle East?" I asked. From the far side of the room, a voice mentioned the Prophet Mohammed under their breath, which was quickly followed by Ghandi. "Ghandi is from India!" one student challenged. "Isn't India a part of the Middle East?" a student asked. "No! That's Asia!" another shouted. "Yeah, but the Middle East is a part of Asia, right?" a student responded. "Umm, no . . . the Middle East is a part of . . . well, the Middle East!" "Oh yeah?!" I heard a student remark from the other side of the room, "Since when was the Middle East a continent? Wait, now I'm confused. Where does the Middle East belong?" "Good question," I said. "Let's start there, friends. Where is the Middle East?"

These class discussions still surprise me. How could individuals, such as mass murderers, be included in the same list of religious and spiritual leaders? Why all men? Not one famous Middle Eastern female? I knew the students could have identified famous Middle Easterners and likely followed many of them on social media, but they probably had no idea of their Middle Eastern roots. TV icons, models, make-up artists, actors and actresses, musicians, artists, politicians, and activists. How could they see Middle Eastern faces and names daily, but not mention them in class?

The need for Middle Eastern studies was incredibly apparent following the events of September 11, 2001. Students tried to comprehend the catastrophic events of that day and the major events that followed, often turning to teachers who struggled to provide answers. However, United States engagement in the Middle East predates the events of 9/11 and continues decades later. As such, the Middle East will continue to be of great importance in our students, lives and our nation's future, further emphasizing the need for Middle Eastern Studies courses and programs. Despite this, the Middle East continues to be overlooked in the social studies curriculum, focusing only on times of conflict and violence (Eraqi, 2014). It is a key factor for the negative responses generated during such classroom activities. I saw this clearly as both a student and a teacher. As a high school senior graduating in 2001, pre-September 11, most of my peers struggled to recognize Middle Eastern countries, let alone who was Middle Eastern. By the time I began my teaching career, post-9/11, it seemed students had only mastered stereotypes and tropes. As an educator, I was determined to make sure that future generations would grow up learning about Middle Eastern culture, history, ancestry, achievements, and contributions in a way that had been absent from my education. This is how the Modern Middle East Studies class was conceived.

Creating a Multicultural/Ethnic Studies Course

"Knowledge of the self is the mother of all knowledge. So, it is incumbent on me to know myself, to know it completely, to know its minutiae, its characteristics, its subtleties, and its very atoms."

—KHALIL GIBRAN

There were mixed reactions when I suggested creating the first multicultural or Ethnic Studies course in our school district, let alone one focused on the Middle East. I initially received support from our social studies department chair, who saw this as an opportunity to create diverse social studies courses. This would keep students engaged, increase student enrollment, and protect social studies teacher placements. The district administration, however, deemed the course unnecessary. First, they argued that there was not a "large enough Middle Eastern population" to merit curriculum development and commit financial resources. Second, they believed Middle Eastern students were already fluent in Middle Eastern culture and history and non-Middle Easterners would not be interested. Third, there were questions about what the curriculum would include, who would teach the course, if other schools offered an Ethnic Studies course, and if not, then why not. The answers to these questions would be vital to garner school board approval.

I spent the next 2 years researching Middle Eastern Studies and drafting a course proposal. I was able to identify only two schools in the state that had a Middle Eastern Studies course listed in their course offerings. Both were private schools (not public schools), and after speaking to the schools, neither had actually run the course. Therefore, I had no prior curricular examples to reference.

Teachers often turn to textbooks in the absence of established curriculums or guides; however, there were almost no books dedicated to a high school audience, let alone an entire course. Additionally, the situation in the Middle East was changing so rapidly that any textbook would be outdated by the end of the semester. Indeed, this is an important factor I learned early in the course development process; one will never be able to teach this course the same way twice.

Thus, the curriculum was developed independently without curricular guides or textbooks, and the course was titled the Modern Middle East. I chose to create a course on the Middle East (which would allow the inclusion of parts of Eastern Europe, West Asia, and North Africa) rather than a course on Arab Studies (which generally focuses on countries in and around the Arabian Peninsula and North Africa). I was concerned that an Arab Studies course would alienate many students who hailed from the Middle East or could relate to Middle Eastern culture, traditions, and history. This choice was also important in highlighting the diversity of the Middle East, making space for the many ethnic, religious, and cultural groups that exist. A Middle Eastern course brought in many students who had historical ties to the Middle East, in particular, the shared histories of my students who hailed from the Balkans or Eastern Europe. Many had historical connections to the former Ottoman Empire, still used Arabic and Turkish phrases in their everyday language, and shared traditions, food, and dress that have been influenced by the Middle East. A Modern Middle East course helps break Western colonial definitions, and as the course progresses, students recognize the lines are certainly blurred between when and where the "Middle East" starts and stops and why some countries are included, and others are not.

How Do You Create Resources for a Course That Has Never Been Taught and Does Not Have a Book?

"Let the beauty of what you love be what you do."

—RUMI

From the start, I created nearly all the resources on my own. I developed the units, assembled the PowerPoints, and created the worksheets, activities, and assessments exclusively. Some of the lessons I had designed for the Arab American National Museum, which is affiliated with the Smithsonian and is the only Arab American museum in the country. I spent years creating lessons and activities for their exhibits and classroom tour groups and led professional development and teacher training. All of this was incredibly time-consuming to create, but also because of the ever-changing situations in the Middle East. The first class I held was in 2008, prior to the Arab Spring, evacuation of U.S. forces from Iraq and Afghanistan, the creation of ISIS, or the Syrian and Yemeni civil wars. It required that I constantly was up to date with the latest developments as these could have serious implications for my lessons.

Although time consuming, the most difficult aspect of lesson planning was the time spent planning in isolation. Modern Middle East is not the only course I teach, but it is the only course where I am a cohort of one. This means that I have no one to collaborate with to develop lessons, activities, or analyze data as I do with any of the other courses that I teach. This will certainly change as multicultural and Ethnic Studies programs continue to grow, even at their current snail pace, but even in year 16 of operation, it is still a challenge.

The number of resources for teaching about the Middle East has also grown exponentially since I first started the course. Today, there are many activities, videos, and lessons available. The challenge now is identifying which are culturally relevant and emphasize culturally responsive teaching and do not reiterate the oft repeated stereotypes and tropes (that all Middle Easterners are Arabs, all Arabs are Muslim, and all Muslims are terrorists).

There are certain lessons and units that serve as the foundation of the course. The introductory unit on stereotypes and biases is one aspect that remains consistent. This unit includes teaching about the diversity of the Middle East, starting first with geography. Geography is a key starting point because it serves as an ice breaker activity to develop student confidence in discussing the Middle East. We focus on the development of the term "Middle East;" the 16 main countries that are generally included in the Middle East; their geography and climate, different ethnic groups and populations, and diverse religious groups. We also discuss how to properly pronounce country names. This is a deeply personal aspect of the course as we begin to focus on Middle Eastern identity and stages of identity development for people of color (please see "Five Stages of Racial-Identity Development for Black People" in Duff, 2023). During this unit we dispel myths and stereotypes about the Middle East and Middle Eastern people and engage in cultural competency. It is an important unit for non-Middle Eastern students who are learning about the region, but equally important for Middle Eastern students who can hold stereotypes and misconceptions about other Middle Eastern groups.

The second part of the course analyzes each Middle Eastern country individually, to further understand its history, culture, ethnic, and religious composition, but also the struggle over Western imperialism and settler colonialism. Through this unit, students easily recognize the struggle of Middle Eastern countries to establish their own democratic governments and connect it to the early years of the United States. They begin to view the Middle East as an ally in the fight for democratic freedom and reform instead of the single-story narrative of anti-democratic monarchies and dictatorships.

The economic and political instability of the Middle East greatly impacts the major waves of immigration to the United States. This leads directly to another unit about immigration and Middle Eastern Americans. Students analyze local and national Middle Eastern communities, understanding push and pull factors, establishments of ethnic communities, contributions to the United States, and yes, famous Middle Eastern Americans. Students are surprised to learn how long these communities have existed in the United States. They are also impressed by the strong educational and political activism displayed by specific waves of immigration. Many of these immigrants had hopes of supporting the development of democratic governments in their home countries. Often, this made them targets of existing regimes and unable to return home (Eraqi, 2014). It also dispels the myth of Middle Eastern immigration as a new occurrence of mostly unskilled, uneducated, and anti-democratic immigrants.

A third aspect of the course is the cultural experience. I work closely with the families of past and previous students who are interested in volunteering to be class speakers, answering student questions, and sharing their experiences. This is always a unique aspect of the course that involves bringing diverse families with different lived experiences from different parts of the Middle East and weaving them into the curriculum. Some are recent immigrants; others have generational roots in America. Some are well-known members of the community, academics, athletes, comedians, and others only known to TikTok.

Many families offer to cook special recipes and meals that hail from their country, region, or are unique to their ethnic group. This gives students a chance to see the diverse cuisine and extends beyond hummus and tabbouleh. Students see pride in the families who put their heart into the preparation of these meals and speak about their culture and heritage with such enthusiasm and passion. Often, non-Middle Eastern students will comment on how similar the stories are to those of their ancestors. It makes the curriculum meaningful and certainly more memorable than any worksheet or reading I could have prepared.

Teachers need not rely on only Middle Eastern families within their own community, although this is always a great start. Southeastern Michigan is blessed to have one of the largest Arab, Assyrian, and Chaldean populations in the country. As mentioned earlier, Michigan has the only Arab American National Museum (AANM) and only Chaldean Museum (located inside the Chaldean Cultural Center) in the country! These provide amazing educational field trips for our students, but they also have online platforms with many of their exhibits available virtually and allow teachers and students to access from around the world.

There has also been astonishing entrepreneurial growth within the southeastern Michigan region throughout much of the country. Numerous restaurants and businesses have opened, which has given our classes access to a greater number of cultural experiences. One class trip was to a Turkish restaurant and included an educational lesson led by a local professor discussing Turkish culture, the growth of the Turkish American community, Turkish cuisine, and dishes that had been prepared by the restaurant's chefs who had been flown in from Turkey!

These class field trips are some of the students' favorite experiences and the ones that they are most excited to share with their families and friends. These experiences allow us to share the cultural aspects of diverse groups, even when we do not have students from these backgrounds in that class. They also provide teachers with the flexibility to collaborate with Middle Eastern families and entrepreneurs to replicate these activities in any part of the country.

These smaller trips serve as excellent ways for students to explore and experience aspects of the Middle East that exist within their own communities. While exploring their own communities offers valuable insights, traveling to the Middle East provides an unparalleled opportunity for students to immerse themselves in its rich culture and history. In 2010, I was able to create the ultimate student trip; a 2-week student tour of Egypt. It was our school's first international trip since 9/11, and we are currently in the process of preparing for another trip in conjunction with neighboring schools.

One challenge of having a Middle East course is that it is currently only offered as a social studies elective. At its inception, the state of Michigan only required global/world history, U.S. history, and U.S. government as part of its mandatory social studies requirements. Shortly after the induction of Modern

Middle East (MME), the state also mandated economics. Students now had more required classes and less room to take exploratory courses (Michigan Department of Education, 2019). Modern Middle East must also compete with students who are interested in taking Advanced Placement courses and the possibility of college credit. In the first year, I taught three sections of MME, with the potential to add more, but after state requirements, and the additional GPA points for those enrolled in AP courses, my sections were reduced to only one section a year. Every year we face the question of whether there will be enough students to run a section of the course.

It Is Still Worth the Fight

"Not everything that is faced can be changed; but nothing can be changed until it is faced."

—JAMES BALDWIN

I'm an optimist and see the value in Ethnic Studies electives. I think back to my high school social studies classes. There were times when Middle Eastern Studies could have been included but was not, either because it was not considered a part of the curriculum, or the teacher did not feel confident in teaching the content. This is why Ethnic Studies cannot be an option, but a requirement. As multicultural education scholar Geneva Gay writes, "Students need a curriculum that allows them to first dissect 'distorted information, prejudices, stereotypes, and other denigrating values associated with an ethnic group,' before then learning about the true narrative of a group, such as cultural, ethnic, religious, and historical context" (2023, p. 39).

Middle Eastern Studies allow students to analyze the impact of settler colonialism and Western imperialism in the Middle East, the history of government imperialism, resource theft, land confiscation, and the development of ethnic identity. Modern Middle East examines the past and present, to understand what is being accomplished now. It challenges racial stereotypes, not just how non-Middle Easterners view Middle Easterners, but also how different ethnic groups in the Middle East view and interact with each other (Eraqi, 2014). Equally important is having a course that provides time, space, and focuses on diverse histories and narratives that will not be included piecemeal as part of another course.

The course is not a utopia either. There are disagreements over human rights, why some countries have been created and others have not, whether some regions deserve autonomy or not. We openly discuss questions about entry into different regional groups, like the European Union. We have disagreements over colonial and Western influence and which country has the greatest influence in the region, and debate the "what your ancestors did to my ancestors" history and who has the right to claim that a particular dish is from this nation and not another. Some teachers shy away from these curricular situations. For me, it shows how important the course is to students; how deeply personal and invested they are in the curriculum that they cannot wait until we study their country, their ethnic group, or religious group. They cannot wait until we reach a particular topic.

Indeed, many of my students have taken the course as a precursor to entering the military or college. I could write another chapter just on the number of emails from previous students who said the course in many ways changed their view of the world and life. There are the personal stories, like how a student took the course just so he could bond with his stepfather and be able to have "conversation at the dinner table." I have countless emails from students who described the class as family and finally feeling like they had a place in the school for the first time. Some wrote passionate emails about their first days in their undergraduate Middle Eastern Studies classes and how they were the only student to recognize historical figures like Mustafa Kemal Ataturk or Gamal Abdel Nasser. They became the base of their new study groups, and this opened a world to making new friends on campus, some even finding their life partners! Students who became doctors and nurses send emails about how they have worked to challenge misconceptions in their workplace or used the class lessons on cultural competency to help support their patients. This demonstrates the long-term value that the curriculum holds, and for many, this is the first time that they have a curriculum that reflects them. This is more important now than ever before as we witness attempts to silence students and teachers who dare to discuss Middle Eastern history and narratives, particularly when it comes to Palestinian Studies.

As I reflect on my 16 years of teaching Modern Middle East, I find myself often returning to a statement made by the former Italian Prime minister, Silvio Berlusconi. During an interview, he was asked about Egypt and the unfolding 2011 Arab Spring. "Nothing has changed in Egypt," he stated, "Egyptians are making history, as usual" (Hasan, 2013). The irony is glaring. Despite all the changes that have occurred in Middle Eastern countries, like Egypt, most students are still meeting a curriculum that perpetuates an outdated single-story narrative not reflective of the world around them. Indeed, nothing has changed. Middle Easterners have been and continue making history, as usual, and now there is a curriculum that reflects those histories.

References

Duff, P. (2023). *Becoming an antiracist school leader: Dare to be real.* Teachers College Press.
Eraqi, M. M. (2014). Arab-Americans and Muslim-Americans in the secondary social studies curriculum. *Arab World English Journal, 5*(3), 45–64.
Gay, G. (2023). *Educating for equity and excellence enacting culturally responsive teaching.* Teachers College Press.
Hasan, T. (2013, June 26). Egypt in the volcano. *Saudi Gazette.* https://saudigazette.com.sa/article/50495#google_vingette.
Michigan Department of Education. (2019). *Social studies standards.* https://www.michigan.gov/-/media/Project/Websites/mde/Academic-Standards/Social_Studies_Standards.pdf?rev=4bab170dd4114e2dbce578723b37ca63.

CHAPTER 8

Learning With and From Student Community Cultural Wealth

Norman Sales

I WAS 19 when I moved from the Philippines to Hawaii with my sister and father after almost a decade of waiting for our green cards to be approved. I brought an undergraduate degree in secondary education with an emphasis in English language teaching from a state university in my rural province of Ilocos Norte. After a year of working shifts at Walmart and a private preschool, I landed my first teaching job as an English language arts (ELA) teacher for English language learners (ELL) at Farrington High School, a large urban high school in Honolulu situated in a predominantly immigrant and low-socioeconomic community. The majority of my students identified as Filipino or Filipino-American.

As a Filipino teacher from the Philippines, I tapped heavily into my knowledge of Filipino and Filipino-American history in Hawaii and the United States. I taught short stories like Saroyan's (1935) "The Filipino and the Drunkard" and showed images of 1920 posters depicting racism against Filipino farmers in California to introduce themes in Harper Lee's (1960) *To Kill a Mockingbird*. We read newspaper archives about the immigration of Hawaii sugarcane plantation farmers while we were reading John Steinbeck's (1937) *Of Mice and Men*. While these were important ways that I drew from many of my students' identities as well as my own history as a person of the Filipino diaspora, I knew not all my students could relate to these Filipino American stories.

In my classroom, I also had students from American Samoa, China, the Federated States of Micronesia, the Marshall Islands, and Vietnam. I had students who were born in Hawaii as well as students who were newcomers to Hawaii and the United States. I had fully bilingual students, students who understood their heritage and home languages but communicated only in English, as well as students who were starting to learn Korean as part of their affinity for K-Pop celebrities. I always wondered how I should teach ELA in a way that represented all my students. There's no singular story that can capture the granularity of experiences brought by my students. More importantly, focusing on the story of the majority reproduced the dismissal of experiences of other students who remained underrepresented or invisible in the curriculum. This wondering was heightened when I met Asian American colleagues at a National Council of Teachers of English (NCTE)Asian American caucus gathering. Unlike me, many of my colleagues belong to minority groups in their school districts.

I started looking into what my students have in common. Opening our classroom to many facets of their identities helped me find an intersection between all the differences that the kids have. Within this intersection is the wealth they bring into the classroom that enhances what we are learning and how they are learning. Dr. Tara Yosso (2005) describes the following six forms of capital in her Community Cultural Wealth model: aspirational, linguistic, familial, social, navigational, and resistance. Zoch and He (2020) offer the following definitions of Dr. Yosso's six forms of capital:

- Aspirational capital—one's ability to maintain aspirations despite barriers and hardships
- Linguistic capital—the multiple language and communication skills that individuals have
- Familial capital—includes kinship ties as well as broader community ties
- Social capital—extends familial capital to include a broader network of people and community resources
- Navigational capital—the skill to navigate social institutions
- Resistance capital—the skill to navigate social institutions (p. 150)

Zoch and He (2020) reiterate Dr. Yosso and Jana Noel's stance that teachers "need to know classroom-based instructional strategies, as well as the dispositions, knowledge, and skills to work with and learn from local communities"

(p. 149). I hope that while you dream about the possibilities of bringing students' cultural capital into your classroom through the lessons I am about to share, you are also examining your beliefs on the importance of providing space for all students' community cultural wealth in your classroom.

Voice: Poetry by the Youth of Kalihi

Voice: Poetry by the Youth of Kalihi (Students of Farrington High School, 2019) is a multilingual poetry and student publication written by culturally and linguistically diverse students. The publication has garnered recognition from both the State of Hawaii Legislature and the Honolulu City Council. In 2019, the publication received a special citation award from the Migration Advocacy Awards of the Philippine government's Commission on Filipinos Overseas. The poems in this anthology were written by 54 ELL students in both English and their home and heritage languages. The students' languages were not used for translation only but as rhetorical devices that helped the kids write poetry that shared their longing for home, love for their families, their healing, and hopes for their future:

> In this anthology, you will find poems sharing the experiences our students wish others knew about them. You will find poems written by students born in Hawai'i while living in multilingual families and who are navigating the disconnect between living in two conflicting cultures. You will find poems written by newcomer students who are adjusting to a new culture, a new school, and a new home. You will also find poems written by 1.5 generation immigrant students who continually grapple with what it means to fit into mainstream American culture while keeping hold of the traditions and values they carried with them into this country." (Students of Farrington High School, 2019)

When we introduced our students to this book publication project, we asked the kids to stand around a circle and step forward when they heard a statement that resonated with them. Our students and three of my colleagues who were part of our English language development (ELD) and 9th grade content-based ELA team moved to the center of our circle when the following statements were called: "I was born outside of Hawaii" and "I speak or understand another language." When we asked if they had a voice, the majority of the kids hesitated to move, and they stayed outside the circle. One student justified his hesitation by announcing, "We are just students." These kids, along with many ELL students, had been exposed to deficit rhetoric ascribed to being an immigrant, a resident of a low-socioeconomic community, and an ELL student.

One of the purposes of this publication is to highlight many of the students' community cultural wealth, which is often overlooked and perceived as deficits: being new to another country, speaking and understanding many other languages while learning English as an additional language, and living in one of the toughest neighborhoods of Oahu in Hawaii.

First, these students speak and understand more than 20 languages. We have poems written in Chuukese, Mandarin, Marshallese, different Philippine languages (Ilokano, Tagalog, and Visayan), Samoan, and Vietnamese. "[L]inguistic capital reflects the idea that Students of Color arrive at school with multiple language and communication skills" (Yosso, 2005). One of the worries of many teachers, not only ELA teachers, is that their ELL students are not yet proficient in English. In the two examples I highlight, two students who are learning English, used their linguistic capitals to write their poetry for the anthology. By deciding to write portions of their poems in their heritage and home languages, the students demonstrated sophisticated authorial choices often seen exclusively in monolingual ELA contexts. In the first poem, a student eulogizes her grandmother. She decided not to italicize her use of Ilokano because she intended her grandma or nanang as her intended audience.

> For you, who sometimes told me "Haan ka pay mangan, annako
>
> ngamin nag lukmeg kan," and I responded "Wen, nanang"
>
> but I still ate because food is life. For you, who let me sleep
>
> between Tatang and you, to whom I said "I love you, Nanang Violet.
>
> I'll see you next year ah, and be careful" and who responded
>
> "Aysus, appo ubbing umay-kayon ah."

Another student uses metaphors to describe his longing for his parents, who he left in American Samoa when he moved to Hawaii to continue his education. The student introduces us to "lua lapoa" (two giants), whose legend explains the origin of American Samoa's tallest mountains. These two mountains are the "most important mountains of all time" similar to how he reveres his parents. He began to conclude his poem by comparing himself to a "va'a" or a boat who is still rowing for answers.

> In American Samoa, in the past, there were two giants
>
> lua lapoa who are brothers, uso
>
> Their names were Matafao and Pioa / but they always argued
>
> Later on, Matafao and Pioa passed away
>
> on the same day
>
> and became the two biggest mountains in American Samoa
>
> They are the most important mountains of all time
>
> because they're big, tall, and beautiful
>
> like my parents who always fight when it comes down
>
> to financial and family issues
>
> I am a va'a who is still rowing to find answers
>
> to help my parents.

While I still struggled to find texts that might represent each student's experience, I pivoted to realize each student could bring their experiences to author powerful texts and teach their classmates (and me) using diverse model texts from other communities. The first poem emulates the style of Sandra Cisneros' (2018) "Abuelito Who." Many of our other students wrote poems in the style of the Marshallese poet Kathy Jetñil-Kijiner, whose anthology *Iep Jaltok Poems from a Marshallese Daughter* (2017) was the first poetry anthology written in Marshallese. The linguistic capital demonstrated and highlighted by the students in their poetry built on the social capital our team also brought into our classrooms. Social capital "can be understood as networks of people and community resources" (Yosso, 2005, p. 79). Although authors like Cisneros and Jetñil-Kijiner are not local to the community where students live, they belong to a community of multilingual writers who serve as models of how multilingualism is an essential aspect of our student identities. When students saw examples of successful writers who share similar traits, they began to let go of the deficit rhetoric they started to believe about their multilingualism and started using their languages as tools for creative expression.

In addition to these authors, our students were also mentored by poets Giovanni Ortega, author of *Ang Gitano* (2017), and Amalia Bueno, a local Hawaii poet who writes about her memories and relationship with Filipino food. Both Giovanni and Amalia ran in-person poetry writing workshops for our students and showed how our kids can use much of their community cultural wealth in their writing. Our students also virtually met with California-based Dwight Ong who, at the time we were starting to write *Voice*, just published *Voices of the New Gen. Fil-Am Community* (2018), a collection of essays by Filipino American college students in California. Our kids were curious about Dwight's motivation and his process, and they asked for his advice as they were about to venture into publishing an anthology too.

The mahalo or acknowledgment page of *Voice* lists over 30 individuals and community groups who served as our editors, heritage language support, volunteer editors, media support, financial donors, book cover designers, reviewers, and photographers. For example, published poets from the Filipino Association of University Women (FAUW) served as book editors. Multilingual staff who speak Chuukese and Marshallese from the Pacific Resources for Education and Learning (PREL) served as language supports, and the Parent and Children Together (PACT) who provide social services to Hawaii's most vulnerable populations helped us bring our book launch to the communities where our students live. When we called for help and support, these individuals and groups contributed their resources, knowledge in publishing and writing, and other skills that paved the way to the publication and celebration of our students' anthology. Most notably, the photographers were photography students at our high school who were also ELL students themselves.

Critical to the anthology's success was looking beyond what was already on our bookshelves and looking into the community's abundant resources. Our poets contributed literature that represents their identities, and through the process, they enriched our communities by becoming social capitals themselves to other students in Hawaii who started studying their poetry and continue to find inspiration in their written work. In all of the poems in *Voice*, students shared the rich stories that were passed down by their families, and they honored their families and friends who continue to give them hope. Their aspirations to finish their education as a vehicle to support their families are evident in many of the poems. Their aspiration to help their peers through their writing is evident in their dedication page: "For those who are about to give up, / And for the troubled youth."

A notable result of *Voice* is it allowed students to demonstrate their resistant capital or "knowledges and skills fostered through oppositional behavior that challenges inequality" (Yosso, 2005) by using and leveraging their linguistic capital to challenge the deficit mindset around their multilingualism in our Western classrooms. *Voice* is a counternarrative, a form of resistance, to all the beliefs that multilingual students should abandon their languages at the door of our classrooms in favor of fluency in English. Turning my team's dream to transform our classrooms where all languages are welcomed and used to learn and form new knowledge is also our form of resistance.

The Potluck Project

I was inspired by an episode from the *School's In* podcast I heard sometime in 2021 for the next example of how we brought in students' community cultural wealth in a mathematics classroom (Schwartz & Pope, 2020). Around this time, two important things happened. First, I joined a group of Hawaii teachers who were designing project-based and place-based lessons and units that will be part of a library of resources for teachers in our state. I was designing a unit with a colleague who teaches mathematics at a different high school. In the podcast episode, Ramón Martínez urged teachers to re-engage multilingual learners while they are learning remotely, at home, by involving their parents in the process. Second, I started learning how to cook Filipino food that I missed eating from home in the Philippines, having just read Michelle Zauner's (2018) essay "Crying in H Mart." The idea of learning and writing about food to re-engage students piqued my interest.

Writing about food is not a matter of dipping into the thesaurus to discover the many ways to say 'tasty.' Instead, it means digging deep into human experience, because tasting, eating, and savoring are very intimate ventures. . . . When one describes food, one does not use words alone, but the reader's remembering as well - of past pleasures, savored sensations. One writes on their reservoirs of pleasures. In effect, one draws on all of the culture that shaped oneself and one's readers. (Fernandez, 2019, p. 1)

Writing about food allows students to bring multiple cultural capitals into our classrooms.

I suggested this idea to a colleague who was teaching math from a neighboring high school, and we started the process of designing an interdisciplinary ELA and math unit where students write about food that reminds them of home, interview a family member to co-write the recipe, and prepare a budget sheet for various serving sizes of their chosen food. We challenged students to write poetry or a short story about the food they were bringing to our virtual potluck. They had the choice to write their pieces, including their recipes, in any language they wanted to use. This was another opportunity for us to partner with local Hawaii poet Amalia Bueno, who virtually spoke to the students about her process of writing about food. After Amalia Bueno modeled her process, the students went to work. I met with the students to help them with their writing, and their math teacher worked with them to prepare their budget sheets.

The students brought in their familial and linguistic capitals during the process. They wrote about memories with their grandparents, attending family gatherings, and even the food they were learning about through their fondness for the emerging Korean pop culture in Hawaii. In writing their recipes, students started the process of preserving family treasures that are passed down in kitchens and between generations. When the students presented their recipe, their creative writing pieces, and their budget sheets with their classmates and a group of community members during our virtual potluck, the students expressed that they learned so much about each other during the writing process. This was surprising for us to hear because the students were about to graduate from high school a few days after the project concluded.

In both examples above, our students' community cultural wealth enhanced how and what they learned in their English and math classrooms. Both examples also challenged the assumptions that students can only demonstrate their knowledge and skills through mastery and proficiency in the English language. We sought the help of community organizations and individuals who modeled possibilities of using community cultural wealth in their chosen professional fields. Most importantly, our students learned more about their identities and celebrated not only their academic achievements but all that makes them who they are. Both *Voice* and the Potluck Project were successful because we had a community of educators who believed in the power of what our students bring to our classrooms.

I have since transitioned from my teaching role into a district educational specialist. I currently facilitate the Hawaii State Department of Education's Na Kumu Alaka'i – Teacher Leader Academy (TLA). I no longer work directly with students, but I emphasize the role of teachers working in communities of practice to address student-centered challenges. As educators, we need to believe that our students' perceived deficits—multilingualism, being an immigrant, from an ethnic minority group, or living in a low socioeconomic neighborhood—are assets and strengths that are as valuable as the knowledge and skills that our content standards dictate us to teach. Honoring our students' cultural capitals requires us, teachers and school leaders, to expand the boundaries of our classrooms and schools until the walls of these physical spaces blend with the communities where the wealth that our students bring with them resides. Our belief that all our students can learn and contribute to their learning is far more important than our knowledge of instructional strategies

References

Cisneros, S. (2018). *Abuelito who*. Teachers and Writers Magazine. https://teachersand writersmagazine.org/wp-content/uploads/2018/04/Cisneros-Abuelito-Who-Poem-and-Bio.pdf.

Fernandez, D. G. (2019). *Tikim: Essays on Philippine food and culture*. Brill.

Jetñil-Kijiner, K. (2017). *Iep Jaltok: Poems from a Marshallese daughter*. University of Arizona Press.

Lee, H. (1960). *To kill a mockingbird*. Lippincott.

Ong, D. (2018). *Voices of the new gen. Fil-Am community: Real Fil-Ams, real stories*. Independently Published.

Ortega, G. (2017). *Ang Gitano*. Carayan Press.

Saroyan, W. (1994). *The William Saroyan Reader*, (pp. 116–118). Barricade Books.

Schwartz, D., & Pope, D. (Hosts). (2020, August 31). Bringing language lessons home (No. 1009) [Audio podcast episode] . In *School's in*. Stanford Graduate School of Education. https://ed.stanford.edu/news/bringing-language-lessons-home

Steinbeck, J. (1937). *Of mice and men*. Penguin Classics.

Students of Farrington High School. (2019). *Voice: Poetry by the youth of Kalihi*. Independently Published.

Yosso, T. J. (2005). Whose culture has capital? A critical race theory discussion of community cultural wealth. *Race Ethnicity and Education, 8*(1), 69–91.

Zauner, M. (2018, August 20). Crying in H Mart. *The New Yorker*. https://www.newyorker.com/culture/culture-desk/crying-in-h-mart.

Zoch, M., & He, Y. (2020). Utilizing community cultural wealth to learn with diverse language communities. *The Teacher Educator, 55*(2), 148–164.

Building an Inclusive Movement: Curricular Re-Memberings

Bic Ngo

NHỚ MÌNH LÀ *người việt* (Remember we are Vietnamese). This was my mother's mantra throughout my years of primary and secondary schooling. My mother understood almost immediately after resettlement that, as refugees to the United States, we would be made to forget Vietnamese culture, identity, language, and heritage. As a technology of the United States empire, education's soft power induces its racialized, ethnic, and Indigenous students to adopt and internalize its hegemonic "values, cultures, knowledges, and practices" (Coloma, 2013, p. 643). In schools, this is reflected in curricula, books, criteria for academic success, legitimized cultural capital, self-image, self-aspirations, and worldview (Maldonado-Torres, 2007). The four chapters in this section recognize the "curriculum as colonizer" (Goodwin, 2010). For example, in Chapter 5, Edward Curammeng, Giselle Cunanan, and Cheralen Valdez point out, "Oftentimes the books that focus on culture and history provide a biased perspective from the dominant culture" (p. 79). In Chapter 6, Ruchi Agarwal-Rangnath contends, "curriculum is framed around the perspectives and experiences of white people" (p. 88). Monica Eraqi suggests, in Chapter 7, the dominance of white perspectives in the curriculum only includes fractured histories or "piecemeal" narratives of diverse groups. Lastly, in Chapter 8, Norman Sales argues, "the story of the majority reproduced the dismissal of experiences of other students who remained underrepresented or invisible in the curriculum" (p. 108). For Asian American students and families, the hegemony of Western cultural logics produces the erasure of culture, ethnicity, and community.

In different ways, each of the four chapters reflects on the possibilities of leveraging ethnic identities and heritages towards decolonial scholar Ngũgĩ wa Thiong'o's (2009) conception of "re-membering." Against the backdrop of dismemberment projects of colonialism that fractured memories, communities, and peoplehood "re-membering" involves practices to regain ethnic memory and membership (Ngo, 2024). Curammeng and colleagues draw on Maria Matsuda's (1992) concept of "multiple consciousness" to explore the ways in which K-12 Asian American teachers engage Asian American Studies in their classrooms. Agarwal-Rangnath explores teaching South Asian American experiences with a focus on *identity and belonging*, one of four elements of Ethnic Studies for the K-12 classroom (others include understanding systems and power, building community and power, and transformation and change) (Agarwal-Rangnath et al., 2022). Eraqi details insights from nearly two decades of teaching a high school elective course on Middle Eastern Studies. Sales elaborates on engaging the community cultural wealth (Yosso, 2005) of Filipino and Filipino American high school students in Hawaii.

Altogether, the four chapters serve as a critical intervention into education as a technology of the U.S. empire (Coloma, 2013) by illuminating insights towards a "re-membering pedagogy" (Ngo & Vang, 2024) for reclaiming and re-storying culture, identity, heritage, and community.

References

Agarwal-Rangnath, R., Yeh, C., & Hsieh, B. (2022). We need to see each other as human: Ethnic Studies as a framework for humanizing K–12 education. In T. K. Chapman & N. Hobbel (Eds.), *Social justice pedagogy across the curriculum* (pp. 217–229). Routledge.

Coloma, R. S. (2013). Empire: An analytical category for educational research. *Educational Theory, 63*(6), 639–658.

Goodwin, A. L. (2010). Curriculum as colonizer: (Asian) American education in the current US context. *Teachers College Record, 112*(12), 3102–3138.

Maldonado-Torres, N. (2007). On the coloniality of being: Contributions to the development of a concept. *Cultural Studies, 21*(2-3), 240–270.

Matsuda, M. J. (1992). When the first quail calls: Multiple consciousness as jurisprudential method. *Women's Rts. L. Rep., 14*, 297.

Ngo, B. (2024). *Re-membering culture: Erasure and renewal in Hmong American education*. University of Minnesota Press.

Ngo, B., & Vang, T. (2024). Re-membering pedagogy: Reclaiming Hmong heritage and belonging within a youth theater program. *Diaspora, Indigenous, and Minority Education,*
1–14.

wa Thiong'o, N. (2009). *Something torn and new: An African renaissance.* Basic Books.

Yosso, T. J. (2005). Whose culture has capital? A critical race theory discussion of community
cultural wealth. *Race Ethnicity and Education, 8*(1), 69–91.

Part III

Extending the Movement

Becoming Justice-Oriented Educational Leaders: Counternarratives and Praxis From Boggs, Kochiyama, and Itliong

Paul Joo Hyun Koh

I WAS BORN in South Korea, and at 6 years old, my family and I immigrated to the United States. From a familiar Seoul to an unfamiliar Seattle, we became "resident aliens." In elementary school, I remember white, male school staff asking, "Are you Chinese?" When I answered "no," they inquired, "Japanese?" When I said "no" again and added "I'm Korean," they followed up with "North Korea or South Korea?" Whiteness likes to determine who we Asian Americans and Pacific Islanders (AAPIs) are, labeling us as model minorities or colonial subjects where "alienage" is our badge (Ngai, 2014).

My parents operated a cafeteria, a video store, and a liquor store so we could survive as a family. Through my parents' sacrifice, I chose education as a career and began teaching at 24 years old. During my first year as a teacher, my resident alien status changed to U.S. citizen. My journey is a speck in the larger history of the Asian diaspora, yet I cannot be Korean, an immigrant, an educator, and American in the eyes of white America.

AAPIs represent 7.7% of the U.S. population, but only 1% of K-12 educational leadership (Budiman et al., 2024; United States Census Bureau, 2021; National Center for Education Statistics, 2020). Similarly, in 2020, while grants that focused on immigrant, Black, and Latinx communities increased by 80% (Immigrant-focused); 64% (Black-focused); 61% (Latinx-focused), those that

are geared towards Asian Americans increased by 30%, and those towards Native Hawaiians and other Pacific Islanders increased by a mere 5% (AAPI Data
et al., 2020). These data points emphasize the degree to which the experiences
of AAPIs are underrepresented and underfunded. When I was a history teacher,
principal, principal supervisor, and then assistant superintendent, I only met
three Korean American educators during this 20-year period.

   With limited examples of critical AAPI leadership in schools, this chapter
lifts up the activism and legacies of Grace Lee Boggs, Yuri Kochiyama, and
Larry Itliong as a way to draw on the cultural community wealth of justice-oriented AAPI activists as a model of leadership. Emphasizing these points, the
chapter is organized into the following sections: AAPI racialization and leadership perceptions; critical race ethnography (CRE) as a way to provide meaning
to the lived experiences of Boggs, Kochiyama, and Itliong; the 11 major leadership tenets of Boggs, Kochiyama, and Itliong; and a synthesis of their leadership
tenets for scholars and practitioners to consider.

AAPI Racialization and Leadership Perceptions

   As an educational leader, I never had a sense of belonging in the schools and
districts I worked for. With no affinity groups for AAPI teachers, principals,
and district leaders, I navigated norms and beliefs that reiterated whiteness and
white-normative behavior as ideal, disappearing my Asian-ness. As a result,
I did not feel self-assured as a leader. For example, at a meeting with school
principals, a San Francisco Police Department (SFPD) representative indicated
school police always considered the safety and well-being of students. Arguing
against that notion, I shared my observations of SFPD officers being aggressive
and, at times, abusive when restraining our students. I noted it was a problem
that such mistreatments stopped only when administrators intervened. The
SFPD representative looked at me and responded, "That doesn't happen. That's
not true," and dismissed my assertions. In that moment, I wished I pushed back
and told the police representative to not gaslight my experiences. Instead, I
looked around and wondered if I was being unreasonable. At the end of the
session, a colleague came up and thanked me for speaking up.

Although I felt validated by a fellow principal, I questioned if my perspective as an Asian male leader carried any authoritative weight, akin to what Eng and Han (2019) assert, that AAPIs are caught in a "suspended assimilation" (p. 36) that splits their psyche between belonging through assimilation and not being allowed to be part of "the larger social body" (p. 43). This dynamic creates an external perception that AAPIs are not strong or effective leaders per white-normative standards, coupled with an internal-psychological perspective that AAPIs lack leadership potential (Balón, 2004).

Critical Race Ethnography

CRE is a framework derived from the body of critical race theory (CRT) in education that shifts the racialized experiences of AAPIs from a place of liminality into liberatory praxis. CRE centers on the analysis of ontologies to understand the ways "race functions as a stratifying force in school and society" and gives meaning to the lived experiences of racialized people (Duncan, 2005, p. 95). CRE "follows the lead indicated by proponents of CRT to take the words of people of colour seriously and, instead of stopping there, to allow these voices to inform how we approach our examination of the material conditions that are basic to and inextricably a part of lived experience" (Duncan, 2005, p. 106). CRE seeks to engage multiple ways of being to give meaning to the lived experiences of racialized people.

In my search for meaning as an assistant superintendent, I engaged fellow AAPI K-12 educational leaders over 2 years to explore our experiences and identities as a research project. As we shared our stories, I offered the lived experiences of Boggs, Kochiyama, and Itliong to participants as a way to share past examples of justice-oriented AAPI leadership. Over the course of our conversations, the project revealed that our experiences strongly connected to Boggs, Kochiyama, and Itliong through the ways each leader intertwined heart, thought, and action to change their communities. Connecting ourselves with each other and to this legacy gave meaning to our lived experiences as leaders. We saw ourselves as part of a lineage of justice-oriented activism and collective critical consciousness that Boggs, Kochiyama, and Itliong exemplified. Honoring these leaders anchored us in the wisdom of AAPI elders and reminded us of our family stories as lived experiences of leadership. In the next section, I discuss my own family experiences in connection to the lives of Boggs, Kochiyama, and Itliong as a way to honor familial leadership experiences.

Honoring Family Leadership

My 외할아버지's (maternal grandfather's) story exemplifies the strength, courage, and resilience of moving through and beyond a war-torn Korea. He stepped off a boat in 부산 (Busan), away from his family in North Korea. A teacher's credential certified under the Japanese government provided a way for him to continue his profession as a teacher and later as a school leader. He met my 외할머니 (maternal grandmother), and together they raised a family with two daughters and two sons. Later in life, he survived a stroke, perhaps the effects of war and restarting of his life. 외할아버지's story is familial love reminding me to persist and transform hardships into a fulfilled life within a U.S. context that diminishes my AAPI identity.

외할아버지's experience is enmeshed within a legacy of AAPIs that is largely hidden or unrecognized in broader U.S. histories. Similarly, the contributions of Boggs, Kochiyama, and Itliong are obfuscated in U.S. historical narratives. They held life experiences, knowledge, and a dedication foregrounded in love for their communities. Amplifying the lives of Boggs, Kochiyama, and Itliong offers a lens of leadership rooted in the cultural wealth of their lived experiences. Their leadership is a model for humanizing and justice-oriented actions that exceed white-centered forms of leadership.

Grace Lee Boggs (1915–2015) asked movements to focus on critical connections instead of critical mass (Boggs & Kurashige, 2012). Critical connections occur as people allow others to be the fullest version of themselves. Through her long-standing activism addressing racial and economic injustice in Detroit, Michigan, Boggs built critical connections through *dialectical humanism,* a process of belief transformation that occurs when people engage with new information and experiences that lead them to reevaluate and embrace positions they once believed to be wrong. Critical connections encourage leaders to embrace the complex dimensions of the people they serve and create spaces to be changed by others.

Yuri Kochiyama (1921–2014) emphasized that individual interests and concerns are as important as the collective struggle against institutionalized racism and state power (Fujino, 2005). This concept of *collective care* emphasized the value in others' well-being in justice-oriented work. Kochiyama exemplified this care for others through activism alongside various communities of color, including Black and Latinx communities in New York. When she was incarcerated in an internment camp, Kochiyama started a letter writing campaign to support the morale of Japanese American soldiers fighting during World War II. Kochiyama's concept of collective care urges leaders to gauge and respond to the wellness and feelings of others. She reminds leaders that engaging with the emotionality of our struggles towards justice is as important as any leadership initiative.

Larry Itliong (1913–1977) came to the United States hoping for a better life. However, seeing his fellow Filipinos struggling, homeless, and jobless in Alaska, Washington, and California, he decided to dedicate his life to create sustainable and humanizing conditions for laborers. Organizing and forging collaborations between Filipino and Mexican workers, Itliong modeled ways to create impact through strategic networking that "helped lead a renaissance of farm labor organizing that is still going on today" (Bacon, 2018, p. 25). Similar to Boggs and Kochiyama, Itliong modeled leadership grounded in connecting with others to change the world through effective action. While change does not occur overnight, creating justice-oriented impact is a process Itliong dedicated his life to up and down the West Coast of the United States.

Figure 9.1 provides an overview of Boggs, Kochiyama, and Itliong's leadership praxis.

Figure 9.1 *Leadership Praxis*

BOGGS
Revolution and Evolution
(Boggs & Boggs, 1974)

Working *with* oppressed people through a lens of activism that is humanizing, filled with struggle, and seeks to resolve a specific societal contradiction.

KOCHIYAMA
Heartbeat of Struggle: The Revolutionary Life of Yuri Kochiyama (Fujino, 2005)

Build our aspirational world through a collective consciousness, through cross-racial coalitions, holding the interests, feelings, concerns of individuals as part of the work.

ITLIONG
How Filipino Migrants Gave the Grape Strike Its Radical Politics (Bacon, 2018)

Leadership is about impact, not notoriety, creates collective power, and builds a pathway for future generations.

Justice-Oriented Leadership Tenets

In my analysis of their life stories and activism, Boggs, Kochiyama, and Itliong collectively promote 11 major tenets for justice-oriented leadership:

1. Project a *more human* human being with a sense of political and social responsibility (Boggs & Boggs, 1974).
2. Work with the oppressed to share a new way of being together and exercise their creativity towards positive societal transformation (Boggs & Boggs, 1974).
3. Develop an ideology to address a specific societal contradiction and create a vision to resolve it (Boggs & Boggs, 1974).
4. Leadership and activism are about struggle with no final solution. The struggle is the work and the highest expression of human creativity (Boggs & Boggs, 1974).
5. Recognize that the interests, feelings, and concerns of the individual within the collective struggle against institutionalized racism and state power are just as important as the struggle itself (Fujino, 2005).

6. Honor cross-racial coalitions to provide organizing approaches that resist gains made at the expense of others (Fujino, 2005).
7. Polarization and racism create artificial divisions on the basis of nationality, race, gender, sexual orientation, and class, impeding any movement's actions towards justice (Fujino, 2005).
8. Build an aspirational world together through the power of collective consciousness (Abdelfatah et al., 2021).
9. Create collective power through strategic networking and organizing to move beyond polarizations (Bacon, 2018).
10. Leadership is about making impact, not notoriety. Leaders must create positive social change with tangible results (Bacon, 2018).
11. Leadership paves the pathway for future generations to build on the work of previous leaders.

Boggs, Kochiyama, and Itliong committed themselves to a collectivist form of leadership that required humanizing relationships and cross-racial coalitions. U.S. K-12 public education is a space where ways of being, ways of knowing, and pedagogy are negotiated through the lens of Western cultures. The 11 leadership tenets of Boggs, Kochiyama, and Itliong push beyond this dynamic and provide tenets for K-12 leaders to center their leadership praxis on humanizing relationships and cross-racial coalitions. Such leadership shifts the core of leadership from an act of doing something to a community into an act of building relational trust with students, families, educators, and community stakeholders to inform the changes needed in public education.

In the next section, I break down the 11 major leadership tenets into three key concepts—withness leadership, alignment of intention and impact, and collective struggle—as a guide for current and future K-12 educational leaders to engage and intertwine their lived experiences with those of Boggs, Kochiyama, and Itliong.

Withness Leadership

Hanold (2017) describes *withness* as a way to tend to the space between self and others, shifting the directionality of one's leadership focus from the interpretation of others into allowing others to shape one's leadership. Withness implores K-12 educational leaders to engage with stakeholders to inform and determine the ways they lead. For Boggs, engaging in withness leadership was about accelerating change efforts to a "higher plateau of [h]umanity" that not only corrects past injustices, but restores relationships with others (Boggs & Kurashige, 2012, p. 70). For Kochiyama, withness leadership echoes her work with the Harlem Parents Committee (HPC) where, as the only AAPI in the group, she demonstrated her commitment to Black and Latinx families through her "hard work, dependability, and enthusiasm" (Fujino, 2005, pp. 116, 122). Itliong's withness leadership derived from his forming of the United Farm Workers union that brought together laborers (Latinx, Filipino, Black) who "lived in different worlds" yet learned to "work together, to know each other, and to begin to fight together" (Bacon, 2018, p. 23).

Leadership is often framed as a solitary and hierarchical process that results in leaders making decisions for others. There are many instances when I felt compelled to abide by such hierarchy, for instance, in budgeting, hiring, or personnel matters. However, Boggs, Kochiyama, and Itliong ask leaders to engage in withness leadership that humanizes and forms cross-racial and other solidarities to break down hierarchies and create change.

Alignment of Intention and Impact

In K-12 education, leadership is often applauded for *trying*. "Well, we're working on it," "we're trying really hard," and "we're in the process of addressing that" are common statements I've made during staff meetings and board meetings to articulate to stakeholders that *something good* is hopefully happening in schools. Boggs, Kochiyama, and Itliong remind us that intention is not enough. In the early 1990s, Boggs worked with community organizers to start Detroit Summer as an action to revitalize the city from the ashes of industrialization by engaging youth in community building activities such as planting community gardens, instituting recycling programs, organizing neighborhood arts and health festivals, rehabilitating houses, and painting public murals (Boggs & Kurashige, 2012). From its inception, Detroit Summer youth have been a part of the program leadership that still exists today as an organization focused on community activism that is responsive to the challenges posed by the conditions and struggles in a postindustrial city. Kochiyama engaged with HPC in the early 1960s to pursue the goal of a quality integrated education centered on the belief that schools in New York City must be both "physically desegregated" and unified through an "integrated curriculum" (Fujino, 2005, pp. 123–124). To achieve this goal, the HPC called for a boycott in every Harlem school on the first day of school in 1963 (Fujino, 2005). This action began a series of boycotts that Kochiyama worked in partnership with civil rights groups in what would become the "largest school boycott in the history of New York City" with 92% of students participating (Fujino, 2005, pp. 123–124). As a way to organize asparagus harvesters, "Itliong would sneak into a camp, crawl under the bunkhouse, and speak to workers through the cracks in the floor" (Bacon, 2018, pp. 9–10). With such actions, Filipino workers began sit-ins at their labor camps to start a strike in Delano, California. Despite some of them being physically assaulted while their gas, water, and lights were shut off at their camps, Itliong worked with fellow laborers to strike for better working conditions and wages through grassroots efforts (Bacon, 2018).

Boggs, Kochiyama, and Itliong lived a leadership that was strategically impactful. Within unjust and unequal educational contexts, their legacy asks K-12 leaders to imagine possibilities and do the work to make impacts grounded in justice. Their leadership is a reminder that leaders cannot engage in such actions on their own and must build coalitions with others to create impactful solutions. For example, if a leader is charged with resolving disproportionate suspension rates of male students of color, they must gather a cross-racial coalition of stakeholders to consider the causes of disproportionality (e.g., relationship of instructional quality and student engagement) and engage in a process of action planning and implementation to reduce these disproportionalities. Thus, if overall suspension rates decrease, districts can report that "things are pointing in the right direction." But if the disproportionality persists, then the leaders in the district must look deep into the initiative and cannot declare success until disproportionality is reduced.

Collective Struggle

Leaders intuitively know that the forces of *-isms*, such as racism, colonialism, and imperialism, impact their work. James Boggs and Grace Lee Boggs (1974) remind us that working through such forces requires a paradigm shift in how we live, while remembering "[w]e are all works in progress, always in the process of being and becoming" (p. xxxiv). In K-12 public education contexts, leaders rarely have time to engage in such reflection. There is a constant urgency that overtakes leaders' abilities to pause, think, and reflect. Boggs, Kochiyama, and Itliong ask leaders to struggle through -isms, knowing that there is no final solution. This type of struggle is a struggle to "find more adequate questions" regarding the nature of humanity which has no "absolute answers" (Boggs & Boggs, 1974, pp. 197–198). Such struggle requires projecting humanity into the future, centering our "creativity, consciousness, . . . a sense of political and social responsibility" as a way to engage in the struggle to change the world (Boggs & Boggs, 1974, p. 19). Similarly, Kochiyama exhibited collective struggling by asking people from opposing sides how they felt after a fierce debate, often listening intently and humanizing their perspectives (Fujino, 2005). Itliong struggled with fellow laborers through violent suppression and inhumane tactics and kept alive their "political and trade union ideas" to lead a renaissance of labor organizing that is still ongoing (Bacon, 2018, p. 25). Each leader reminds us that leadership is about struggle with no final solution. Through questioning, tending to others' feelings, and taking action within coalitions, Boggs, Kochiyama, and Itliong demonstrate the ways leaders can struggle through together to create paradigms beyond the -isms.

Windows to Another World

> You grow up hearing two languages. Neither fits your fits
> Your mother informs you "moon" means "window to another world."
> —JOHN YAU FROM *MUSIC FROM CHILDHOOD*

Withness, alignment of intention with impact, and collective struggle underscore the praxis that Boggs, Kochiyama, and Itliong used to lead. This chapter delineates major leadership tenets drawn from these Asian American social justice warriors: engaging in humanistic activism, working with the oppressed, developing ideologies to address societal contradictions, recognizing the emotionality of justice-oriented work, building cross-racial coalitions, acknowledging the realities of polarization and racism, and building an aspirational world with others in service of future generations. Boggs, Kochiyama, and Itliong represent a humanizing and collectivist form of AAPI leadership, underscoring the strengths that AAPI leaders bring to the work. In K-12 public schools where various ways of being, knowing, teaching, and leading are constantly negotiated, Boggs, Kochiyama, and Itliong provide windows into another world beyond Western ways of leadership. They exemplify justice-oriented leadership and remind us that Asian Americans and Pacific Islanders have been and will continue to be effective leaders.

References

AAPI Data, Center for Social Innovation, & AAPIP. (2020). *State of philanthropy among Asian Americans and Pacific Islanders: Findings and recommendations to strengthen visibility and impact.* https://aapidata.com/wp-content/uploads/2024/02/aapi-state-of-philanthropy-2020-report.pdf

Abdelfatah, R., Arablouei, R., York, J., Caine, J., Kaplan-Levenson, L., Wu, L., Shah, P., & Yvellez, V. (2021, April 1). *Our Own People.* NPR. https://www.npr.org/2021/03/29/982274384/our-own-people

Bacon, D. (2018). How Filipino migrants gave the grape strike its radical politics. *Dollars & Sense 336.* https://search.proquest.com/docview/2069032921

Balón, D. G. (2004). *Racial, ethnic, and gender differences among entering college student attitudes toward leadership, culture, and leader self-identification: A focus on Asian Pacific Americans.* (Publication No. 3139101) [Doctoral Dissertation, University of Maryland, College Park]. ProQuest.

Boggs, G. L., & Kurashige, S. (2012). *The next American revolution: Sustainable activism for the twenty-first century.* University of California Press.

Boggs, J., & Boggs, G. L. (1974). *Revolution and evolution.* Monthly Review Press.

Budiman, A., Passel, J. S., & Im, C. (2024). *Key facts about Asian American eligible voters in 2024.* Pew Research Center. https://www.pewresearch.org/short-reads/2024/01/10/key-facts-about-asian-american-eligible-voters-in-2024/

Duncan, G. A. (2005). Critical race ethnography in education: Narrative, inequality and the problem of epistemology. *Race, Ethnicity and Education, 8*(1), 93–114. https://doi.org /10.1080/13613320520003410 15

Eng, D. L., & Han, S. (2019). *Racial melancholia, racial dissociation: On the social and psychic lives of Asian Americans.* Duke University Press.

Fujino, D. C. (2005). *Heartbeat of struggle: The revolutionary life of Yuri Kochiyama.* University of Minnesota Press.

Hanold, M. (2017). Toward a new approach to authentic leadership: The practice of embodied dialogical "thinking" and the promise of shared power. *Advances in Developing Human Resources, 19*(4), 454–466. https://doi.org/10.1177/1523422317728940

National Center for Education Statistics. (2020). *Characteristics of public school principals.* https://nces.ed.gov/programs/coe/indicator_cls.asp

Ngai, M. M. (2014). *Impossible subjects: Illegal aliens and the making of modern America.* Princeton University Press. https://doi.org/10.1515/9781400850235

Abdelfatah, R., Arablouei, R., York, J., Caine, J., Kaplan-Levenson, L., Wu, L., Shah, P., & Yvellez, V. (2021, April 1). *Our Own People.* NPR. https://www.npr.org/2021/03/29/ 982274384/our-own-people

United States Census Bureau. (2021). *Race and ethnicity in the United States: 2010 Census and 2020 Census.* https://www.census.gov/library/visualizations/interactive/race-and-ethnicity-in-the-united-state-2010-and-2020-census.html

Mapping Consequential Geographies: Examining the Model Minority Racial Project in Teacher Education

Lawrence Teng, Cathery Yeh, and William Bae

SPACE MATTERS IN our racialized lives. As Asian Americans, we have been conditioned with the mentality of "knowing our place," expected to be a quiet, apolitical racial minority without taking up space. The authors identify as Taiwanese, Chinese, and Korean Americans, and as East Asians, we recognize that our social locations have historically occupied majoritized status in Asia, minoritized status in North America, and an increasingly "model minority" status around the world. Our identities and those of other Asian Americans are profoundly shaped by the histories of migration, colonization, and imperialism that shape our parents' and ancestors' stories. This awareness has empowered our work as educators and community members, pushing us to build solidarity with our students and to embody the understanding that learning, living, and dreaming require us to examine our lives and those of our students within and beyond school walls. Our origins, locations, and interactions with our environment and each other are all part of the spatial dimension of our reality.

In this chapter, we explore how space is a crucial sociopolitical factor in shaping racial identity, particularly as Asian Americans in educational systems. We begin by linking space and race through the works of Du Bois (1903), Soja (2010), and Coloma (2017). Using AsianCrit (Iftikar & Museus, 2018) and Critical Race Spatial Analysis (Morrison et al., 2017) as frameworks, we examine how Education Journey Mapping (Annamma, 2018) and digital multimodal storytelling facilitate individual and collective counterstorytelling. Spatial methodologies allow students and teachers to analyze racial identity in relation to location and sense of belonging. Through two case studies, we illustrate how spatial counterstorytelling both documents Asianization and serves as a form of resistance and self-narration for Asian Americans. This has significant implications for racial advocacy in both educational settings and beyond.

Mapping the Connections Between Race and Space

Our conception of space refers most directly to how people, locations, and objects relate to each other within geographical settings. Du Bois (1903) described the intersection of space and race as the "color line." In describing how Blacks and whites are "separate not simply in the higher realms of social intercourse, but also in church and school, on railway and street-car, in hotels and theatres" (Du Bois, 1903, p. 96), Du Bois highlights how racism and physical/ social separation can be mutually reinforcing. Forcible manipulations of space such as segregation, colonization, and imperialism contribute to racism and racial inequity—and vice versa—forming a mutually constructive interchange which Soja (2010) terms the "socio-spatial dialectic." The influence of space exists at all scales, from electoral gerrymandering and neighborhood resource distribution, to how students navigate classrooms and school. Regardless of context or scale, spatial arrangements both shape and are shaped by our social reality, reflecting the presence of oppression or justice.

Spatial racialization is central to the Asian American experience. From the onset of Asian immigration to the United States, groups such as Chinese, Japanese, and Indian immigrants were racialized as transient alien labor and perpetually foreign (Au, 2022; Kim, 1999). This spatial othering was reinforced by legal barriers to citizenship, access to schooling and other public spaces, and immigration restrictions such as the Chinese Exclusion Acts. Asians and Asian Americans have been depicted as undesirable immigrants and dangerous foreign agents, all consistent with the historical "yellow peril" narrative (Au, 2022). Recently, this othering has intersected with religion through travel bans targeting nationals from Muslim-majority Asian countries like Iran, Syria, and Yemen as well as African nations like Libya and Somalia (ACLU, 2024). Utilizing a transnational framework by Coloma (2017) helps us to recognize and challenge these spatial processes of othering, which demarcate Asia and the Pacific as "over there" and the United States as "over here." With an understanding of spatial racialization, we can better advocate for inclusion and support of Asian Americans through curricular representation and political activism.

AsianCrit

AsianCrit (Iftikar & Museus, 2018) provides an essential framework for understanding the issues and oppressive structures faced by Asian American communities. We focus on three of its seven tenets to shape our theoretical framework: *Asianization, transnational contexts,* and *strategic (anti)essentialism. Asianization* helps us identify specific racialization patterns of Asian Americans, such as the forever foreigner trope, yellow peril narrative, and the model minority myth (Au, 2022). Examining *transnational contexts* reveals how global economic and socio-political processes, including imperialism and colonialism, influence the daily experiences of Asian Americans (Coloma, 2017). Finally, with *strategic (anti)essentialism,* we can counter monolithic stereotypes by highlighting diverse Asian American voices and critically examining the social construction of race and the model minority myth. These tenets guide our application of Education Journey Mapping to explore how socio-spatial experiences shape racial identities throughout educational journeys.

Our application of AsianCrit to education responds to the reality that education is a consequential arena in which Asians and Asian Americans encounter racialization processes, influencing overall racial equity (Coloma, 2017; Iftikar & Museus, 2018). The model minority myth (MMM) is a key concept in this context, portraying Asians and Asian Americans as a socially and academically successful racial group, which other minority groups should emulate to succeed (Au, 2022). By positioning Asian American students as model minorities and, consequently, non-Asian students as "problem" minorities, the MMM supports racial hierarchy and weakens race-based coalitions essential for racial justice (Kim, 1999). It advances a false meritocratic image of education that attributes racial inequality to individual or cultural deficiencies rather than the need to examine how spatial environments, like schools, inscribe and are inscribed by social inequalities (Yu, 2006). Additionally, the MMM conflates diverse Asian

American experiences—from well-educated East Asians who benefited from the Immigration and Nationality Act of 1965 to Southeast Asian refugees fleeing war in their homeland—erasing distinct histories and socio-spatial inequities. A dominant form of Asianization, the MMM encourages the essentialization of all racial groups and works against racial justice overall.

Critical Race Spatial Analysis

To understand how space shapes the racialized experiences of Asians and Asian Americans, we integrate AsianCrit with Critical Race Spatial Analysis (CRSA). Building on critical race theory's (CRT) analysis of race as endemic, CRSA focuses on the "socio-spatial dialectic" (Soja, 2010), examining how space constructs race and interacts with other systems of oppression. Vélez & Solórzano (2017) describe CRSA as a framework and methodology for "identifying and challenging racism and white supremacy within these spaces [geographic and social]" and "to spatially examine how structural and institutional factors influence and shape racial dynamics and the power associated with those dynamics over time" (p. 20). Combined with AsianCrit, CRSA reveals the socio-spatial nature of *Asianization*. For example, CRSA, when used with a focus on *transnational contexts* and *strategic (anti)essentialism*, sheds light on how immigration histories of Asian American subgroups—such as those from the Philippines—are shaped by colonization and imperialism, affecting their educational experiences in the United States (Coloma, 2017). The absence of their narratives in curriculum is implicated in a process of empire-building in which students are educated to forget that *"we are here because you were there"* (Coloma, 2017, p. 98). Thus, AsianCrit and CRSA work in tandem to reveal how space mediates the unique racialization processes of Asian Americans.

Education Journey Mapping With Geographic Information Systems

In this chapter, we apply AsianCrit and CRSA to Education Journey Mapping (EJM) (Annamma, 2018). EJM examines the physical, social, and personal geographies in one's educational trajectory to uncover the power dynamics encountered along this path. Participants create visual representations of their educational journeys, including physical spaces, social environments, their personal growth, and anything else they deem important to their learning. They then explain and discuss their maps, providing insight into their experiences.

Annamma (2018) developed the method of EJM with incarcerated girls of color to explore their experiences with (in)justice in education over time. By hand-drawing and discussing their EJMs, they highlighted "consequential geographies, the physical and social spaces in their education trajectories that transmitted injustice and justice" (Annamma, 2018, p. 29). Findings included over-surveillance in incarceration, punitive treatment by educators, and restricting access to resources or privileges. EJM can reveal intimate personal insights and foster self-reflection and resistance, offering a multimodal approach that uncovers aspects of racial identity not captured by interviews or written accounts alone.

When combined with the digital mapping technologies of geographic information systems (GIS), EJM becomes a powerful tool to reveal how racism manifests over time and space and how individuals engage in resistance. We detail below how we adapted GIS to create digital EJMs with teachers and students and investigated patterns in them using CRSA and AsianCrit. Our examples demonstrate that EJM is a promising tool for uncovering socio-spatial experiences of racialization and resistance among students, teachers, and educators.

Education Journey Mapping With Teachers

In early 2024, we began Zoom meetings with six Asian American mathematics teachers across California, Texas, and Illinois who are committed to social justice teaching and organizing. The six teachers were chosen by the second author, who knew them through previous collaborations on social justice mathematics and other education and community organizing efforts, such as Creating Balance for an Unjust World, National Council of Teachers of Mathematics, and the miseducAsian community.

This group formed to center Asian American identities, histories, and complexities and to explicitly attend to mathematics education as a racial project. Our goal was to create an environment and process to explore the role of space, place, and belonging in our education and racial formation. Using EJM as our primary method, we asked the teachers to respond to the following prompt:

> *From your time as a student to your time now as a teacher, please indicate*
> *and detail important spaces that have had influence on you. Focus on*
> *how your racial identity evolved or changed through time, especially with*
> *respect to moments of interaction/contestation/acceptance with the model*
> *minority myth, and how that leads to your work and commitments as a*
> *justice-oriented math teacher. You can include photos, videos, gifs, certain*
> *color or font, or whatever that speaks to you in your map.*

The teachers used StoryMap, a publicly available mapping software from Northwestern University Knight Lab (https://knightlab.northwestern.edu/) that allows the integration of storytelling and GIS. Since this technology was new to them, we took steps to ensure they were comfortable with its use. In our initial meeting, we debriefed the teachers on the software, providing them with a reference presentation for later use (Figure 10.1).

Figure 10.1 *StoryMap Getting Started Page*

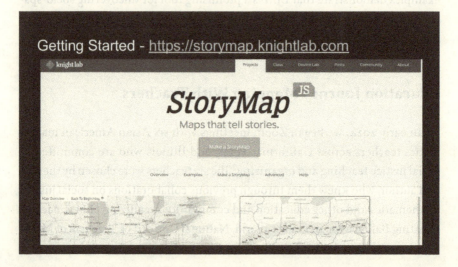

To document their stories on StoryMap, they added locations, images, videos, and optional text (Figure 10.2). We encouraged them to adapt the technology to suit their needs so they could fully illustrate the intimate nature of their stories. Importantly, we shared our own EJMs to both provide illustrative examples as well as to foster a communal environment conducive to sharing and trust.

Figure 10.2 *StoryMap Adding Locations, Images, Videos, and Optional Text*

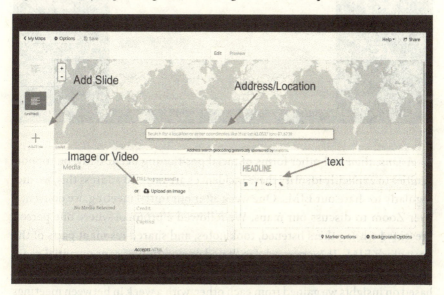

We then showed the teachers how to duplicate their EJMs after each meeting to track changes over time and observe how our discussions added depth, realizations, or connections to their own understanding of space's role in their racial identity formation (Figure 10.3). Discussing each other's EJMs, for example, allowed teachers to identify and interrogate shared spaces and dynamics they had not realized before as racializing factors in their lives, such as being used as "diversity pawns" in predominantly white spaces or having to navigate lack of Asian American curricular representation in school. It was powerful for us to see how the dynamics of our conversations shaped each iteration of the process.

Figure 10.3 *StoryMap Copying/Duplicating*

Asianization and other forms of racial positioning occur daily, but opportunities to explicitly identify these incidences are rare. To address this, we met regularly to share our EJMs. One week after our initial meeting, we convened over Zoom to discuss our maps. We followed a protocol where one person presented while others listened, took notes, and shared resonant parts of the presenter's EJM. This approach facilitated exploration of consequential geographies and intimate sharing in a communal space. We then revised our maps based on insights we gained from each other, with a week in between meetings to reflect and incorporate new understandings. These reflection periods between meetings were essential for recognizing the various ways we embodied and resisted spatial inequities throughout our journeys. Through our discussions and reflections, we identified shared themes around how transnational family immigration, racial segregation in childhood cities, and underrepresentation in school curriculum contributed to our racialized identities, as well as how we each uniquely navigated these experiences in different locations and communities to form our social justice and activist orientations towards mathematics teaching.

With this process, each teacher was able to paint a detailed portrait of their educational journeys that, through spatial analysis, revealed how space and place mediated racialization, resistance, and healing. For example, one of the teachers, Michael (pseudonym), shared that as a middle and high schooler, he used to judge how "Asian" he was with constructed standards of cultural authenticity. With ancestors from Indonesia and China, but being born and raised in the United States, Michael struggled with his racial identity during childhood. In his EJM, he writes that this changed when he discovered Asian American Studies during his high school years:

> *I read about Wong Kim Ark, I read about Japanese Internment, I read about Yuri Kochiyama and Grace Lee Boggs and Vincent Chin and realized that there have been Asian people in this country for a long time. And they haven't just been here passively, but they've been loud and active and controversial and deeply political. A friend and I learned a bunch of this and we made a presentation for a high school conference for Asian Americans on Asian American Activists, and I think I saved myself doing this.*

Michael's reflection reveals many elements of space, place, and belonging in relation to his racialized identity and the racialization of Asian Americans in the United States. In learning about these prominent Asian Americans, he was able to form a personal ancestral lineage local to the country in which he was born and raised, developing a strong "Asian *American* identity distinct from an 'Asian' identity . . . related to the continent." Moreover, these prominent individuals' political activism inspired him to perceive Asian Americans as deserving to live, be seen, and be heard in this country in their full humanity. He realized that Asian Americans counteract socio-spatial patterns of racial othering and silencing—such as through the MMM—that have discriminated against Asian Americans throughout history (Au, 2022). Putting this conviction into action, Michael became determined to make space and take up space as an Asian American, first by making a presentation on Asian American activists, and now as an Asian American mathematics teacher active in the local Asian American community, including teaching STEM-integrated Asian American Studies on weekends. Other teachers in the group also shared stories of making space and taking up space as Asian Americans in their own lives and work as teachers, from engaging in labor organizing with their teacher's union to facilitating discussions around immigration justice as part of teaching mathematics in the classroom. Through their visible activism, they have exercised a stance of spatial ownership and belonging that directly counters the racialization of Asian Americans as the forever foreign, quiet, and apolitical model minority (Au, 2022; Kim, 1999). EJMs have been invaluable for sparking discussion and self-reflection on such pivotal moments in the teachers' racial identity formation, which continue to influence their work today.

Education Journey Mapping With Students

We have also used digital EJM with K-12 students to enhance accessible storytelling and to align with common forms of youth self-expression such as drawing, collage, emojis, videos, photos, and music. Below is an EJM prompt the second author used with K-12 students in Seattle, Austin, and California schools to explore their sense of belonging in and outside of school and the social-spatial mechanisms that constrain or support it:

> Who we are is shaped by our experiences in and out of school. Map your education journey. Include people, places, discoveries, wonders, obstacles, and opportunities on your way. Include your experiences inside and outside of school. What place supports your sense of belonging? Where do you feel most at home? Use different color, videos, gifs, images, and the map to show different feelings and to share your story. These are just suggestions. Be as creative as you like. We will later share our maps with each other and get to add to it throughout the year.

Student EJMs provide deep insights on their experiences inside and outside of school and how one's sense of belonging is not fixed but situated in context and place. Similar to using EJM with teachers, we also have students go through rounds of refining their EJMs in which they listen to others' journeys and add to their own EJMs in response. Since the concept of belonging may not be as immediately articulable to students, providing an opportunity for students to hear others' experiences and meaningful places allows them to be able to identify their own places of connection and their characteristics.

As students share their maps publicly, the socio-spatial characteristics across maps emerge. The second author conducted a pilot study as part of a university-school research partnership on students' sense of belonging in mathematics classrooms using EJM with fourth grade students. Figure 10.4 shows the spaces identified by Avi, an Indian American student. Avi was in a classroom with 34 students, all of whom were Black, Indigenous, and other people of color. However, Avi was one of only three students who identified as Asian American. Avi's EJM included photos and videos of his favorite places and activities (e.g., a short video of him counting while walking across the bridge, keeping track of his shots in basketball) and provided images of the places he identified as sites of belonging within the community.

Figure 10.4 *Student Example of StoryMap*

Young people make meaning of race, racism, and racial formation through their daily interactions. Despite being in a class where all students identify as students of color, Avi felt excluded. Moreover, his Asianness was something he often hid, and the experiences shared on his EJM were to showcase his "Americanness," from playing basketball to hanging out at "UT" (the University of Texas at Austin). Asian Americans must navigate different forms of racialization than other people of color (Iftikar & Museus, 2018), such as the MMM (Au, 2022), which helps to explain why Avi felt excluded in his class and highlighted his "Americanness" on his EJM. Yet when interviewed, he shared that all the photos captured sunny days, as his name, Avi, in Sanskrit means sun and air. Avi, being the firstborn son, was the family "sun." Taking pride in his racial and ethnic identity shows that Avi also drew strength from his family connections and cultural roots. Through creating and discussing his EJM, Avi illustrated how his socio-spatial surroundings—from the racial makeup of his class to the physical environment around his home—mediate the ways in which he has made sense of his racial identity.

Avi's sharing of basketball, a shared interest among many in the classroom, also allowed his teacher, Ms. Zúñiga (pseudonym), to introduce Wataru Misaka. Misaka was selected by the New York Knicks, breaking the color barrier in professional basketball as the first non-white player to play in the National Basketball Association in 1947, the same year that Jackie Robinson broke the baseball color line (Johnson & Johnson, 2010). Misaka's accomplishments occurred during World War II as the U.S. government forced Japanese Americans into internment camps across the country. Despite Utah having its own internment camp in Topaz, Misaka was not interned since he had lived in Utah and not a coastal state. In fact, he played in the 1944 NCAA Basketball Championship game while the internment camps were still in operation. Misaka's story highlights how our social realities both shape and are shaped by spatial arrangements. The example of Avi showcases how teachers can intentionally build on student stories and experiences in their curricular and pedagogical decision making in ways that make Asian American stories and contributions visible.

Final Thoughts

Education Journey Mapping counters the silencing and invisibilization of Asian American stories, providing a mechanism for making and taking up space. The sharing of personal instances of belonging, racism, and resistance when combined with GIS mapping allow for exploration of the ways in which spatial and geographic factors impact social dynamics, identities, and power structures in our everyday lives. For example, Michael reflected in his EJM that the space of a high school conference for Asian Americans "saved" him, while Avi's teacher used shared experiences to highlight Asian American history and contributions of relevance to her students. As EJMs combined with GIS are used to elevate more Asian American stories and make visible the socio-spatial dimensions and consequential geographies important for racial justice, they can inform, shape, and empower efforts to pursue racial justice in education, local communities, and society at large.

References

ACLU. (2024). *Living with the Muslim ban*. American Civil Liberties Union. https://www.aclu.org/issues/immigrants-rights/living-muslim-ban

Annamma, S. A. (2018). Mapping consequential geographies in the carceral state: Education journey mapping as a qualitative method with girls of color with dis/abilities. *Qualitative Inquiry, 24*(1), 20–34. https://doi.org/10.1177/1077800417728962

Au, W. (2022). Asian American racialization, racial capitalism, and the threat of the model minority. *Review of Education, Pedagogy, and Cultural Studies, 44*(3), 185–209. https://doi.org/10.1080/10714413.2022.2084326

Coloma, R. S. (2017). "We are here because you were there": On curriculum, empire, and global migration. *Curriculum Inquiry, 47*(1), 92–102. https://doi.org/10.1080/036267 84.2016.1254505

Du Bois, W. E. B. (1903). *The souls of black folk: Essays and sketches*. A. C. McClurg & Co.

Iftikar, J. S., & Museus, S. D. (2018). On the utility of Asian critical (AsianCrit) theory in the field of education. *International Journal of Qualitative Studies in Education, 31*(10), 935–949. https://doi.org/10.1080/09518398.2018.1522008

Johnson, B. A, & Johnson, C. T. (Directors). (2010). *Transcending: The Wat Misaka story* [Film]. Moongate Artists.

Kim, C. J. (1999). The racial triangulation of Asian Americans. *Politics & Society, 27*(1), 105–138. https://doi.org/10.1177/0032329299027001005

Morrison, D., Annamma, S. A., & Jackson, D. D. (Eds.). (2017). *Critical race spatial analysis: Mapping to understand and address educational inequity.* Stylus Publishing.

Soja, E. W. (2010). *Seeking spatial justice.* University of Minnesota Press. https://doi. org/10.5749/minnesota/9780816666676.001.0001

Vélez, V. N., & Solórzano, D. G. (2017). Critical race spatial analysis: Conceptualizing GIS as a tool for critical race research in education. In D. D. Jackson, D. Morrison, & S. A. Annamma (Eds.), *Critical race spatial analysis* (pp. 8–31). Routledge. https://doi. org/10.4324/9781003443896-3

Yu, T. (2006). Challenging the politics of the "model minority" stereotype: A case for educational equality. *Equity & Excellence in Education, 39*(4), 325–333. https://doi.org/ 10.1080/10665680600932333

CHAPTER 11

"Activism can be the journey rather than the arrival": Organizing for Teaching Asian American and Pacific Islander History in Michigan

Roland Sintos Coloma

ACCORDING TO THE 2020 Census, Asian Americans constitute 4.1% of Michigan's total population, with Asian Indian, Chinese, Filipino, Korean, Japanese, and Vietnamese Americans as the six largest Asian American ethnic groups in decreasing order of size. Native Hawaiians and other Pacific Islanders comprise 0.1% of the state population (U.S. Census Bureau, 2020). In spite of their small numbers, Asian Americans and Pacific Islanders (AAPIs) are the fastest growing racial minority group in Michigan, with the number of Asian Americans increasing by 42.2% and Native Hawaiians and other Pacific Islanders by 20.4% from 2010 to 2020. The transnational linkages between Michigan and Asia as well as the migrations, community formations, and socio-cultural, economic, and political contributions of AAPIs in Michigan are critical histories that need to be documented, taught, and learned. The first recorded Asian migrant in the state arrived in 1872, and Michiganders have been actively involved in Asian politics and economy, for instance, in the U.S. colonial administration in the Philippines in the early 1900s and in U.S. "modernization" initiatives in Vietnam in the 1950s (Wilkinson & Jew, 2015). AAPIs organizing for curricular and epistemic justice in Michigan demonstrates the transformative power of mobilization, resilience, and solidarity.

I write this chapter as a fairly new transplant to Michigan. Born in the Philippines and raised in California, I have lived and worked in the U.S. Midwest and Canada since 2000 as a graduate student and then university faculty member interested in the cultural histories of race, intersectionality, and education. In 2018, I joined Wayne State University as a teacher education administrator and faculty and began to immerse myself in historical and contemporary issues impacting AAPIs and other communities of color in Detroit. Among my intellectual guides in this journey is the late Grace Lee Boggs whose theorizing and political analysis of Detroit, racial and economic justice, and youth and community development continue to inspire, challenge, and hold me accountable. In honor of Boggs, I draw insights from her book *The Next American Revolution* with Scott Kurashige as signposts in my accounting of recent campaigns to require the teaching of AAPI history in Michigan. Boggs' idea that "activism can be the journey rather than the arrival" (Boggs & Kurashige, 2012, p. 48) not only serves as the chapter title, but also delineates the importance of "how" we get to "where." As of this writing, Michigan has not passed a legislative bill to mandate the teaching of AAPI history in schools. Even when such a bill becomes law, the journey towards a more inclusive history will be continuously paved by educators, students, and community members committed to curriculum and pedagogical transformation.

Histories of Asian American communities and activism generally privilege the coastal states. For AAPIs who live "east of California" and especially in the Midwest, we share our work and perspectives to intervene and broaden our views on anti-racist and social justice organizing. To narrate the counterstories of AAPI advocates in Michigan committed to integrating AAPI history in schools, this chapter will unfold with the following goals: (1) to contextualize this curriculum struggle within the current socio-political climate; (2) to highlight legislative actions in Michigan that would require the teaching of AAPI history; and (3) to promote institutional, community, and cultural resources for AAPI history. This chapter foregrounds various initiatives and resources that I am familiar with, mindful that my rendition is limited and does not include other important efforts that positively contribute toward our shared goals.

Visionary Organizing in a Climate of Fear and Hostility

Every crisis, actual or impending, needs to be viewed as an opportunity to bring about profound changes in our society. Going beyond protest organizing, visionary organizing begins by creating images and stories of the future that help us imagine and create alternatives to the existing system.

—BOGGS & KURASHIGE (2012, P. XXI)

Organizing for teaching AAPI history is not new. Its genealogy draws from a history of student protests for Ethnic Studies in California in the late 1960s, to more recent Ethnic Studies campaigns of street marches, sit-ins, online petitions, and hunger strikes led by students of color across the country. Activists recognize that for AAPI and Ethnic Studies to be taught in schools, they need to put in place legislative laws, curriculum standards and materials, pedagogical training of preservice and in-service educators, support from teachers and administrators, and advocacy from students, parents, and community leaders. Such organizing needs to take place at the local, state, and national levels with different stakeholders: elected legislators, departments of education, school boards, teachers unions, as well as parent and student groups. In documenting and analyzing campaigns to develop AAPI studies in schools, we account for the ways power, knowledge, and subjects shape the cultural politics of curriculum policy, development, and implementation.

To date, only six states have passed laws that mandate the teaching of AAPI history in public schools: Illinois (2021), New Jersey (2022), Connecticut (2022), Rhode Island (2022), Florida (2023), and Wisconsin (2024). In 2021, California became the first state to require Ethnic Studies, which includes AAPI history, for high school graduation, starting with the class of 2030. Other states, such as Oregon (2017), Vermont (2019), and Washington (2019), mandate the inclusion of Ethnic Studies in their school curriculum.

The recent campaigns to integrate AAPI history in Michigan's PK-12 school curriculum need to be understood as taking place within a socio-political climate of hostility toward marginalized groups. For Asian Americans, the COVID-19 pandemic elicited a compounded fear of being infected by the coronavirus and being targeted for anti-Asian racism (Coloma et al., 2021). The

shooting rampage in Atlanta in March 2021 that killed six Asian women highlighted intersectional violence that renders Asian Americans as yellow perils
and foreign contagions targeted for elimination. This period saw more vitriolic
movements against diversity, equity, and inclusion, against critical race theory,
and against African American, immigrant, and lesbian, gay, bisexual, and trans-
gender communities. The radical right ideologies have manifested in the U.S.
Supreme Court with majority rulings that overturned reproductive rights and
affirmative action, in many state legislatures with prohibitive education laws,
in school board meetings with protesting audiences, and in social media with a
conservative brand of cancel culture. The latest rise of anti-Asian racism in the
United States emerged within an era of "anti-woke-ness" that yearned for the
return of a hegemonic status quo.

In January 2022, Stephanie Chang, the first Asian American woman to serve
in the Michigan legislature, introduced Senate Bill (SB) 797 to "ensure that 1
unit of instruction of age- and grade-appropriate instruction concerning Asian
American and Pacific Islander history is incorporated in the history curriculum" (Mich. 2022). The bill provided a curricular scope of "historical Asian
American and Pacific Islander events," such as their contributions in "government, the arts, humanities, and sciences" and to the "economic, cultural, social,
and political development of the United States;" their history in Michigan and
the Midwest including "past policies that were discriminatory" toward AAPIs;
and their roles in "advancing civil rights from the nineteenth century onward"
(Mich. 2022). The "1 unit of instruction" means a "minimum amount of instructional time" (Mich. 2022), which can range from a mini-lesson or a class activity,
to a multi-day unit or an entire course on AAPI history. SB 797 was part of a
package of bills that simultaneously advocated for the teaching of Latinx and
Caribbean American (SB 798), African American and Native American (SB
799), as well as Arab and Chaldean American (SB 800) histories. Consistent
with Boggs' concept of visionary organizing, Chang collaborated with fellow
Democrat senators in proposing bills that would teach comprehensive histories
of racialized minority and Indigenous communities.

Democrat Ranjeev Puri introduced House Bill (HB) 6166 in June 2022 as
the House counterpart to SB 797. Chang's SB 797 and Puri's HB 6166 were
referred respectively to the Senate Committee on Education and Readiness

and the House Committee on Education, but did not move forward in the Republican-majority committees. The Republican chair of the Senate Committee on Education and Readiness, Lana Theis, led an anti-CRT (critical race theory) legislative campaign in schools by introducing SB 460 in May 2021 that prohibited the "coverage of the critical race theory, the 1619 project, or any of the following anti-American and racist theories," including that the "United States is a fundamentally racist country" (Mich. 2021b). A month later, fellow Republican Andrew Beeler introduced HB 5097 that mandated schools to "not, in any way, include any form of race or gender stereotyping or anything that could be understood as implicit race or gender stereotyping" (Mich. 2021a). In response to accusations that those who promote CRT and Ethnic/Feminist Studies and queer studies are anti-American radicals, Boggs' stance serves as an astute comeback: "We are not subversives . . . We are struggling to change this country because we love it" (Boggs & Kurashige, 2012, p. 175).

Since these bills did not pass in 2022, Chang co-sponsored a set of Senate bills in November 2024 that would mandate the public school teaching of one unit of instruction in Asian American and Pacific Islander history as well as the histories of African American, Indigenous, Latin American, Hispanic American, Caribbean American, Arab American, North African, Chaldean American, and Jewish American communities, starting in the 2027-28 school year (SB 1145). It will also provide resources to public schools to support professional learning related to cultural competency (SB 1146) and create a statewide cultural history advisory board in the Michigan Department of Education (SB 1147). In December 2024, Puri co-sponsored a similar set of House bills that would mandate the teaching of age- and grade-appropriate diverse histories in Michigan public schools (HB 6248), provide resources for cultural competency (HB 6246), and create a statewide cultural history advisory board (HB 6247). As of this writing, the Senate and House sets of legislative bills have been referred to their respective Committees on Education, but no public hearings have been scheduled.

Narrating Histories Differently in Schools and Universities

History is not the past. It is the stories we tell about the past. How we tell these stories . . . has a lot to do with whether we cut short or advance our evolution as human beings.

—BOGGS & KURASHIGE (2012, P. 79)

Top education leaders in Michigan have taken significant public positions in support of teaching inclusive and justice-oriented histories. State superintendent Michael Rice (2021) emphasizes educators' right and responsibility to teach the breadth and complexity of U.S. history, including race and racism. While other administrators have denied the use of CRT in schools, Nikolai Vitti, superintendent of the state's largest district, Detroit Public Schools Community District, embraces and promotes it in the teaching of social studies, English language arts, and other disciplines (Bakuli, 2021). These leaders are notable examples of employing not only their prominent roles and platforms, but also their privileged identities as white men to speak truth to power and advocate for curriculum deemed controversial by others.

With forward-thinking leadership, the Michigan Department of Education (MDE) launched a free webinar series in 2022 on "comprehensive history instruction" (Michigan Department of Education, 2022b) for school teachers and administrators. The series included a wide range of topics, including Indigenous history, the Holocaust, and civil, disability, and labor rights. The MDE webinars on "Asian Americans and the United States" (Michigan Department of Education, 2022a) in September 2022, led by Naoko Wake and Andrea Louie of Michigan State University, focused on three themes: immigration and citizenship, model minority myth, and Asian American movements. In 2024, MDE administered a grant competition on "Teaching Diverse Histories" based on a $6 million appropriation from the state school aid fund (Section 99d) aimed to "develop and implement plans for professional learning concerning the teaching of the fullness of American history, including, but not limited to, the teaching of the history of communities of color and other marginalized communities" (Michigan Department of Education, 2024). Through this funding, Democrats have proactively provided state resources that would facilitate the teaching and learning of diverse histories in schools.

Two Michigan school districts have official courses on AAPI studies. Plymouth-Canton Community Schools, with a student population of 15% AAPI, began offering an elective high school course titled Asian American History, Culture, and Issues, developed and first taught by Richard Mui (see Chapter 1 of this volume) during the 2023-2024 school year. Ann Arbor Public Schools, with a student population of 13.6% AAPI, has a high school course titled Asian/Pacific Islander American Studies, developed by Joslyn Hunscher-Young. Moreover, the state's major universities have long-standing and new programs in AAPI studies that can provide curriculum and pedagogical resources for PK-12 school teachers. University of Michigan established its Asian/Pacific Islander American (A/PIA) Studies program in 1989, with course offerings at the bachelor's and graduate levels, including an undergraduate minor in A/PIA Studies. Michigan State University started its Asian Pacific American (APA) Studies program in 2004 with undergraduate course offerings including a minor in APA Studies. Wayne State University offered its first course of Introduction to Asian American Studies that I developed and taught in winter 2024.

Enacting Public Pedagogies in Communities

If we want to see change in our lives, we have to change things ourselves.
—BOGGS & KURASHIGE (2012, P. XV)

Various community organizations have mobilized to address the need to teach and learn AAPI history in schools. Rising Voices, led by co-executive directors Regina Tsang and Jasmine Rivera, is a nonprofit organization that fosters leadership among Asian American women and youth. In 2022, it launched a Youth Leadership and Civic Engagement Fellowship program that provided young activists with knowledge, skills, and networks for the PK-12 Ethnic Studies and Language Justice campaigns. Asian Pacific Islander Vote Michigan, led by executive director Rebeka Islam, is a nonpartisan nonprofit committed to grassroots mobilization, leadership development, and coalition building. It organizes the annual advocacy day in the state capitol where community members meet with elected legislators and their staff on AAPI issues. At the

2024 Day at the Capitol, API Vote Michigan brought hundreds of community members across the state to voice support for the teaching of diverse histories and for other pertinent matters, such as the voting rights act, family leave optimal coverage, and allowing community members without official paperwork to apply for a driver's license.

To promote awareness about the significance of teaching AAPI history in schools, the Michigan Asian Pacific American Affairs Commission (MAPAAC) convened a series of statewide virtual town halls for schoolteachers, teacher educators, students, parents, and community members. Appointed by the governor and led by chair Ayesha Ghazi-Edwin, MAPAAC serves as a vocal statewide advocate to raise concerns and provide sustainable solutions for AAPI constituencies. For 3 years, I co-organized the town halls on "Addressing Anti-Racism in Schools" (2021), "Beyond Model Minority: Asian American History in Michigan's K-12 Schools" (2022), and "Where are you from?: The Role of Asian American Studies in K-12 Curriculum" (2023). Speakers included the state superintendent (Michael Rice), elected legislators (Stephanie Chang, Ranjeev Puri, and Lori Stone), schoolteachers and administrators (Richard Mui and Suchiraphon McKeithen-Polish), university faculty (Manan Desai, Noreen Naseem Rodriguez, and Naoko Wake), students (Kathryn Ocomen, Neha Rao, Ally Wang, and Haidy Zhang), parents (Neeraja Aravamudan), and union leaders from the American Federation of Teachers Michigan and the Michigan Education Association (Meenakshi Mukherjee and Chandra Madaferri). The town halls drew hundreds of online participants from Michigan and across the country who have subsequently become more informed in their advocacy to integrate AAPI history in the school curriculum (Coloma et al., 2022).

As I highlight the important work of Rising Voices, API Vote Michigan, and MAPAAC, I am mindful that many AAPI organizations across the state have enacted various forms of public pedagogies in their social, cultural, and other activities. Ranging from ethnic performances and food festivals, to youth programming and professional networking, these groups teach and provide important lessons on culturally sustaining support, resilience, and belonging in a state with a small but engaged AAPI community.

Cultivating an Epistemology of Compassion in Public Spaces

It goes back to an epistemology, a theory of knowledge that is not just of the brain but of the heart. An epistemology of compassion that recognizes how we belong to each other, that recognizes we are each other's harvest, we are each other's business.

—BOGGS & KURASHIGE (2012, P. 211).

To elaborate on what Boggs means by an epistemology of compassion in the section epigraph above, I highlight a documentary film, a commemoration, and a museum exhibition created by Asian Americans in Michigan.

In the film *Bad Axe*, director David Siev (2022) narrates intimately the trials and tribulations of his close-knit, multi-racial family as a symbolic love letter to rural Michigan that they call home. He tackles trauma from war and genocide, survival and resilience, and the inexplicable feeling of loving a place that doesn't love them back. The documentary features his Cambodian refugee father who fled the Khmer Rouge regime and his Mexican American mother who, together, established a restaurant in 1998 in a town of about 3000 people who are mostly white and politically conservative. Filmed in 2020 in the midst of the COVID-19 pandemic and anti-Asian racism, it showcases how racism impacted their family when their restaurant's social media posted support for the Black Lives Matter movement and they participated in a BLM rally in their downtown. Consequently, they received hostile phone calls, threatening letters, and angry social media comments. When the Siev family stood up against white supremacy and refused to comply with assimilationist expectations to conform, they received immediate and virulent backlash. But they remained resolute and found support locally and nationally in their American dream that embraces diversity, equity, and justice. The film offers poignant lessons on how an Asian American family in a small town can promote social change in spite of racial and political differences.

In June 2022, prominent leaders Helen Zia, James Shimoura, Roland Hwang, and Rebeka Islam organized the 40th year commemoration of the tragic murder of Vincent Chin. Chin was killed by two white men who racially profiled and scapegoated him as the cause of large-scale layoffs and unemployment in Detroit's automobile industry in the 1970s and 1980s. The miscarriage of justice that enabled his murderers to be given only a 3-year probation and $3000 in fines galvanized Asian Americans in Michigan and nationally to launch a renewed Asian American civil rights movement. The four-day 40th year commemoration brought hundreds of people to Detroit and online to attend an interfaith ceremony, a filmmakers' convening, and public showings of the *Bad Axe* and *Who Killed Vincent Chin?* documentaries. It included a celebration of arts and culture and a national conversation on race and democracy that featured the American Citizens for Justice co-founders. It also gathered diverse leaders of color in panel discussions to analyze the legal battles, community campaigns, and lessons learned from the 1980s and to link them to current movements for multi-racial justice. The commemoration spotlighted the persistence of anti-Asian racism and the significance of AAPI organizing to build understanding and coalitions within and across communities.

From October 2023 to March 2024, the Detroit Historical Museum displayed the "Detroit's Chinatowns" exhibit, and curator Lily Jiale Chen gathered artifacts and oral histories from previous residents to uncover a nearly-forgotten history. Marking the 150-year history of Chinese Americans in Detroit, the exhibit highlighted the first recorded Chinese in the city named Ah-Chee in 1872 and the establishment of its first Chinatown just west of downtown. By the 1930s, the neighborhood was bustling with restaurants, laundries, and other businesses. The exhibit also noted how "urban renewal" and the construction of the Lodge Freeway starting in the late 1950s demolished the flourishing ethnic enclave, similar to what occurred in the Black Bottom and Paradise Valley neighborhoods that served as cultural and economic centers of the African American community. Consequently, displaced residents and businesses developed a smaller Chinatown in Cass Corridor close to the Wayne State University campus. However, the decline of the automobile industry starting in the 1960s, which resulted in unemployment, economic instability, white flight, and escalating violence, contributed to the eventual waning of Detroit's second Chinatown. The exhibit captures the rise and fall of an ethnic neighborhood with a small pagoda as the fading marker of a previously vibrant area.

Conclusion

In his memoir *Everything I Learned, I Learned in a Chinese Restaurant,* Curtis Chin (2023) narrates his experiences growing up as a gay, working-class, Chinese American in Detroit in the 1980s. Chung's, his family's restaurant in Chinatown, closed in 2000 after operating for 40 years. As he struggled with his racial and intersectional identities, he gained a better understanding of being Asian American through his activism and courses at the University of Michigan. For many, our first educational exposure to critical readings and discussions on race, racism, and anti-racism takes place in college. Current organizing for teaching AAPI history in Michigan promotes such engagement earlier, in PK-12 school classrooms and beyond in age-appropriate and culturally relevant ways. Inclusive and justice-oriented pedagogies will benefit both AAPI students who will finally see themselves represented in the school curriculum and all students who will gain fuller and more complex perspectives on our diverse society. In her vision of what education ought to be, Boggs offers this insightful counterstory: "when Education involves young people in making community changes that matter to them, when it gives meaning to their lives in the present instead of preparing them only to make a living in the future, young people begin to believe in themselves and to dream of the future" (Boggs & Kurashige, 2012, p. 151).

References

Bakuli, E. (2021, November 15). *Detroit school district pushes back against anti-CRT legislation.* Chalkbeat. https://www.chalkbeat.org/detroit/2021/11/15/22784151/detroit-school-district-pushes-back-against-anti-crt-bills-black-history/

Boggs, G.L., & Kurashige, S. (2012). *The next American revolution: Sustainable activism for the twenty-first century.* University of California Press.

Chin, C. (2023). *Everything I learned, I learned in a Chinese restaurant: A memoir.* Little, Brown and Company.

Coloma, R.S., Chang, S., Rice, M.F., Mui, R., Ocomen, K., Rao, N., McKeithen-Polish, S., Desai, M., & Palepu, K. (2022). Beyond model minority: Asian American history in Michigan's K-12 schools. *The Great Lakes Social Studies Journal, 2*(2), 27–32.

Coloma, R. S., Hsieh, B., Poon, O., Chang, S., Choimorrow, S. Y., Kulkarni, M. P., Meng, G., Patel, L., & Tintiangco-Cubales, A. (2021). Reckoning with anti-Asian violence: Racial grief, visionary organizing, and educational responsibility. *Educational Studies, 57*(4), 378–394.

H.B. 5097, 101st Leg., Reg. Sess. (Mich. 2021a). http://legislature.mi.gov/doc.aspx?2021-HB-5097

Michigan Department of Education. (2022a). *Asian American history a focus in MDEs next comprehensive history webinars.* https://www.michigan.gov/mde/news-and-information/press-releases/2022/08/30/asian-american-history-a-focus-in-mdes-next-comprehensive-history-webinars

Michigan Department of Education. (2022b). *Teaching comprehensive history.* https://www.michigan.gov/mde/services/academic-standards/teaching-comprehensive-history

Michigan Department of Education. (2024). Section 99d teaching diverse histories grant. https://www.michigan.gov/mde/services/academic-standards/section-99d-teaching-diverse-histories-grant

Rice, M. F. (2021). *Reflection on critical race theory, race, racism, other isms, and the teaching of history.* Michigan Department of Education. https://www.michigan.gov/-/media/Project/Websites/mde/Year/2021/08/10/Race_and_Racism_August_2021.pdf?rev=d6626b10e32d42f09c07ca41a2f70c2a

S.B. 460, 101st Leg., Reg. Sess. (Mich. 2021b). http://legislature.mi.gov/doc.aspx?2021-SB-0460

S.B. 797, 101st Leg., Reg. Sess. (Mich. 2022). http://legislature.mi.gov/doc.aspx?2022-SB-0797

Siev, D. (Director). (2022). *Bad axe* [Film]. IFC Films.

U.S. Census Bureau. (2020). *Michigan: 2020 census.* https://www.census.gov/library/stories/state-by-state/michigan-population-change-between-census-decade.html

Wilkinson, S., & Jew, V. (Eds.). (2015). *Asian Americans in Michigan: Voices from the Midwest.* Wayne State University Press.

CHAPTER 12

The Fight for Asian American Studies in a "Red State": Voices From Texas

Indira Moparthi, Annie Nguyen, and Mohit Mehta

TEXAS HAS THE nation's third largest Asian American population, and Asian Americans are the state's fastest growing demographic group (Budiman & Ruiz, 2021). The Center for Asian American Studies (CAAS) at the University of Texas at Austin, the first Asian American Studies (AAS) program in the U.S. South, was established in 1999 after 4 years of organizing and activism led by students and faculty. Recently, CAAS collaborated with a Texas high school teacher and Asian Texans for Justice (ATJ), a statewide nonprofit organization, to pilot the state's first AAS high school course. The 2-year journey from conceptualizing the course, writing the course framework, developing curricular materials, recruiting students, and advocating at the state and district level for its approval has been an arduous process and met by many instances of institutional opposition. In this chapter, we share our collective narratives as a student who advocated for the course at her high school and later completed the pilot (Indira), the primary course teacher (Annie), and the course co-teacher (Mohit). We reflect on the emotional, physical, and mental labor of fighting white supremacist institutions and practicing care through ancestral strength, seeking guidance from movement elders, and foregrounding youth care and well-being. In sharing our collective experiences in bringing a critical Ethnic Studies course to fruition in a state mired by right-wing politics, we hope to equip other teachers and student activists with practical tools and inspire others in the ongoing fight for educational justice.

The Fight for More Inclusive Education and Red State Politics

In recent years, conservative politicians and right-wing groups have grown in influence. They have organized to criminalize the rights of trans children and teachers, ban and remove books from school libraries, insert religious doctrine in schools, and lead efforts to privatize public education through voucher schemes (López, 2022a; Winter, 2024). Texas was one of the first states to pass a so-called anti-critical race theory (CRT) law that dampens discussions about race, gender, and sexuality in public schools (Kunzman & Allen, 2024). Texas social studies standards propel a whitewashed history that celebrates settler colonial exceptionalism (Valenzuela, 2019). Furthermore, these standards have not been revised since 2008. In 2022, the State Board of Education, under conservative leadership, vetoed changes recommended by historians, educators, and community members that would provide students with a more inclusive social studies curriculum (López, 2022b).

At the same time, Texas has a long history of resistance against education injustice. In 2018, after a decade of advocacy by scholars, teachers, and community members, Mexican American Studies was finally approved as a high school elective course (Puente & Alvarez, 2021; Saldaña, 2022). Two years later, it was joined by African American Studies. But the struggle for educational justice goes back even further. Mexican American students and teachers in Texas have a sustained history of demanding equity and more inclusive education (Gutiérrez, 1998; San Miguel 1983; Sinta & Rivas-Rodríguez, 2023). More recently, Native American tribal leaders and Indigenous scholars have struggled for more than 4 years with political obstacles towards the approval of an American Indian Native Studies course (Xia, 2024). As students, scholars, and teachers of Asian American Studies in Texas, we draw inspiration, organizational strategy, and practice *solidaridad* with both national movements for Asian American Studies and from our colleagues and friends across Ethnic Studies disciplines who have sustained the battle in Texas for generations.

Asian American Studies in Texas: A Journey in Persistence

In 2022, we set out to join the political and social momentum across the nation for Asian American curricular inclusion. We were grounded in the belief that Ethnic Studies and access to community-centered, inclusive histories benefit all students. As part of the 2022 social studies revision process in Texas, a member of the State Board of Education (SBOE) invited the proposal of an Asian American Studies course. Asian American curricular inclusion, although uneven and rife with controversy in some states, was gaining traction across the country. During the spring and summer of 2022, several teachers, community leaders, and scholars came together to draft an inclusive high school AAS elective course that would meet the requirements set forth by the SBOE and Texas Education Agency in terms of breadth and sequence. Since narratives from geographic peripheries are often not included in dominant narratives of AAS, we made sure to include local histories. We were also intentional about including the histories and experiences of diverse Asian American communities. We carefully debated about the inclusion of Pacific Islander histories, cultures, politics, and communities and ultimately honored the calls from Pacific Islander communities about the need for an independent course that follows the intellectual traditions of Pasifika scholars and community leaders. Acknowledging the challenges of establishing such a course in Texas, we intentionally included course objectives that address the U.S. colonization of Hawai'i and the inherent challenges present in identity terms like Asian American Pacific Islander (AAPI) and Asian American Pacific Islander Native Hawaiian (AAPINH).

Lily Trieu of Asian Texans for Justice (ATJ) organized with Woori Juntos and colleagues at OCA-Houston to bring more than 60 K-12 and university students, recent graduates, and families to testify in front of the SBOE in August 2022. Many students shared highly emotional testimonies of being bullied and feeling uncared for in schools. When the SBOE was scheduled to take an initial vote on the Asian American Studies course and other social studies revisions, conservative forces, led by Moms for Liberty and Texas Values, convinced the largely conservative SBOE to halt the revision and new course adoption process.

Lily and Mohit continued to meet and organize to bring the AAS course to fruition through another process set forth by the Texas Education Agency.

They consulted with movement elders and colleagues. A veteran teacher, Annie Nguyen, agreed to help pilot the AAS course and conferred with her school administrators. Lily, Annie, and Mohit subsequently met with district officials. Some were encouraging, while others did not see the value of the course. Youth began to organize and spread awareness about a potential AAS course. After an entire semester of organizing, the course was approved with a few caveats. Annie would have to teach the AAS course during her off period and would not be compensated for it. In summer 2023, Annie and Mohit met regularly to write grants and lesson plans. During the 2023-2024 school year, they co-taught the AAS course to 29 students. For their culminating projects, students showcased their learning with thoughtful presentations about Vincent Chin, techno-Orientalism, the model minority myth and its impact on mental health, and the aesthetics of dance in Asian American communities. From the dreams of developing an AAS course in the red state of Texas to the last day of the course in June 2024 was a long journey in persistence. After the course was successfully implemented for a full year, we faced another period of uncertainty. Luckily, our collective advocacy with the district superintendent resulted in course approval for a second year.

Finding Care and Community Against White Backlash

The white backlash against educational justice has a long history. Despite understanding historical cycles of history and resistance, it's hard not to take institutional obstacles personally. The ongoing legitimization of Ethnic Studies in general and AAS in particular has mental, emotional, and physical consequences on well-being. Yet the field of critical Ethnic Studies is built on the ethos of radical care. In this section we, Indira (Indu), Annie, and Mohit, share our personal journeys and the ways we find strength, solidarity, and communal care to sustain ourselves.

Indu's Story

I am a rising senior at a large high school in Austin, Texas. I was born in Cupertino, California and raised in Chicago, Illinois. Our family ended up moving to Texas for a change in scenery in contrast to the harsh winters of Chicago. I'm a South Indian young woman, and I'm extremely passionate about political and social advocacy, which originally started with a love for public speaking and evolved into a bigger purpose. Throughout my life, my identity was a source of hatred from others. At first, I felt helpless, but I then learned about various affinity groups that worked towards creating social change like Asian Texans for Justice. Being exposed to fellowship groups that taught information while also being able to create tangible change was exciting and made me find my passion. I initially learned about Asian American Studies because Ms. Nguyen was my English teacher at the time, and I remember how stressful the environment seemed. However, I learned the specifics of the course after I got connected with ATJ, and I felt so empowered by the nuanced curriculum the course presented.

I began helping to advertise the Asian American Studies course by posting flyers and speaking in classes alongside a few friends. We spoke on a student panel, and circumstances began to look more hopeful. However, difficulties arose when school counselors began encouraging students to opt out of the AAS course and to take more career-oriented courses like Principles of Information Technology or Money Matters. The official approval of the AAS course seemed ambiguous, and the counselors' lack of support deterred students from taking the course, and they began looking for alternatives. Nevertheless, the unwavering support of many organizations, and the continued recognition of being the first Asian American Studies course in high school in Texas, gave hope to us as students and encouraged us to keep fighting for such a revolutionary course.

It's daunting to fight against such a repressive system when it's clear that powerful and influential figures are not in support of our actions. Change can be a disdainful concept because it can insinuate that there are flaws within our current system, and that can be a hard notion to digest. This may be the reason as to why Texas is so quick to resist ideas geared to improve our society because it means we must make changes in our current way of doing and governing. It is discouraging when our state does not support movements like teaching Asian American Studies in schools and in fact has tried to suppress other Ethnic Studies movements. It makes me wonder if the state targets me and other activists, and that's quite a scary thought to have as a girl and as a teenager.

Persistence is key to bringing about any change. If you keep saying something loud enough, someone will hear you. Whether it's out of curiosity or annoyance, recognition is imperative in this work. During the time of establishing the AAS course, there were many times I felt like I was parroting myself, but I still had a sense of motivation to keep going because the more persistent you are, the more opportunities are opened. As a young woman, I also wanted to see myself and my cultural roots depicted in history. It's disheartening to know that the stories of my life and my ancestors will be peculiar and foreign to many individuals. That's where my motivation towards advocacy started: the lack of nuance and representation in our current educational curriculum. I wanted to create a place where I felt happy to learn and proud to share with my friends. Through this course, it's happening, and I'm so thankful to let the inner child within me to grow and heal.

Annie's Story

Figure 12.1 *Annie's Illustration of Intergenerational Knowledge and Community Care*

My name is Annie Aí Hiền Nguyễn. I am a daughter of Vietnamese refugees who settled in Palacios, Texas. Growing up in a small town with a predominantly Vietnamese Catholic community, I often felt lost as a second-generation Vietnamese American. However, I found escapism in education. I come from a lineage of educators: my bà nội (paternal grandmother) in Bến Tre, my Grandma Ann (my father's sponsor) in Carroll, Iowa, and my mother in my hometown in Vietnam. Learning was my family's love language.

My experiences with AAS, however, were nonexistent in Palacios. Although surrounded by my Vietnamese community, I only knew of white, colonial U.S. history. It wasn't until I attended the University of Texas at Austin and took an Introduction to AAS course that I realized there was Asian American history. After graduating with a B.A. in English and teaching for 9 years, I reunited with AAS again to reimagine new possibilities.

In December 2022, ATJ and Mohit from CAAS invited me to pilot the first AAS high school course in Texas—aiming for the SBOE's approval statewide. Despite initial fear, my commitment to belonging and justice pushed me to recognize the need for AAS. Piloting a course that centers an ignored history would be revolutionary for our students who often feel invisible. To offer a nuanced lens to critically examine the United States, foster a greater global understanding, and promote an empathetic and just society is all I wanted for my community.

In January 2023, with ATJ, CAAS, and my students, I organized for flyers to be hung in hallways and for hundreds of red envelopes to be distributed throughout the school as advertisements for the Lunar New Year. I presented to classes, filmed promotional videos, and met with administrators. Mohit and I co-hosted a successful informational night with over 30 guests. Despite this collaborative joy, we faced administrative pushback and funding threats. It was draining to witness such clear community interest, yet be restrained by financial concern and a lack of prioritization from administration. However, the students' dedication was empowering. They knew the importance of AAS and were willing to take up space, speak up, and act. Their solidarity was healing and gave me hope to continue to disrupt and resist. As a result, we had over 70 students interested in taking the course and 30 students willing to change their schedules despite AAS being non-credit bearing. The pilot course became a reality. However, it came with sacrifices. I lost a planning period, taught an extra class, and received no compensation from my district. Fortunately, ATJ secured grants to cover my unpaid time, and CAAS provided curriculum support.

During the 2023-2024 school year, the inaugural class of AAS, with the interactive lessons provided by Mohit's expertise and co-teaching, dove into primary sources, engaged in critical discussions, and nurtured curiosity. From connecting through community circles and inviting guest speakers to celebrating cultural holidays, taking local field trips, and convening an end-of-year student showcase, we always centered one another's voices and joy. After this year, I cannot fully express how meaningful this course has been. I am profoundly grateful for a community that made this course possible—a long acknowledgement page of ancestors, activists, students, teachers, friends, therapists, scholars, and local leaders. I have never felt so connected to such a beloved community, and being part of this collective is my greatest joy and hope.

Even before AAS, being an Asian American woman teaching English in Texas has been challenging. I encountered parental unrest, harassing emails, and accusatory meetings, questioning my professional legitimacy. I felt fearful in planning my lessons and exerted extra effort in striking a balance between featuring diverse narratives and taking precautions to protect myself. Not only was it time consuming, but it often led to censoring myself to make lessons more "palatable" to prevent conflict. So when I was first approached to pilot AAS, I was hesitant because I didn't want to be a target. Even when the class started, I feared gaining too much coverage where conservative organizations could jeopardize the class. However, I am learning how visibility is foundational for change. Despite the risk of being attacked by ignorance, there is a chance to be seen, understood, and embraced by those who uphold values of belonging and care. With this courageous collective, we pave towards a more liberated education and a path for meaningful societal change.

Mohit's Story

Like many others, I came to Asian American Studies later in life. In one of my last years as an elementary bilingual teacher, Noreen Naseem Rodríguez, who was working on her doctoral research on the enactment of Asian American history in the elementary social studies classroom, invited me to be part of her research. For the first time in 2015, I taught about Japanese American incarceration to 3rd and 5th graders.

During the COVID-19 period of school shutdowns, distance learning, and estrangement from community, Leila Grace Pandey from the Asian American Resource Center in Austin and I organized an online storytelling series with Asian American children's book authors in an intergenerational setting (Mehta & Pandey, 2022). We later designed a Saturday program for youth to learn about Asian American histories in a community setting. In late spring 2022, Lily Trieu, the ATJ executive director, and I started working with students, allies, and community partners to develop an Asian American Studies course for Texas high schools. After meeting with district and state officials, co-writing curriculum, and seeking grants with local and national organizations, Annie and I were able to teach the course to 29 students during the 2023-2024 school year.

In navigating the political complexities of Texas, our colleagues across other Ethnic Studies disciplines served as movement elders that provided encouragement and advice. That year, state law SB 17 went into effect, forcing several student-facing services associated with "Diversity, Equity and Inclusion" to be shut down. By April 1, 2024, 60 of my university colleagues and friends were fired. The pilot year of the AAS course coincided with the genocide in Gaza and the protests across university campuses. Many of the students I worked with on campus were arrested and faced academic sanctions. It felt as if we were facing assaults from the state against equitable, truthful teaching of history on multiple fronts. There were times I was overwhelmed by the intensity of assaults on multiple fronts. As co-teachers, Annie and I checked in with each other during class. Lily and I had frequent check-ins on Zoom where we provided meaning and strength to each other. In the end, none of us wanted to let our youth down.

Finding Care Against Oppressive Systems

As a 17-year-old high school student, Indu wanted to see educational justice for her younger self and for other women like her who have been absent from history books. Annie connected to the maternal lineage of educators and caregivers who have come before her. As a female Asian American teacher who faced microaggressions and challenges from some parents, the fight to bring AAS to her campus was intensely personal. She sought care and affirmation from friends, family, and allies across the nation who encouraged and provided her with teaching materials and supplies. For Mohit, it was extremely important to maintain relations of reciprocity and care with colleagues in other Ethnic Studies areas and movement elders. This was especially true given political moves in other states where laws mandating Asian American history were passed, while African American Studies was being criminalized by the state governor. We also found care with each other. We all knew that we were advocating for the well-being of Asian American youth in Texas who were asking for an AAS course and provided emotional testimonies in front of the SBOE.

Conclusion

In this chapter, we shared our collective triumphs and challenges in advocating for Asian American Studies for Texas schools. The fight for educational justice generally, and Ethnic Studies in particular, has a particular set of obstacles in "red" states like Texas that are intensifying attacks against public education and criminalizing inclusive, accurate teaching of history. Our narratives provide insights into the emotional, mental, and physical consequences of fighting for AAS during the past several years. We are continuing the fight, just like our Asian American ancestors and our local Texas ancestors in previous decades. After all, each of us will eventually become somebody else's ancestor.

References

Budiman, A., & Ruiz, N. G. (2021, April 29). *Key facts about Asian Americans, a diverse and growing population.* Pew Research Center. https://www.pewresearch.org/short-reads/2021/04/29/key-facts-about-asian-americans/

Gutiérrez, J. A. (1998). *The making of a Chicano militant: Lessons from Cristal.* University of Wisconsin Press.

Kunzman, H., & Allen, D. (2024). *Beyond the sound and fury: The landscape of curricular contestation in Texas.* Ash Center for Democratic Governance and Innovation,

Harvard Kennedy School. https://ash.harvard.edu/wp-content/uploads/2024/06/Beyond-Sound-Fury-Allen-Lab-Occasional-Paper.pdf

López, B. (2022a, September 19). Texas has banned more books than any other state, new report shows. *The Texas Tribune.* https://www.texastribune.org/2022/09/19/texas-book-bans/

López, B. (2022b, September 22). Conservative backlash pushes Texas social studies curriculum review to 2025. *The Texas Tribune.* https://www.texastribune.org/2022/09/02/texas-state-board-social-studies-review/

Mehta, M., & Pandey L. G. (2022). Stories of our elders: Creating an online space to safeguard our stories in response to anti-Asian xenophobia. *Language Arts, 100*(1), 63–67.

Puente, J., & Alvarez, S. (2021). Texas resistance: Mexican American studies and the fight against whiteness and white supremacy in K-12 at the turn of the 21st century. *Association of Mexican American Educators Journal, 15*(2), 64–84.

Saldaña, L. (2022). The struggle for Mexican American Studies in Texas K-12 public schools: A movement for epistemic justice through creation/resistance. In R. Rosales (Ed.), *Making citizenship work* (pp. 96–111). Routledge.

San Miguel, G. (1983). The struggle against separate and unequal schools: Middle class Mexican Americans and the desegregation campaign in Texas, 1929–1957. *History of Education Quarterly, 23*(3), 343–359.

Sinta, V., & Rivas-Rodríguez, M. (2023). The 1970 Uvalde school walkout. *US Latina & Latino Oral History Journal, 7*(1), 4–37.

Valenzuela, A. (2019). The struggle to decolonize official knowledge in Texas' state curriculum: Side-stepping the colonial matrix of power. *Equity & Excellence in Education, 52*(2-3), 197–215.

Winter, J, (2024, May 25). The Texas school district that provided the blueprint for an attack on public education. *The New Yorker,* https://www.newyorker.com/books/under-review/the-texas-school-district-that-provided-the-blueprint-for-an-attack-on-public-education

Xia, A. (2024, April 1). The State Board of Education again delays discussion on whether to approve new Native studies course. *The Texas Tribune.* https://www.texastribune.org/2024/04/01/texas-sboe-native-studies-course-delayed/

At the Wonton-making Table: On Belonging and Resistance

Edwin Mayorga

THE AFTERNOON SUN was setting as my tía Leonor coordinated our wonton-making factory at her small and cozy dining table. "Mojen las esquinas (wet the corners). A si no (not like that)," she would say sharply, as she chatted with my mom (her sister) and other relatives. My tía Leonor passed away in 2022, and it has been over 35 years since our familia sat around the table. As a child of intergenerational migrations from China to Nicaragua, Nicaragua to Southern California and Miami, and (for me) to New York City and Philadelphia, those moments of wonton making, of Spanish chatter and chisme (gossip), of belonging stay with me.

As I read the contributions to this section of the book, I was immediately brought back to the warmth and creativity of tía Leonor's wonton-making table. Across these chapters, these educator-scholar-changemakers have compassionately gathered and told stories of Asian American educators, history, curriculum, pedagogy, leadership, and activism. In doing so, the authors are inviting readers to sit at a table where "freedom is a place" (Gilmore, 2023, p. 474) to be created through teaching, learning, and advocacy. There are many lessons through these chapters, but here I will focus on belonging and resistance.

On Belonging

Belonging is a spatial and relational set of processes that is inextricable from the long history of Asian America, and these complexities were present throughout the chapters. Today, Asian Americans make up 7% of the overall U.S. population, but only 2.5% of U.S. teachers and less than 2% of school leaders (Superville, 2023). As both Koh and Teng et al. show, for the too few Asian American educators who sustain in the field, the desire for belonging is, at least in part, a response to intergenerational processes of exclusion, displacement, and systemic racism that persist in educators' everyday lives. Koh notes how much he struggled to feel as though he belonged when he repeatedly found himself the only Asian American educational leader at work. Teng et al. spotlight how belonging, exclusion, and space are bound to processes of Asianization, or racialization, within a racial field defined by systems of white supremacy and empire.

Moparthi et al. and Coloma document ways that various curricular and social movement initiatives have been advanced from classroom and community to state policy advocacy to ensure the histories of Asian Americans and Pacific Islanders are included in K-12 school curricula. These two pieces amplify how the curriculum becomes a key site of struggle over belonging for Asian Americans where we are superficially present, at best, or completely erased, at worst.

Resistance

Koh asks directly, "where do we find belonging?" Across these chapters, the response to this question is resistance as a means to create spaces of belonging, rather than belonging to something not of our own making. To Lee (2017), resistance refers to "[collective and] active efforts to oppose, fight, and refuse to cooperate with or submit to . . . abusive behavior and . . . control" (p. 44). In these chapters, resistance takes on many forms, including connecting to histories of Asian American resistance (Koh and Coloma), storytelling and story mapping (Teng et al.), and pedagogical experiments (Moparthi et al.). A unifying thread across the pieces is the practice of resistance storytelling (Bell, 2019; Goulding, 2015). Educational story mapping and advocacy for statewide inclusion of Asian American studies in schools function as ways to resist being made invisible. By engaging in resistance storytelling, these authors are not only ensuring Asian American stories are included in statewide curricula, but also providing inspiring examples of how to resist white supremacy in our bodies, in our classrooms, and in policy.

Closing Breaths

These works raise the question of "with whom are Asian Americans seeking belonging?" In the years since the tragic anti-Asian spa shootings in Atlanta in 2021, there has been a surge in initiatives around combating anti-Asian hate and asking for a more profound appreciation of the long history of Asian Americans within the fabric of U.S. society. What is less examined is whether these initiatives advocate for inclusion into U.S. society for the sake of belonging to a profoundly oppressive society or something else.

Certainly, Asian America is not a singular story, and thus motivations that undergird visions of belonging are also not singular. In loving ways, each of these chapters remind us that resistance is not only fighting for belonging to this world, but belonging to a process of creating another world. It is a world vision that signals entry into an era of what Boggs and Kurashige (2012) describe as "an epoch of responsibilities, which requires new, more socially-minded human beings and new, more participatory and place-based concepts of citizenship and democracy" (p. xviii). It is a world where Asian Americans find themselves cozied up at a wonton-making table, where people are creatively making freedom to breathe into existence a world of belonging, safety, borderlessness, mutuality, and freedom. Roy (2004) reminds us this world "is not only possible," but that "she is on her way," and "on a quiet day, we can hear her breathing" (p. 86). These four chapters are traces of that breath, and for that I am ever so grateful.

References

Bell, L. A. (Ed.). (2019). Resistance stories: Drawing on antiracism legacies to map the future. *Storytelling for social justice* (2nd ed., pp. 71–83). Routledge.

Boggs, G. L., & Kurashige, S. (2012). *The next American revolution: Sustainable activism for the twenty-first century*. University of California Press.

Gilmore, R. W. (2023). Abolition geography and the problem of innocence. In B. Bandar & A. Toscano (Eds.), *Abolition geography: Essays towards liberation* (pp. 471–495). Verso.

Goulding, C. (2015). The spaces in which we appear to each other: The pedagogy of resistance stories in zines by Asian American riot grrrls. *Journal of Cultural Research in Art Education, 32*(1), 161–189.

Lee, D. W. (2017). Resistance dynamics and social movement theory: Conditions, mechanisms, and effects. *Journal of Strategic Security, 10*(4), 42–63.

Roy, A. (2004). *An ordinary person's guide to empire*. South End.

Superville, D. R. (2023, February 28). Why aren't there more Asian American school leaders? Here's what we heard. *Education Week*. https://www.edweek.org/leadership/why-arent-there-more-asian-american-school-leaders-heres-what-we-heard/2023/02

Part IV

Envisioning New Worlds

CHAPTER 13

Am I a Model Minority?: Critical Reflections on Asian American Pasts and Futures

Wayne Au

I'VE BEEN THINKING and talking a lot about model minority and Asian American education over the last few years. The spikes in anti-Asian violence since the early 2020s have compelled me to try and understand Asian American racialization—what it is, what it has been, and how it has positioned us as Asian Americans[1] within the politics of education. The model minority stereotype remains the dominant way that many in the United States make sense of supposed Asian American achievement in education. In what follows, I discuss the origins of the model minority stereotype and how it is grounded in anti-Blackness, the diversity found within the racial category of Asian American, my own relationship with Asian American identity, and the kinds of expansive solidarities and critical identities we need if we are going to divest from the destructive nature of the model minority stereotype.

The Birth of the Model Minority

The concept of Asian Americans as model minority originated with the January 1966 article entitled "Success Story: Japanese-American Style" (Peterson, 1966). In this article, the author lauded Japanese Americans for their ability to overcome the racist discrimination of being illegally incarcerated during World War II. He also praised Japanese Americans as self-respecting, disciplined citizens who believed in education and hard work. Even though the article never used the term "model minority," it did uphold Japanese Americans as a racial model in contrast to what the author termed as "problem minorities" (Peterson, 1966, p. 40): specifically Black Americans, Mexican Americans, and Native Americans. The article closed by claiming that, unlike Japanese Americans, Black people had been unable overcome racial discrimination.

In December of that same year, a second model minority article was published entitled "Success Story of One Minority Group in the U.S." (*U.S. News & World Report*, 1966). Unlike its predecessor, this article focused on Chinese Americans. However, similar to the earlier piece, it claimed that Chinese Americans overcame a history of anti-Chinese discrimination and were successful because of their cultural values, self-respect, achievement, discipline, respect for authority, and hard work. While upholding Chinese Americans as a racial model, this article also took direct aim at Black Americans, for instance, claiming that "At a time it is being proposed that hundreds of billions be spent to uplift Negros and other minorities, the nation's 300,000 Chinese-Americans are moving ahead on their own-with no help from anyone else" (*U.S. News & World Report*, 1966, p. 73).

The 1966 formation of the Asian American model minority stereotype as an extension of anti-Blackness is not mysterious. The Voting Rights Act of 1965 had been recently passed, and the racial uprising of the Watts Rebellion had occurred in 1965, as well. Additionally, the *Moynihan Report*—which offered the racist argument that Black families were weak and that a culture of poverty was the reason for their social and economic status—was published in the same year (Jun, 2011; Museus et al., 2019). The Black Power movement was also building nationally such that by 1968 there was a widespread radical anti-imperialist and anti-war movement in the United States (Taylor, 2016).

The model minority was a crafted narrative of successful Asian American assimilation that served as an argument either that racism did not exist in the United States or that racism was best overcome through hard work, the right cultural values, and working nicely within the system to advance racial equality. Thus, the model minority stereotype of Asian Americans as hard-working students, educational whiz kids, and academic hyper-achievers (Au, 2025; Lee, 2009) is not a "good" or "positive" stereotype because such construction is predicated on other racial groups, particularly Black Americans, as "problem minorities" (Peterson, 1966). Simply put: To uphold the model minority stereotype is to uphold anti-Blackness (Au, 2022). Not surprisingly, a 2021 study found that for some Asian American college students, stronger internalization of the model minority stereotype predicted stronger feelings of anti-Blackness (Yi & Todd, 2021). What many don't get is that the model minority stereotype also strikes fear in white people, just as it ultimately hurts Asian Americans too.

The Model Minority Threat

The root of a lot of anti-Asian racism is the threat of an Asian takeover, and the model minority stereotype only serves to buttress these fears among white people. For instance, during the 1980s, Asian American students were regularly described as "surging" like a "tidal wave" into top universities, and white university students joked that MIT (Massachusetts Institute of Technology) was short for "Made in Taiwan" and UCLA (University of California, Los Angeles) stood for "University of Caucasians Living among Asians" (Allred, 2007; Osajima, 2005). In 2011, a white student at UCLA went viral after she posted a video complaining about the Asian "hordes" of students and did a racist mimicking of Asian languages (Poon, 2011). Other research finds that white students still view Asian students as overrepresented in U.S. universities (Cabrera, 2014).

The model minority stereotype also operates as a threat against Asian American students because it creates a racial exceptionalism for Asian Americans that is impossible to live up to (Eng & Han, 2002). Research shows that Asian American students who do not fit the model minority stereotype often silence themselves, face feelings of inadequacy and self-hate, and experience strong feelings of being an impostor or inauthentic Asian (Lee, 2009; Ninh, 2021; Rivera, 2022). The perceived "success" of Asian Americans as model minority has led many to presume that Asian Americans face fewer psychological issues than other racial groups—which in turn has also led to underdiagnosis and misdiagnosis of psychological issues among Asian Americans (Cheng et al., 2016). The outcomes of these issues on Asian American mental health are quite concrete: suicide is the second leading cause of death for Asian Americans ages 15 to 34, with the highest concentration between ages 20 and 24 (Cheng et al., 2016; Kim et al., 2021). As one Asian American psychologist explains, "We self-harm. We quietly continue to do our homework, even though we're super depressed or anxious. We act out inside the house, but it never shows outside the house. . . . So this system of schools has . . . always been like, 'Oh, you're good, you're fine'" (Chen & Doherty, 2023, n.p.).

What Is "Asian American"?

In addition to mental health issues, the model minority stereotype poses a threat to Asian Americans because it hides the staggering diversity that falls under the racial category itself. The United States Census Bureau (2023) estimates there were almost 24 million people of Asian or mixed Asian descent in the United States, constituting 7.2% of the total population and spread across 21 different ethnic groups. Chinese Americans make up the largest segment (22%), followed by Indian Americans (20%), Filipino Americans (19%), Vietnamese Americans (10%), Korean Americans (8%), Japanese Americans (7%), and all other groups making up the rest in smaller percentages. Asian Americans are also multiracial, with 15% (over 3.6 million) identifying as being "mixed" Asian.

Importantly, there is diversity within these categories, as well. Take, for instance, the category of "Chinese." In China, the Han ethnic group officially makes up over 90% of the population. While Mandarin is the official language, even amongst the dominant Han ethnic group, there are at least 1500 "dialects" (French, 2005). This linguistic and cultural diversity does not include the other 55 non-Han ethnic Chinese minorities, like the Uyghurs, Tibetans, Buyi, or Miao (Luo, 2018; Montefiore, 2013). So, when we say someone has Chinese heritage, we have to recognize that category is not specific enough to fully capture its nuances and complexities. From many Asian nations, such as India, Vietnam, Japan, and the Philippines, similar histories and complexities exist. So, not only is Asian America extremely diverse, but the individual "ethnic" groups within Asian America also have their own depths of diversity (Au, 2025).

In this regard, the model minority stereotype does exactly what all racist stereotypes do: it covers over the immense complexity of a racial group in favor of an oversimplified narrative that flattens the reality of experience. It dehistoricizes and decontextualizes Asian Americans in ways that mask how histories and conditions of immigration play a significant role in the Asian American experience. Since Asian immigration to the United States was reinstated in 1965, the vast majority of Asian immigrants came with higher levels of income and college degrees (Budiman & Ruiz, 2021), with most recent Asian immigrants coming to the United States on H1 visas connected to the technology and banking industries (Watsky et al., 2020). This explains why almost 60% of Asian Americans hold a bachelor's degree (United States Census Bureau, 2020).

Given that research has consistently shown that college attainment and test scores correlate most strongly with family income and education levels of parents (Au, 2023; Berliner, 2013), it is no wonder large numbers of Asian American students are getting high test scores and attending college. The "educational success" of Asian Americans reinforces the ways the U.S. education system reproduces social and economic inequities and privileges those who already have higher levels of education and financial resources. In creating the stereotype of Asian Americans as model minority, we've taken the selective sample of highly educated Asian immigrants and their children and substituted them for all Asian Americans (Au, 2025).

In stark contrast to flattened narratives of Asian American model minority success, nationally, almost 1.1 million Southeast Asian Americans are designated "low income," with 460,000 of them living in poverty. At 58% low income and 26% living in poverty, Hmong/Hmoob Americans are economically one of the poorest groups in the country: their poverty rates essentially double that of whites and equal that of Black Americans (SEARAC & AAJC Los Angeles, 2020). Data from California (with the highest concentrations of Southeast Asian Americans) shows that almost 30% of Southeast Asian Americans have not earned a high school diploma, and their college attainment rates are as low as 14% (SEARAC & AAJC Los Angeles, 2020).

Am I a Model Minority?

Am I, then, a model minority? I'm a Chinese American with a particular history within the broader Asian American transnational diaspora. My Chinese family first came to Hawai'i in the 1880s when it was still the Native sovereign kingdom of Hawai'i. One thing I've learned in my life as a "mixed" person is that race—and whatever meaning is drawn from it—is always in the eye of the beholder. My Asian family in Hawai'i used to argue if I looked white or Asian, with my Korean auntie saying I looked more Asian and my Chinese grandmother (my popo) calling me a "haole boy" (aka "white boy"). Things were markedly different in super-white, suburban Connecticut where my white family lived. Any ambiguity about me being Asian was cleared up on my first day of elementary school after moving there. As I climbed the school bus steps, I heard a white student say, "Look at that Chink." From then on, I knew where I fit (or didn't) in suburban Connecticut. I know I'm talking about being "mixed," but in reality, whether or not I am a model minority hinges on whether or not I am perceived as an Asian American. Since racial purity is a governing tool of white supremacy, I strive to claim who I am as an Asian American who is part of a diverse, transnational, diasporic community.

Early on as a student, I might have been a model minority. I was placed on the "gifted" track in 2nd or 3rd grade because I was a good reader and I apparently answered correctly on some ink blot test given by a school psychologist. In high school, I was enrolled in all honors courses, but I found them to be alienating and entirely uninteresting. They also did not engage my own growing politicized consciousness—which was in part due to the influence of my radically leftist Chinese father and in part due to the influence of politicized hip-hop of the late 1980s. I then de-tracked myself throughout the years, enrolling myself in "regular" courses one by one until I gave up my Advanced Placement Calculus course during my senior year (Au, 2005). Instead, I sought out more meaningful educational and politically academic experiences at my school by enrolling in Black Studies courses (Au, 2009). My SAT scores were middling at best, and I did go to college.

My sense of politics meant that I knew I could never go into business or anything corporate, and I knew I liked to help people. Plus, both of my parents had been educators. So, as early as 9th grade, I knew I wanted to become a teacher, and that became what I pursued. However, originally I wanted to be a science teacher, but seeing films like *Who Killed Vincent Chin?* and taking part in protests against the first U.S. war on the Persian Gulf changed my consciousness, and I decided to become a history teacher instead. For me, being an educator has always been a political act, as the point of education at all levels is to help students develop clearer, more critical understandings of the world. I carried this belief into and through getting my PhD, manifest it in all of my publications, and still hold this to be true as a university professor and dean today. In the end I came out with a resistant Asian American identity, sort of an anti-model minority. I followed the path laid out by radical, leftist, activist Asian Americans before me, such as Yuri Kochiyama, and took up struggles for racial justice in education, including making Black Lives Matter in schools, supporting K-12 Ethnic Studies, and working through a politics of solidarity with working people of all races (Au, 2024).

Divesting From the Model

My connection with radical Black politics played a significant role in keeping me from investing in the model minority stereotype. Investment in the Asian American model minority is ultimately an investment in the same white supremacy and anti-Blackness that birthed it. If we are interested in racial justice for Asian Americans or any other racial groups, then we need to divest from the stereotype entirely. Such divestment requires developing more critical understandings and solidarities between Asian Americans and non-Asian Americans alike. For Asian Americans, such expansive solidarities (Nguyen, 2024) would push us to continually uncover, radically reconstruct, and relearn our Asian American histories because our actual identities far exceed our current racialization.

In order to divest from the model minority stereotype, we need to understand Asian Americans historically, including following in the footsteps of radical, leftist Asian American individuals and organizations that have called for critical solidarities and understandings of Asian America since the late 1960s (Ishizuka, 2016). Further, we need to recognize where these legacies are being carried forward today by those doing Asian American Studies in the K-12 curriculum (Au, 2025; Rodriguez et al., 2024), demonstrating how Asian Americans are deeply connected to all racial groups who have struggled against settler-colonialism, anti-Black racism, racial capitalism, and white supremacy. In this regard, as Asian Americans, we need to divest from model minority as a useful identity and fight it at every turn because it only serves to dehumanize us. In kind, we need to foster more critical, expansive solidarities and identities so that we are poised to challenge racial capitalism for its unending degradation of humans and the environment (Au, 2025).

Endnotes

1. I do not believe in grouping Indigenous Pacific Islanders/Pasifika peoples together with Asians and Asian Americans because the racialization of the two groups is entirely different and because historically the broad grouping of the two typically results in the marginalization of Pasifika peoples.

References

Allred, N. C. (2007). Asian Americans and affirmative action: From yellow peril to model minority and back again. *Asian American Law Journal, 14*(1), 57–48.

Au, W. (2005). Power, identity, and the third rail. In P. C. Miller (Ed.), *Narratives from the classroom: An introduction to teaching* (pp. 65–85). Sage.

Au, W. (2009). Decolonizing the classroom: Lessons in multicultural education. *Rethinking Schools, 23*(2), 27–30.

Au, W. (2022). Asian American racialization, racial capitalism, and the threat of the model minority. *Review of Education, Pedagogy, and Cultural Studies, 44*(3), 1–25. https://doi.org/10.1080/10714413.2022.2084326

Au, W. (2023). *Unequal by design: High-stakes testing and the standardization of inequality* (2nd ed.). Routledge.

Au, W. (Ed.). (2024). *Rethinking multicultural education: Teaching for racial and cultural justice* (3rd revised ed.). Rethinking Schools Ltd.

Au, W. (2025). *Asian American racialization and the politics of U.S. education*. Routledge.

Berliner, D. C. (2013). Effects of inequality and poverty vs. teachers and schooling on America's youth. *Teachers College Record, 115*(12). https://doi.org/10.1177/016146811311501203

Budiman, A., & Ruiz, N. G. (2021, April 29). *Key facts about Asian Americans, a diverse and growing population*. Pew Research Center. https://www.pewresearch.org/fact-tank/2021/04/29/key-facts-about-asian-americans/

Cabrera, N. L. (2014). Beyond Black and white: How white, male, college students see their Asian American peers. *Equity & Excellence in Education, 47*(2), 133–151. https://doi.org/10.1080/10665684.2014.900427

Chen, S., & Doherty, E. (2023, February 25). *Schools unprepared to help Asian American students navigate racial trauma*. Axios. https://www.axios.com/2023/02/25/asian-american-mental-health-schools

Cheng, A. W., Change, J., O'Brien, J., Budgazad, M. S., & Tsai, J. (2016). Model minority stereotype: Influence on perceived mental health needs of Asian Americans. *Journal of Immigrant and Minority Health, 19,* 572–281. https://doi.org/10.1007/s10903-016-0440-0

Eng, D. L., & Han, S. (2002). A dialogue on racial melancholia. In D. L. Eng & D. Kazanjian (Eds.), *Loss: The politics of mourning* (pp. 343–371). University of California Press.

French, E. (2005, July 10). Uniting China to speak Mandarin, the one official language: Easier said than done. *The New York Times.* https://www.nytimes.com/2005/07/10/world/asia/uniting-china-to-speak-mandarin-the-one-official-language-easier.html

Ishizuka, K. (2016). *Serve the people: Making Asian America in the long sixties.* Verso.

Jun, H. (2011). *Race for citizenship: Black Orientalism and Asian uplift from pre-emancipation to neoliberal America.* NYU Press.

Kim, J. M., Kim, S. J., Shin, G. H. R., Lee, C. S., He, W., & Yang, N. (2021). The "Let's Talk!" conference: A culture-specific community intervention for Asian and Asian American student mental health. *Community Mental Health Journal, 57,* 1001–1009. https://doi.org/10.1007/s10597-020-00715-3

Lee, S. J. (2009). *Unraveling the "model minority" stereotype: Listening to Asian American youth.* Teachers College Press.

Luo, Y. (2018). Alternative indigeneity in China? The paradox of the Buyi in the age of ethnic branding. *Verge: Studies in Global Asias, 4*(2), 107–134.

Montefiore, C. S. (2013, December 15). How China distorts its minorities through propaganda. *BBC News.* https://www.bbc.com/culture/article/20131215-how-china-portrays-its-minorities

Museus, S. D., Wang, A. C., White, H. H., & Na. (2019). A critical analysis of media discourse on affirmative action and Asian Americans. *New Directions for Higher Education, 2019*(186), 11–24.

Nguyen, V. T. (2024, January 23). Palestine is in Asia: An Asian American argument. *The Nation.* https://www.thenation.com/article/world/palestine-asia-orientalism-expansive-solidarity/

Ninh, E. K. (2021). *Passing for perfect: College impostors and other model minorities.* Temple University Press.

Osajima, K. (2005). Asian Americans as the model minority: An analysis of the popular press image in the 1960s and 1980s. In K. A. Ono (Ed.), *A companion to Asian American studies* (pp. 215–225). Blackwell Publishing Ltd.

Peterson, W. (1966, January 9). Success story, Japanese-American style. *New York Times,* 21, 33, 36, 38, 40–41, 43.

Poon, O. (2011). Ching chongs and Tiger moms: The "Asian invasion" in U.S. higher education. *Amerasia Journal, 37*(2), 144–150.

Rivera, T. (2022). *Model minority masochism: Performing the cultural politics of Asian American masculinity.* Oxford University Press.

Rodriguez, N. N., An, S., & Kim, E. J. (2024). *Teaching Asian America in elementary class-rooms*. Routledge.

SEARAC, & AAJC Los Angeles. (2020). *Southeast Asian American journeys: A national snapshot of our communities*. The Southeast Asian Resource Action Center & Asian Americans Advancing Justice - Los Angeles. https://www.searac.org/wp-content/uploads/2020/02/SEARAC_NationalSnapshot_PrinterFriendly.pdf

Taylor, K. Y. (2016). *From #Blacklivesmatter to Black liberation*. Haymarket Books.

United States Census Bureau. (2020). *U.S. Census Bureau releases new educational attainment data*. https://www.census.gov/newsroom/press-releases/2020/educational-attainment.html

United States Census Bureau. (2023). *Asian American and Pacific Islander heritage month: May 2023*. https://www.census.gov/newsroom/facts-for-features/2023/asian-american-pacific-islander.html

U.S. News & World Report. (1966, December 26). Success story of one minority group in U.S. *U.S. News & World Report, 61*(26), 73–76.

Watsky, C., Ishimatsu, J., Harrison, A., & Nieves, E. (2020). *The economic reality of the Asian American Pacific Islander community is marked by diversity and inequality, not universal success* [FactFile]. Prosperity Now & the National Coalition for Asian Pacific Americans Community Development. https://prosperitynow.org/sites/default/files/PDFs/Policy/CAPACD-PN_AAPI_Fact_File_FINAL_11.10.20.pdf

Yi, J., & Todd, N. R. (2021). Internalized model minority myth among Asian Americans: Links to anti-Black attitudes and opposition to affirmative action. *Cultural Diversity and Ethnic Minority Psychology, 27*(2). https://doi.org/10.1037/cdp0000448

CHAPTER 14

Homeplace: Finding a Sense of Self Among Shattered Realities

Sawsan Jaber

"The entire narrative of this country argues against the truth of who you are."

—TA-NEHISI COATES

Ancestors, Birthing a Pride in Identity

I ASKED LITTLE Sawsan, "What does it mean to be Palestinian?" She shrugged her shoulders, knowing the complexity of that response even as a child. Today, I know that the version I was then and the skin I wear now would offer two different answers. This question elicits responses that vary depending on one's stage in life.

As Little Sawsan, that question takes me back to warm summer nights with all of the grandchildren sitting around my sido (grandpa) as he fed all of us and told us stories about how he escaped the massacre of Deir Yassin, our village in Palestine, in 1948 as a 15-year-old boy saving two of his sisters. We craved stories of Palestine before the occupation. He told us about the trees his father planted and how he found life tending to the gardens of figs, oranges, lemons, pomegranates, and so much more. He talked about olive picking season and the songs his mother and grandmother would sing during those times of celebration. He described a time inscribed with joy, a generous people, a time where people from all faiths lived together and had access to the beauties and wonders of the Holy Land. He planted in us a love and desire for justice and liberation, a responsibility to revive the joy. We were not free and he wanted us to know that our freedom and self-determination were our responsibility and our moral imperative.

Palestinians have always questioned their homeplace. Forcefully extracted from their own lands for more than 76 years, the international diaspora continues to grow exponentially. As refugees, they have never been welcomed anywhere. But also as refugees, their survival was contingent on their attachment to their ancestral identities.

Today, we watch as the most livestreamed genocide in history continues for 11 months as much of the world watches in silence. The trauma on Palestinian bodies, the erasure of their identities, the dehumanization of the people in educational institutions, and the media for over 75 years has contributed to the normalization of the violence alongside the silence. So many view the violence and erasure as deserved. So many feel so strongly about it that they do not contest billions of American tax dollars endorsing the ongoing occupation and genocide. The hidden curriculum of the world has been internalized by the Palestinian diaspora in all places. How can we ever begin to feel the value in our own lives when our death does not bat an eye? How can I ever feel like I belong in a context that is funding the killing of my people? How do I reconcile my identities when what they stand for is so conflicting?

Family, My First Homeplace

When reflecting on all the aspects of my identity, I always say with pride that I grew up in a Palestinian home in the heart of Brooklyn, New York. While my peers in school listened to Madonna, Michael Jackson, and the Backstreet Boys, I grew up listening to Palestinian dabke (traditional step dance) music and mawaweel (folklore music) that echoed the resilience of my ancestors and weaved a tale of resistance, patriotism, and unwavering love for our land. I remember my father, a refugee, getting out of his car at red lights to dance the dabke outside in the street with music blasted, my mother in the front seat, and all of us clapping along. I don't recall ever taking a peanut butter or cold-cut sandwich for lunch. I craved and enjoyed my labna with mint leaves in pita or my hummus sandwiches.

I always say that my journey is literally mapped on my parent's hands. My parents worked tirelessly with their hands to actualize their radical dreams (Safir & Dugan, 2021) of getting an education through their children. Their calloused hands are a result of decades of physical labor, a labor of love, a required labor if their children were going to have the education that was stolen from them by the occupation, displaced again and again. They were both children of war. Yet, despite the traumas and tragedies they witnessed, they decorated our childhood with joy. Their children were their biggest achievements and a source of immeasurable pride. The opportunity of education would never surface for them, so it was a dream that we inherited. We could never afford to visit Palestine, a privilege members of the diaspora who held American or European passports had. But we could not love Palestine any more if we did. Our ancestors made sure of it. We lived and breathed Palestine in our heart and our veins. It was baked into our being in my mother's womb.

Navigating the Macroaggression of Erasure

We grew up experiencing Palestine through our screens, following massacres, kidnappings, illegal settlement growth, more Palestinians displaced with time, Palestinian territories shrinking, more children jailed, more restrictions on Palestinians in movement, less access to natural resources like water, and less access to jobs. We grew up watching peaceful Palestinian protests in Palestine met with Israeli violence and the disconnect of the media calling Israel's army "the most moral army." Was our definition of morality different? How could you build a country on the corpses of an Indigenous people and still claim morality? We grew up living Palestine through our screens and growing more and more confused as we were able to developmentally process the differences in the narratives we were told and experienced with criticality. Our home was not unique. This was the experience of so many first- and second-generation Palestinians. Experiencing Palestine alongside the war on drugs and the war on crime as the number of young Black men filling American jails grew, birthed a passion for justice. Justice was the thread that connected all members of marginalized groups. We all yearned to be seen as human. The work necessary to humanize ourselves had to be collective. Justice was collective.

This made it even more difficult to reconcile our American intersectionality as Palestinian Americans. The complexity of my identity in the United States became more apparent as I continued my journey through school. I recall a first-grade experience of having to put a thumbtack on my country of origin on a map. I was so frustrated and confused when Palestine was nowhere to be found. My teacher was equally frustrated with my confusion. Why was she not as upset as I was? I felt her irritation with me and retreated.

Little did I realize that this would become a common theme in my life, especially in educational spaces throughout my doctoral studies, even as a professional. It felt like identifying as a Palestinian publicly was an audible statement that I was not American even though I was born in Chicago. After all, the media and curriculum did a great job painting a picture that those two identities were in direct contradiction to each other. I would eventually learn that one in three Arab students is bullied by a teacher (Bajaj et al., 2016). With education and a deeper understanding of the interconnectedness of oppressive systems, so much began to make sense. Yet, it continued to contradict my own self-concept. I took pride in my intersectional identity, but in hindsight, I can name the microaggressions I faced by educators throughout my educational career: Each time that I lost a small piece of myself in a school space, the first time that I was labeled and placed in a box. Each time it added to the larger macroaggression of erasure. How was I to exist in a world that could not allow me to claim my identity with pride without some level of reprimand? How would I model the abandonment of double consciousness to my students when I struggled to bring my whole self into spaces that insisted who I was was not good enough?

The Penalties of Palestinian Identity

As I grew older, being different was frowned upon and came with an aura of negativity. Being Arab and Muslim was perceived by many in positions of power as a threat to American values and ways of being. Being Palestinian often came with an additional label of antisemite, also by design. Decades of conflation of anti-Zionism with antisemitism blurred the lines for many. Ironically, there are laws in the United States censoring Americans from criticizing the Israeli government while no such laws exist for criticizing our own government.

No government responsible for serving its people should be free from accountability nor criticism, especially not when Israel is considered "the only democracy in the Middle East." What interest does the United States have to protect the Israeli government from criticism at the expense of our first amendment rights? These are fear tactics used to create a smoke screen around understanding political and social realities in the region and halt pro-Palestinian activists and Palestinians from telling their stories and speaking their truths in turn, erasing the Palestinian narrative from schools and from media for so long.

Social media has put a dent in the government's ability to control such narratives. We are witnessing the story of Gaza shared from the phones of the people in Gaza, their trauma on display to educate the world. We are also witnessing the intentional murder of our storytellers in Gaza as journalists are targeted one by one. Today, people have access to truths that were once secrets to so many. If people don't know today, it is because they have chosen ignorance.

In Palestine, being Palestinian means existence in occupation and in an apartheid state. Their identity is grounded in their endurance to stay steadfast on the land and continue to live and love despite the threat of constant and consistent violence as a form of resistance. It is living under military rule in your ancestral homeland when your oppressor would like to see nothing more than your exodus. It is to that end that Israel has enacted an apartheid state; a Palestinian staying is resistance, and resistance is clasping to identity.

As we witness the atrocities happening in Gaza today while world leaders watch and support financially, politically, and militarily, those words could not be more true. Banks (2017) called Arabs failed citizens—not because we failed to become citizens, but because the social and political context of the United States failed us then and continues to fail us today. No matter how many generations of Palestinians exist in the United States, we are seen as perpetual foreigners and are one of the most hypervisible and invisible marginalized communities (Jaber, 2023) living in a social third space. I cannot recall how many times I have been told to go back to my country and how that violent statement never fails to confuse me. Isn't this my country too? It is the only home I have ever known.

Refusing Silence

What does it mean to be an American? My answer today is different than it would have been before October 7, 2023. Today, being an American means I am complicit with the massacre and genocide of the Palestinian people. My tax dollars fund the weapons making this genocide possible. My president vetoed humanitarian aid and conflated, justified, and reinforced Israeli rhetoric normalizing the terrorism in a current-day holocaust happening on our screens. The carnage and screams of children decapitated and orphaned as we watch; to date, 20,000 babies have been murdered, not accounting for those under the rubble. Twenty thousand! My heart shatters every time I think about those children. Twenty-five thousand are the only survivors of their parents. Twenty-five thousand! Does anyone understand what it means to lose your parents as a child? Many of these children have lost both parents and entire families, left to navigate the world alone. Forty percent of Gaza's population is under 15. These numbers do not include the children and babies who have been buried under the rubble. Our hands are just as bloodied. If we stay silent, our silence is complicity and treachery to our shared humanity. If we look away, we are complicit with the collective world powers acting to erase Palestinians.

What does it mean to be an American? It means a new Nakba for Palestinians, a genocide. And for Americans, a chapter in history that we will be held accountable to and will have to face in our lifetime. Those pictures and videos of human beings decapitated by the thousands and displayed in the streets of Gaza will haunt us as a country if we do not act now to liberate the people. We cannot claim that we did not know. This truth will follow us. We will never be able to escape it.

A few years ago, an administrator came to my classroom and asked me if he could talk to me. He sat across from my desk and said, "Sawsan, your Palestinian identity is offensive. Can you tone it down?" It took me a minute to register what he actually said. My first thought is always about the Palestinian students in our school. What would their experiences look like if this was the way the gatekeepers viewed their identities? My response to him was, "Your white privilege is offensive. Can you tone it down?" Given the positionality of the administrator, a white male with direct power over me, I knew I was taking a risk through my response. But I knew that I owed it to my students and my ancestors to challenge his implicit bias. The way he viewed my identity was a projection of how he viewed all of my students. His negative connotation to my Palestinian identity could not be dismissed as a personal opinion or deficit, rather, it was a racist construct of a group he had the power to impact directly.

As I am shamed, punished, my integrity questioned, my reputation slandered, and speaking events I have been contracted for months ago are canceled because of my pro-Palestinian stance, I realize that the first amendment right is reserved for some as is the American dream. Did I have to be pro-genocide for my identity to be acceptable? Did I have to condone the senseless murder of tens of thousands by a settler colonial entity as an entry point into Americanness? Did I have to abandon my claim to the stories, legacies, and dreams of my ancestors to survive?

Cole Arthur Riley (2023) in *This Here Flesh* says, "Our liberation begins with the irrevocable belief that we are worthy to be liberated, that we are worthy of a life that does not degrade us but honors our whole selves" (p. 15). This question makes me consider what it means to be a Palestinian American educator in the public sector. Ironically, I live in the largest Palestinian community in the country in Illinois. One would think that would add a layer of belonging or create a sense of community; however, we all know that segregation, redlining, and siloing groups never led to community. On the contrary, it leads to othering, and whenever we have othering, we have fear of "the other." The humanity of people is lost when they cannot interact regularly, and they are reduced to stereotypes and single stories.

Our Existence is Resistance, Our Education Must be Loving and Liberatory

Dr. Bettina Love (2019), a leading abolitionist scholar, says "Abolitionist teaching is built on the creativity, imagination, boldness, ingenuity, and rebellious spirit and methods of abolitionists to demand and fight for an education system where all students are thriving, not simply surviving" (p. 11). This quote resonates with me as I reflect on my evolution as an educator. What does it mean to teach and how has that evolved with me? How have my educational experiences shaped my ideology and pedagogy as an educator? I grew up being taught to comply and conform, to never disrupt, to sit in my assigned seat, and to never challenge authority. This left me being subjected to what I know now are anti-Arab tropes by educators and even the punishment and exclusion of Palestinian stories and perspectives. Educators failed me time and time again, yet their failure became my fuel. It would not be an exaggeration to say that teaching saved me, and I was good at it.

Education is often perceived as a tool of liberation. In my educational career, I am proof that it can also be a weapon of oppression, exclusion, and conformity. I remember hearing, "students don't care what you know until they know that you care," at the beginning of my career, which became a standard and foundation of my own educational philosophy. While teaching in my own community, I came to learn that caring for my students would mean that I would have to unlearn much of what I was taught, remove myself from the center, and elevate my students and their stories. My classroom would be as diverse and complex as they were, and that would mean that their voices, stories, cultures, lived experiences, and histories would be reflected in all spaces of my classroom. While I came to the field with a focus on American literature and history, I could no longer live in that box. I began learning about marginalized communities, our intersectional struggles, our hopes and dreams, and our exclusion from the traditional curriculum. I began to shift my thinking about learning. I saw it as a process of excavating identities, cultivating passions, reflecting on our experiences, and considering our positionality in the context of the world and others.

While teaching became an embodiment of justice, I could not teach in a way that excluded or dehumanized my students. I had to create learning spaces and experiences that cultivated and empowered their greatness. In doing so, I evolved as an abolitionist educator, redefining education for myself and for my students. I didn't need to follow a curriculum or set standards. Rather, I co-designed experiences with my students that would center on their growth and engagement. I focused on their strengths and built experiences around their greatness. I learned that my teaching was a reflection of my love for them. I was the teacher I needed and wanted as a child. Teaching could no longer be about compliance, conformity, and passing tests; teaching needed to be about reflecting, critiquing, growing, creating, and imagining a world where we would all thrive, not just survive.

I knew that to be a Palestinian educator was a rebellious act in itself. Despite the consistent attempts to eradicate the Palestinian people, I existed, and my very existence was an act of resistance. As the world watches the genocide happening in Gaza, my responsibility is even greater. With 1.1 million children displaced, tens of thousands of people murdered (over 6000 children), schools bombed, no access to clean water, and a communication blackout, I am proof that they are not alone. In the midst of so much death and destruction, I carry the burden of hope. My students depend on me to create spaces where they can dream, imagine, and build the world they want to live in.

Teaching for me has become about centering my students and creating spaces where they are seen and loved. It is about deconstructing and abolishing what is no longer serving us and constructing what we need. Teaching is the process of humanizing education and seeing our humanity in each other. It is about building spaces of connection, joy, and peace. It is knowing that while I am fighting for my students' rights to learn and grow, I am also honoring my ancestors and resisting oppression. It is knowing that I am not alone and that our collective humanity and dignity are what we all need to build a world where we all belong and are valued.

Being Palestinian is not just an identity; it is a lived experience of resilience, resistance, and a relentless pursuit of justice for all. From the oral histories shared by my grandfather to the daily struggles and microaggressions faced in educational spaces, the Palestinian identity is deeply rooted in a collective memory of displacement, yet it is also a source of immense pride and strength. It is an identity that demands recognition and respect, not just in the context of the Israeli-Palestinian conflict but also within the broader tapestry of American society. As we navigate these complexities, it is crucial to hold onto the stories, the truths, and the unwavering spirit that define what it means to be Palestinian.

References

Bajaj, M., Ghaffar-Kucher, A., & Desai, K. (2016). Brown bodies and xenophobic bullying in US schools: Critical analysis and strategies for action. *Harvard Educational Review, 86*(4), 481–505.

Banks, J. A. (2017). Failed citizenship and transformative civic education. *Educational Researcher, 46*(7), 366–377.

Jaber, S. (2023). Invisibility and hypervisibility of Arab American female students in times of heightened Anti-Arab and Anti-Islamic sentiment. In K. Monkman, A. Frkovich, & A. Proweller (Eds.), *Navigating precarity in educational contexts* (pp. 34–49). Routledge.

Love, B. L. (2019). *We want to do more than survive: Abolitionist teaching and the pursuit of educational freedom.* Beacon Press.

Riley, C. A. (2023). *This here flesh: Spirituality, liberation, and the stories that make us.* Convergent Books.

Safir, S., & Dugan, J. (2021). *Street data: A next-generation model for equity, pedagogy, and school transformation.* Corwin.

CHAPTER 15

River of Collective Struggle: Intergenerational Fugitivity

One Heartbeat Collective

Ethnic Studies: Journeys in Fugitivity, Empowerment, and Care

EUNICE HO (EH): My journey as an Ethnic Studies (ES) practitioner started as a student before I became a teacher. I first discovered ES in 2012 as a sophomore at the University of California, San Diego through a Diversity Equity Inclusion graduation requirement, which emerged from Black Student Union organizing (UCSD Black Student Union, 2010). This signified my entry point into a river of collective struggle made of ordinary people, starting with my mentor Dr. Dennis Childs, who modeled intergenerational prison abolition community organizing that held youth in high esteem.

During the 2022-2023 school year, I taught an ES elective in a district that had recently passed an ES graduation requirement as a result of student organizing in 2020 which preceded the 2021 California Assembly Bill 101 ES graduation requirement. I am a Taiwanese, Asian American woman. The district's student demographic was mostly East, Southeast, and South Asian Americans, followed by Latinx and a few Black and white students. Unlike the previous schools where I taught, the majority of my students looked like me.

After being painfully pushed out of the teaching profession in 2023, I found healing by organizing with youth outside of a traditional classroom setting. In this historical moment of ES legislation and institutionalization, I invited 13 youth, most of them Asian American, to tell this story with me about how we practiced fugitivity together both in and out of the classroom to maintain the spirit of ES. With much gratitude, we lean on fugitive pedagogy (Givens 2021), a framework and practice of Black educators navigating anti-Blackness in education. Because white supremacy culture racializes Asian bodies in particular ways in service of anti-Blackness, our liberation is intimately tied with Black siblings in the struggle. Exploring how we challenge racialized scripts may offer some direction in how we move towards freedom, together. Perhaps an Asian American ethic offers an invitation for all to remember our interconnected past, present, and future; to reject being used to buttress white supremacy; and to continually practice solidarity towards healing and liberation.

Some of these youth used community grants to initiate student-led Asian American Studies PhotoVoice (de los Ríos, 2020) programs during the 2023-2024 school year. Others were part of the inaugural 8-week online program hosted by the Coalition for Liberated Ethnic Studies in fall 2023 where 23 youth organizers from across the country met weekly to build community, engage in political education, and organize local ES efforts. These students were navigating districts (four in Southern California, one in the Midwest) that didn't have ES, actively removed ES, or were developing ES.

On the way to building new worlds, youth throughout the generations have employed practices of fugitivity by creating healing, refuge-like spaces for subversive organizing outside the watchful eyes of the institution. ES experts know that with the recent legislated ES mandates nationwide, institutions will sanitize and misrepresent ES. Practicing fugitivity within this backdrop feels especially urgent. How do we navigate this moment with clarity and precision, guided by the wisdom of forebears and the passion of youth, to shape the future of the ES movement?

Amy Nguyen (AN): It was the last semester of high school, and ES was one of the most impactful, empowering classes I had ever taken. My classmates and I created a safe space to foster learning and community within a competitive school. We were grateful to be under the guidance of Eunice, a compassionate, patient, and passionate teacher.

Sarah Pollyanna Cardenas-Agudelo (SPCA): When I first started at the school as a Latina student, I immediately noticed the disproportionate number of

Asian American students compared to my elementary school. Throughout my years, I often felt like an outsider at this school even though I passed the entrance exam. In junior year I signed up for an ES class, not knowing what it entailed but curious regardless. I remember Eunice immediately created a personable environment with her heartwarming vulnerability.

EH: The school functions as a magnet school within a predominantly Latinx school district. It uses an entry exam to siphon "high-performing" students through anti-Black, model minority myth logics. Most faculty were white. When I was hired, colleagues repeatedly said that I ought to be grateful because this school had less issues (read: Asians are compliant). Although this was a harbinger for what was to come, I poured my heart, time, and labor into building humanizing classroom spaces. This, too, was an act of fugitivity.

SPCA: Our first class circle involved everyone sharing the story of their name. This changed my view on how classes should operate because I learned beautiful, funny stories from classmates, many of whom I was unfamiliar with. Circles were fundamental to my ES experience. I grew compassion for my Asian American classmates through learning about how the model minority myth harms them, too—especially at this school.

AN: Unlike a traditional classroom where teachers lecture while students listen, Eunice invited students to shape the direction of the curriculum, co-creating the classroom experience and tearing down power dynamics. This humanizing experience created interconnectedness, something our school district didn't value. In January 2023, we received bad news.

EH: As counselors were building the schedule for the following school year, the ES elective was removed from the offerings. I began mobilizing with students to collect names of those interested to reinstate the class. I leaned on allies, while other colleagues told me "don't mistake incompetence for malice" and "don't worry, we already do ES anyways." Earlier in the year, my principal told me to "not offend" my colleagues. District personnel told me "We'll reinstate the class if you get enough interest. Nobody is out to get you." Counselors told me "removing ES was an honest mistake." Behind this "honest mistake" belies a culture that, at its roots, did not value the transformative power of ES. I tried to feign a collected facade, but my body remained hypervigilant in this hostile environment.

Figure 15.1 *Microaggressions*

AN: Our entire class felt the substantial weight of the school's actions. We heard anonymous stories of blatant microaggressions (Figure 15.1) from Eunice's colleagues while we mobilized together. The experience was emotionally taxing.

SPCA: I was frustrated by the devaluing of the ES class because I was learning so much about U.S. history that was not covered elsewhere. AP classes, for example, force teachers to gloss over so many stories for the sake of an expensive test. There are also politicians nationwide actively trying to censor or erase stories about systemic racialized violence. We were determined to keep the ES class.

EH: Despite our collective efforts to gather interest, it was an uphill battle to keep counselors accountable to their word to change student schedules. It culminated in a conversation with the superintendent who told me, an untenured 29-year-old Asian American woman with her job at risk, to "Let it go. Play the long game. Do it for the love of the students." What I heard was: be the obedient, token Asian, sacrifice myself, shoulder racialized emotional labor, and acquiesce to the institution's terms and timeline.

AN: This couldn't stop us though. During the final weeks of school, we presented our Youth Participatory Action Research (YPAR) projects to peers on topics like abolition, redlining, foster care, pushout rates, microaggressions, and more.

SPCA: I wouldn't have learned about abolition or transformative justice without this class. ES must be taught by those who are passionate and properly trained. Embedding ES into other subjects, if done poorly, is a disservice to the ES discipline and its passionate educators. We as students lose out.

EH: During our YPAR unit, I was told I would be moved to another school. The students gave me the courage to name the district's untenable maltreatment and practice my own exhortation: "ES is about loving ourselves and each other and re-imagining to build alternative worlds." I was pushed out of the teaching profession for *doing* ES: practicing fugitivity grounded in the community care of not only my teacher-activist community, who lent wisdom, encouragement, and material support, but also the students who sent me off with their blessings.

SPCA: We had a final circle on the last day, hours before our graduation ceremony. Many of us were tearing up or crying as we reminisced. ES was the best class I'd ever taken. I had learned so much about the origins of ES and my classmates' lives, which helped me feel closer to them. I am thankful to Eunice and my classmates for creating a fugitive class community that I always looked forward to: a space for healing within a larger, harmful culture.

EH: After being pushed out, I was recovering from the adrenaline and rage I used as protection from the institution's gaslighting mechanisms. I struggled to imagine an alternative world to still "do" ES. In my grief, I temporarily forgot the youth-led spirit of ES that initially brought me to the profession. I felt powerless, economically vulnerable, and worthless in the eyes of the institution. But over the next year, community organizing with former and new students outside a traditional classroom setting helped me compost this grief into new life. Just as I was expected to comply with a particular racialized script for Asian women, the Asian American students were also experiencing parallel racialized, gaslighting expectations to be high achieving, compliant, and race blind.

Love Through an Asian American Lens: A Youth-Led Asian American PhotoVoice Program

Karina Li: In Spring 2023, I participated in an Asian American PhotoVoice youth program hosted outside of school. I felt so empowered that I took the initiative to ask Eunice to help me to start our own PhotoVoice program, Love through an Asian American Lens, which ran during the 2023-2024 school year after Eunice left the school. Although the youth participants were from different grades and schools throughout the district, we created a safe space to learn about Asian American resistance groups or intersectionality between race and gender. We discussed how the "model minority myth" harmed us and how it's weaponized against the Black community. The school is toxic because it defines success through test scores, instead of valuing ES.

Gina Ngo: This school taught me to prioritize "important" subjects that were supposed to build my future career. Anything else was deemed insignificant, including ES and exploring my ethnic identity. I experienced a change of heart because through this student-led program I realized that education should be for personal transformation. The essential question was "How can we transform ourselves and our communities?" It culminated with a community showcase. I embraced my ethnic identity, grew a deeper understanding of the history of people of color, and most importantly, gained stronger empathy for others experiencing similar struggles.

Victor Do: I often felt my history classes and textbooks didn't reflect any of the faces in my class. Through this program outside of a traditional classroom, I learned history that resonated with my own personal experiences. I talked with my elders at the dinner table, sharing stories that were never included in my history classes that typically only taught dominant narratives.

Erin Kim: Being taught outside an official classroom also allowed us to learn how the genocide in Palestine is connected to Western imperialism in Asia, a topic considered "too controversial" in normal classrooms. I learned about racist micro- and macro-aggressions. We dug deep into the truth. We claimed the freedom to learn.

Karoline Nguyen: It was a safe space because no one was silenced. I felt comfortable and respected by everybody. Being there with students with strong personalities and voices helped me find my voice and engage both in and outside of the program. I was no longer afraid to express myself.

Coalition for Liberated Ethnic Studies Youth Organizing Cohort

EH: The Coalition for Liberated Ethnic Studies (CLES) hosted an online youth organizing cohort in fall 2023. I was grateful to be in community with fellow ES educators and organizers who lovingly put this program together. I was also excited to continue working with youth as a mentor.

Justin Le: We not only learned about our ancestral roots but also connected with others across the country. I saw the perspectives of cohort mates and learned how their lives influenced their commitment to ES. We are connected in solidarity by our practice of advocacy and justice. ES pulls us outside of the bubble-like comfort zones we live in and closer to each other in the world.

Jennifer Nguyen: Through terms like "coalition" and "solidarity," I realized that fugitivity was based in *community*. Within this community, I heard about the experiences of other students without fear of judgment. Mentors and peers were patient, supportive, and understanding about our situations and opinions, something I never felt in official classrooms that limit knowledge taught to students, sticking to subjects that "should" be taught: math, English, science, and history. Instead of waiting for opportunities to contribute to society, we took initiative to create our own ES projects in our local contexts rather than waiting for outside powers to do so.

Justin Parnjan: "Official" classrooms rarely mentioned the land we were on and who its original caretakers were, often keeping to a tight agenda to cover what was "more important" and rarely covering current social issues. In CLES, we started by centering the original caretakers of the land. Even though we had an agenda, we had space to discuss Palestine. Learning outside of restrictive "official" spaces is where we learned the uncensored truth. ES does not fear the "controversial," and neither should we. We should not be deterred or limited by institutions that say otherwise. I realized that it is not just our small home communities fighting for change. People across the country were fighting in solidarity so that OUR communities can be transformed through OUR studies.

Other Asian American Youth Organizing

EH: Through word of mouth in the ES community, I heard of two other students in other districts bravely navigating institutional bureaucracy to create fugitive spaces. They, similar to me, were activated and ushered into the struggle by mentors. I felt deeply resonant with their stories, too.

Lauryn Chew: Inspired by my mom's involvement in Asian American activism, I joined a local PhotoVoice program during my freshman year in spring 2023. Our instructor, Phúc Tô, created a fugitive space for us to heal by interrogating the dominant narratives. Unlike most of my K-12 teachers, Phúc modeled courage by vulnerably sharing their stories. Through Phúc's example, I began challenging my teachers and peers to consider whose stories were centered or erased. I sensed that my questioning made many uncomfortable. I wondered if it was because my actions directly confronted their internalized expectations of Asian American girls to be compliant.

After the program, there was a grant for youth to build their own programs. I applied, explicitly focusing on cross-racial solidarity, hoping to create similar fugitive, healing spaces for my peers to understand how systems of power, including white supremacy, racism, xenophobia, classism, and sexism, work in tandem to reinforce harmful stereotypes and expectations. With this grant, I founded OC Focus, a student-led, ES nonprofit that amplifies youth stories through multimedia such as photography and artwork. We initially intended to start a club at my school because a teacher had agreed to be our advisor. However, the teacher did not respond to our emails, and our club was rejected by our school's Associative Student Body, so we pivoted to a district-wide virtual format as an act of fugitivity.

Although I received guidance from several community mentors, we crafted our curriculum and ran our sessions without "official" teachers. Being student led dismantled the power dynamic where "students" are expected to unquestioningly absorb and accept the "facts" that "teachers" feed them even if what is taught contradicts students' lived experiences. We created a space of refuge, kinship, and creative resistance without the institution's help.

Kai Yamamoto: I was born in China during their One-Child Policy and taken to an orphanage. A third-generation Japanese/Okinawan American family adopted me and tried their best to incorporate Asian traditions while raising me. Attending dual immersion, predominantly Latino schools made it difficult to feel belonging. The only things I learned about Asian American histories were the Transcontinental Railroad, the Chinese Exclusion Act, and Japanese incarceration.

Everything changed when, in response to the COVID-19 pandemic, a teacher named Ms. Nguyen formed an online webinar for Asian American youth to share their experiences with racism. I joined as a curious freshman. Ms. Nguyen became my mentor "in the system," supporting me with my Girl Scout Gold Award project. I started with a Student Interest Survey at the beginning of my sophomore year. Out of 256 survey respondents, 76% indicated interest in an AAPI course. I scheduled multiple appointments with district staff. After tenaciously sending follow-up emails and waiting outside the principal's office, the course was temporarily approved. We started class with journal prompts such as "Why do you think you and your families' stories matter in the context of ES? What stories do you want to see reflected in your education?" ES was where I first learned about my Chinese American identity and truly accepted myself. We shared laughter, sadness, and understanding.

Every week of class was precious. At its conclusion, I was excited and hopeful for the class to continue. I sent multiple emails asking the district about the necessary steps for a permanent course. The ES coordinator indicated that the curriculum is "in draft form and it is too early to share," although they would "extend an invitation" my way. I never heard back. My principal offered "providing the space," but said the course proposal and implementation was on me.

A little voice in my head began saying, "It's not worth it. The course isn't *that* important." Aware of my rapidly approaching graduation, I felt embarrassed and thought I had failed. Knowing the project I worked on for my entire high school career wouldn't be available anymore was disheartening.

In writing this, Eunice helped me realize I'm not a failure. The school system failed me. How do we create belonging for each other to heal when school systems fail us?

EH: The school system failed me, too—but the students created belonging for me. The youth in the PhotoVoice program at the district I was pushed out from, youth across the nation in the CLES organizing program, and students like Lauryn and Kai who initiated other programs in their local contexts all practiced fugitivity by carving out spaces for themselves—just as the Third World Liberation Front strikers demanded a space in the academy. In particular, as many of these youth were Asian American, practicing fugitivity was both an important challenge to the racialization they experience to be the passive, obedient model minority as well as a loud assertion of solidarity with other communities of color.

I was honored to be part of their journeys and hoped that I supported them with the same spirit that Dr. Childs supported me with. The students showed me a beautiful web of hyperlocal organizing that institutions don't recognize or celebrate, and illuminated the importance of intergenerational healing and mentorship. How might educators model vulnerable, fugitive spaces like Phúc did for Lauryn? How might educators pave the way alongside them and make their paths easier when navigating institutional bureaucracy like Ms. Nguyen did for Kai? How might educators learn from the youth and follow their lead?

One of my former students, Freddy, is now eager to join the struggle as an educator.

Freddy Netto: To future me, an Ethnic Studies Educator: I'm excited and apprehensive about what lies ahead. The impact I can have on students is something I *know* is worth fighting for, just as I have been revolutionized by educators. However, I've witnessed the pain that can be inflicted. The fight to transform the education system that encloses us cannot be endured alone. As a Hispanic American student in a predominantly Asian American student population, I was socialized to believe that our struggles were isolated and only ours to bear; Asian American stories revealed to me that because we ultimately operate under the same system, our isolation is just another tool to prevent our joint liberation. While these conversations were relegated to outside the classroom throughout high school, Eunice's class showed me otherwise.

Despite possible hurdles like admin curbing freedom, colleague ostracization, parents questioning competence, and constant self-doubt or pressure to conform, I want to create a fugitive classroom space, and I know it will be worth it.

One Heartbeat Collective

The institution can revoke its "permission" for us to exist in its halls—like when Eunice was pushed out, when ES legislation rejects the true spirit of ES, or when student initiatives are rejected—but truthfully, it cannot take anything away from us. It had nothing to give us to begin with. We are the ones who sustain this work by practicing fugitivity as we carry each other towards new worlds. This is a poem our collective wrote together as a celebration of our continued struggle.

> Solidarity . . .
> smells like the powerful fragrance of fresh kimchi filling the room
> looks like a rising tide, a wave of empowerment and unconditional love
> sounds like laughter from memories and silence
> that we share as we process and move through pain

feels like a warm embrace
  when we unite as one, liberated community

Fugitivity . . .
feels like gripping your dreams and never letting go, chasing the North
Star
reaching out your hands to those before and after you

Transformation . . .
feels like the first droplets of rain, as summer turns into fall
sounds like a song, sung by those who yearn for change
looks like dandelions blown by the wind
  carrying the will of those who seek change
feels like finding chosen family

Liberation . . .
tastes like the sweet nectar of honeydew and sunlight
looks like a paper boat that traveled through raging sewer water and
out into the ocean
feels like knowing your presence and stories are precious

Healing feels like . . .
  giving ourselves permission to rest, play, live
  peace after a long, strenuous war
and sounds like the music of one heartbeat

References

de los Ríos, C. V. (2020). Writing oneself into the curriculum: Photovoice journaling in a
  secondary Ethnic Studies course. *Written Communication, 37*(4), 487–511. https://doi.
  org/10.1177/0741088320938794

Givens, J. R. (2021). *Fugitive pedagogy: Carter G. Woodson and the art of Black teaching.* Harvard University Press.

UCSD Black Student Union. (2010). *State of emergency: The UCSD Black Student Union
  address.* UC San Diego Library. https://pages.ucsd.edu/~rfrank/class_web/
  BSUresearch/Black%20Student%20Union%20at%20UC%20San%20Diego-State%20
  of%20Emergency-Demands022510.pdf.

Centering RADical Asian American Epistemologies to Envision New Worlds

Allyson Tintiangco-Cubales

ARE ASIAN AMERICANS—AND those adjacent or placed under the Asian American umbrella—allowed to have epistemologies? The first time I heard the word "epistemology" was in the early 1990s in Ronald Takaki's Introduction to Asian American Studies course at the University of California, Berkeley. We were in a large lecture hall known as Dwinelle 145. On the classroom stage, he stood with great confidence emitting from his petite body, crowned with a salt and pepper feathered bob, eyes framed by large black glasses, a big smile before he spoke, "In this class, we are going to learn about the epistemologies of Asian Americans." I looked around checking to see if any of the other 200 students knew what he was talking about. Before anyone could ask, he explained, "Epistemology is how you know you know what you know." I remember writing that definition of epistemology in the margins of my hardcover copy of *Strangers from a Different Shore*. I wrote it over and over again in my Bay-Area-Pinay-bubble-writing font as if to convince myself that I understood what he meant, maybe also to convince myself that I had an epistemology. But did I really know how I knew what I knew? See, I was a transfer student, not really a model minority, but definitely with a classic case of impostor syndrome, trying to figure out my sense of self and my place in the world called higher education.

Little did I know that this core moment in Takaki's class was going to be my life's study and an integral part of what I know as my own radical Ethnic Studies epistemology. In this section of *Moments and Movements: Journeying Towards Critical Asian American+ Studies in Education*, the focus on *Envisioning*

New Worlds is a centering of RADical Asian American Epistemologies (RAAE). The notion of being radical can hold a multitude of meanings. As Angela Davis (1990) describes it, "Radical simply means 'grasping things at their root'" (p. 14). As racialized beings, grappling with the roots of our oppression means grasping the violent epistemicide that we and our ancestors have suffered through and resisted in dehumanizing systems such as colonialism, racial capitalism, and white supremacy. In Ethnic Studies, a reclaiming of epistemology is a political act of defiance and is inherently radical. Because RAAE emerges from critical pedagogy, critical race theory, Ethnic Studies pedagogy, community responsive pedagogy, womanist/Pinayist pedagogies, queer theory and pedagogies, and disability critical race theory, it pushes us to be committed to centering epistemologies and envisioning new worlds that value:

1. **Reflection:** Reflecting—personally and collectively—on the historical roots and contemporary experiences of Asian Americans.

2. **Relationships:** Relating Asian Americans' experiences to each other, to the narratives of communities of color, and demonstrating our interconnectedness; this includes being in the right relationship with the natural world and all relations.

3. **Analysis:** Analyzing systems of oppression that shape the experiences of Asian Americans and similarly racialized and marginalized groups.

4. **Dreaming:** Dreaming about how we can take the learnings from Asian American Studies and activists to support the self-determination and community actualization of Asian Americans and our co-conspirators.

5. **Determination:** Determining our lives and taking direct and collective action toward solidarity and unity with Indigenous peoples and all communities of color. (Tintiangco-Cubales, 2020; Sacramento et al., 2023)

The chapters in this section of the book are examples of applications and expansions of RAAEs. While I was writing this commentary, I was in conversation with a doctoral student, Castro, and serendipitously they mentioned the desire to include Glenn Omatsu's (2016) conceptualization of "community-based" epistemology in their literature review. I was led back to revisit his chapter, "Militant Humility: The Essential Role of Community Engagement in Ethnic Studies Pedagogy" in *"White" Washing American Education: The New Culture Wars in Ethnic Studies*. In rereading this seminal piece, I learned that not only does he provide a strong case for rooting ourselves in community, but there is also a need to think about the breadth, depth, and plurality of our epistemologies as we begin to think about dreaming about the worlds ahead of us.

This section begins with an essay from Wayne Au entitled "Am I a Model Minority?: Critical Reflections on Asian American Pasts and Futures," where he encourages us to divest from the hegemony of the model minority myth as a useful tool in the "achievement" of Asian Americans. Au resurfaces a counter-epistemology from the radical legacies of Asian American politics rooted in the actions and solidarities of activists and organizations in the 1960s. He then connects this history to the current movement of Asian American and Ethnic Studies K-12 curriculum efforts as acts of resistance to settler colonialism, anti-Black racism, racial capitalism, and white supremacy. Reminiscent of Vijay Prashad's call to "commit model minority suicide" in *The Karma of Brown Folk* (2001), Au courageously proclaims that investment in identifying as a model minority is the same as investing in "the white supremacy and anti-blackness that birthed it" (p. 185). To further personalize this call to divest, Au shares his epistemological journey to answer the question: am I a model minority? Resisting the staticity of identity, he courageously admits to being a "model minority" early in life because that was what was expected of him, and then gradually detracked himself and became politicized through enrolling in Black Studies. He literally took control of his epistemology and followed "the path laid out by radical, Leftist, activist Asian Americans" before him.

In Sawsan Jaber's "Homeplace: Finding a Sense of Self Among Shattered Realities," she grapples with the question, "What does it mean to be Palestinian?" She traces her ancestor-guided epistemology as a grandchild of her sido (grandpa), whose stories before and during the occupation shaped her imagined Palestine filled with "gardens of figs, oranges, lemons, pomegranate and so much more." Embedded in the stories she learned from her ancestors was the responsibility of fighting for self-determination. Although she had a sense early on that Palestinians were not free, her sido "planted in us [them] a love and desire of justice and liberation, a responsibility to revive the joy." Her vivid and beautiful descriptions of growing up Palestinian in Brooklyn is juxtaposed to "penalties of Palestinian identity" as automatically "antisemitic." As she shares her dehumanizing experiences as a Palestinian American educator in Illinois with the largest Palestinian community in the United States, her ancestral-guided epistemology is about remembering their stories, and she is armed with the resistance and responsibility to respond. When an administrator literally called her Palestinian identity offensive, she felt that she owed it to her students and her ancestors to challenge him. Unfortunately, part of her epistemology was the punishment for her resistance, but this did not stop her. She evolved into an abolitionist educator and created liberatory learning spaces. She writes, "I knew that to be a Palestinian educator was a rebellious act in itself. Despite the consistent attempts to eradicate the Palestinian people, I existed, and my very existence was an act of resistance."

The concluding chapter in this section, "River of Collective Struggle: Intergenerational Fugitivity" by One Heartbeat Collective, embodies Omatsu's conceptualization of community-based epistemologies both in its purpose and pedagogy. In his own reflection, Omatsu (2016) offers,

> ... learning occurs not within the individual person but for a person
> within a web of social relationships. Thus, if I want to increase learning
> outcomes for each student in a classroom, I need to enhance human
> relationships. My mentors taught me that a major responsibility of
> teachers, whether in schools or in community settings, is to promote
> healthy group dynamics—essentially, community building. (p. 171)

In the "River of Collective Struggle" chapter, Eunice Ho, an amazing Ethnic Studies teacher, provides a space where the youth she has worked with in and outside of the classroom learn to unearth their epistemologies while also connecting them to the epistemologies of those who share space with them. Unjustly, Eunice was pushed out of teaching, but this did not stop her from working with youth. She found herself immersed in organizing with youth, and in the spirit of Ethnic Studies, they collectively created fugitive spaces. This was inspired and guided by Black scholars and activists who fought against anti-Blackness in and outside of schooling. Through PhotoVoice projects and through the Coalition of Liberated Ethnic Studies youth organizing development series, Eunice and the 13 youth whom she invited to share community-based epistemologies that tell stories of how refuge-like spaces are necessary for both individual and collective healing and liberation. In many ways, the One Heartbeat Collective lives what Steve Louie (2001) asserts in his introductory remarks in *From Asian Americans: The Movement and the Moment*, "When we wanted it done, we did it ourselves" (p. xv). So much can be learned from the ways fugitive spaces resist systems and institutions that are harmful. One Heartbeat Collective teaches us that "The institution can revoke its 'permission' for us to exist in its halls . . . but truthfully, it cannot take anything away from us. It had nothing to give us to begin with. We are the ones who sustain this work by practicing fugitivity as we carry each other towards new worlds."

Envisioning new worlds requires us *to know how we know what we know.* But how, where, and from whom we choose to root our knowledge matters. It is our choice. As you will read in various chapters in this book, RADical epistemologies require us to divest from epistemologies imposed on us, to return to the epistemological teachings of our ancestors, and to commit ourselves to community-based and culturally-rooted epistemologies. Ultimately our freedom is bound with each other and in solidarity with communities that have also experienced epistemicide. To envision new worlds is a political act of taking back our epistemologies because they belong to us and we get to decide where our knowledge comes from.

References

Davis, A. Y. (1990). *Women, culture, and politics*. Vintage.

Louie, S. (2001). When we wanted it done, we did it ourselves. In S. Louie & G. Omatsu (Eds.), *Asian Americans: The movement and the moment* (pp. xv–xxv). UCLA Asian American Studies Center Press.

Omatsu, G. (2016). Militant humility: The essential role of community engagement in ethnic studies pedagogy. In D. M. Sandoval, A. J. Ratcliff, T. L. Buenavista, & J. R. Marín (Eds.), *"White" washing American education: The new culture wars in ethnic studies* (vol. 2, pp. 167–178). Praeger.

Prashad, V. (2001). *The karma of brown folk*. University of Minnesota Press.

Sacramento, J., Curammeng, E. R., Diego, R. S., & Tintiangco-Cubales, A. (2023). Toward a radical Asian American studies pedagogy. *Journal of Asian American Studies, 26*(2), 207–219.

Tintiangco-Cubales, A. (2020, Dec. 5). *Teaching in a time of lovelessness: A proposal for a RADical ethnic studies pedagogy* [Online Presentation]. Pin@y Educational Partnerships Annual Winter Retreat.

Editor Biographies

Betina Hsieh is the Boeing Endowed Professor of Teacher Education at the University of Washington (Seattle). Her teacher education work is informed by 10 years of urban middle school classroom experience and work with literacy professional learning among K-12 educators. Dr. Hsieh is deeply committed to creating more equitable spaces in education and amplifying the voices of Asian Americans, teachers of color, and communities of color doing solidarity work in education. She is the former chair of the AERA Research on the Education of Asian Pacific Americans Special Interest Group and co-author of *The Racialized Experiences of Asian American Teachers* with Dr. Jung Kim.

Roland Sintos Coloma is a professor and associate dean of Faculty and Staff Affairs in the College of Education at Wayne State University in Detroit, Michigan. His research and teaching on the cultural politics of difference in education pursues critical questions on race, gender, and sexuality from historical, intersectional, and transnational frameworks. His publication record consists of 4 books and over 40 articles and book chapters, and he has garnered over $3 million of funding from federal, foundation, education, and philanthropic agencies. He served in the statewide Michigan Asian Pacific American Affairs Commission in 2020-24.

Author Biographies

Ruchi Agarwal-Rangnath is an associate professor at the University of San Francisco and faculty coordinator of the South Bay Masters of Arts and Teaching Credential program, Project H.E.A.L. (Humanizing Educators and Learners). She is deeply committed to centering the work of Ethnic Studies and humanizing education in teacher preparation. Her research focuses on critical literacy, social studies, Ethnic Studies, and social justice learning and teaching in the elementary classroom. She is author of the books *Planting the Seeds of Equity: Ethnic Studies and Social Justice in the K-2 Classroom; Social Studies, Literacy, and Social Justice in the Elementary Classroom: A Guide for Teachers*; and co-author of *Preparing to Teach Social Studies for Social Justice: Becoming a*

Renegade, as well as numerous journal articles and book chapters. She is executive director of CARE-ED (California Alliance of Educational Researchers) and founding member of the National Association of Multicultural Education, California Chapter.

Sohyun An is a professor of social studies education at Kennesaw State University. Her teaching and research centers on issues of racism, war, migration, imperialism, and citizenship within the context of social studies education. Her recent works include *Asian American Studies K-12 Framework* co-authored with Dr. Noreen Naseem Rodríguez and *Teaching Asian America in Elementary Classroom* co-written with Dr. Noreen Naseem Rodríguez and Dr. Esther June Kim.

Wayne Au is dean and professor in the School of Educational Studies at the University of Washington Bothell. He is a former public high school social studies teacher and a long-time editor for the social justice teaching magazine *Rethinking Schools*. His work focuses on high-stakes testing, teaching for social justice, critical pedagogy, and anti-racist education. Author or editor of over 100 publications, his recent books include *Unequal by Design: High-Stakes Testing and the Standardization of Inequality* (2nd ed.) and the upcoming *Rethinking Multicultural Education* (3rd ed.). An award-winning teacher and scholar, he was named the 2023 Weissberg Chair for Human Rights and Social Justice at Beloit College and honored with the UW Bothell Distinguished Teaching Award in 2015.

William Bae, a Korean-American, is a current PhD candidate at the University of Texas at Austin in the Department of Curriculum & Instruction, focusing on secondary social studies. He received his Bachelor of Arts degree at Baylor University in political science (2015) and his Masters of Education degree in curriculum & instruction at the University of Texas at Austin (2017). He is a former classroom teacher of 4 years, having taught middle school and high school social studies courses in Katy, Texas. His research interests focus on how the racial identity of Asian American teachers and educational stakeholders influences curricular decisions and classroom practices and understanding the process and decisions of curricular reclamation for Asian Americans in the social studies curricula.

Sarah Pollyana Cardenas-Agudelo (she/her) (One Heart Collective) is a second-year college student at Fullerton College pursuing a BA in psychology. She is passionate about Ethnic Studies, particularly inequity in education.

Theodore Chao is an assistant professor of mathematics education at California State University, Fullerton. His research involves video storytelling to engage students and teachers in sharing counterstories of mathematics that push back on harmful stereotypes, particularly within Asian and Asian American communities. His projects have been funded through the IES, NSF, and Fulbright. He is currently the host of the *TODOS: Mathematics for All* podcast with Shari Kaku. He also produced the *Radical Cram School* web series and is an author (with Kristina Wong, Anna Michelle Wang, and Jenessa Joffe) of the forthcoming book *Auntie Kristina's Guide to Asian American Activism*.

Lauryn Chew (she/her) (One Heart Collective) is a high school junior from California who is passionate about uplifting others' voices and exploring the intersections of race, gender, and migration. An advocate for social change through community building, she is the founder and president of OC Focus, a student-led, Ethnic Studies-based nonprofit organization that amplifies youth stories of love, community, and resilience through multimedia.

Giselle Cunanan is an assistant professor of Ethnic Studies at California State University, Sacramento. Her work examines the limits and possibilities of working for social justice within settler colonial institutions and the afterlives of empire as it relates to U.S.-based Filipinos.

Edward R. Curammeng is an associate professor in the College of Education at California State University, Dominguez Hills. His teaching and research interests include Ethnic Studies education and critical race theory in education to examine the experiences of students and teachers of color. His recent research can be found in *Review of Educational Research*, *Teacher Education Quarterly*, *Educational Studies*, and *Journal of Asian American Studies*.

Victor Do (he/him) (One Heart Collective) is a high school sophomore in California attending Oxford Academy. He is passionate about Ethnic Studies advocacy, particularly promoting Vietnamese and Asian American Studies in K-12 education. He hopes to continue organizing for inclusive curricula, gain more experience in policy making, and make a meaningful impact to represent minority communities in the United States.

Monica Eraqi is currently in her 18th year as a high school social studies teacher, teaching U.S. history, economics, and Modern Middle East, a course that she designed 16 years ago. She has also served as an adjunct assistant professor teaching multicultural education at the graduate level. She holds a doctorate in curriculum and instruction and her research is concentrated on multicultural education, with a specific focus on Arab American and Muslim American studies at the secondary social studies level. She has lived, worked, and studied in 34 countries and is a regular presenter at the Arab American National Museum.

Eunice Ho (she/her) is an Ethnic Studies practitioner and practices humanizing, healing-centered, praxis-driven, and place-based critical pedagogy. She is a former Ethnic Studies high school and middle school teacher who taught in Los Angeles and Orange County. She received her BA in Ethnic Studies from UCSD and her M.Ed with an emphasis in Ethnic Studies from UCLA.

Dr. Sawsan Jaber is a global educator, presenter, equity strategist, curriculum designer, community activist, and keynote speaker of 20+ years. She has held a variety of leadership positions both in the U.S. and abroad. Dr. Jaber is currently a high school English department chair, district equity leader, and teacher at Maine West High School in Park Ridge, IL. Dr. Jaber founded Education Unfiltered Consulting and works with schools nationally and internationally. She completed her Ph.D. in curriculum and instruction primarily on inclusion and belonging of students from marginalized communities, with a focus on Arab American students in historically homogenous communities Sawsan was one of the ten finalists for Ilinois State Teacher of the Year. She was awarded the Cook County Teacher of the Year in 2023, ISTE 20 to Watch Award for 2023, the CEL Teacher-Leader of Excellence Award in 2023, and IDEA Teacher of the Year in 2022.

Dr. Jaber is a board director of Our Voice Alliance (OVA) charged with amplifying the voices of teachers of color to create more equity for students of color. Additionally, Sawsan is one of the founders of the Arab American Education Network (AAEN). She is a member of the International Society for Technology in Education's (ISTE) Community Leader Network. She is a member of NCTE's Committee Against Racism and Bias in the Teaching of English. Dr. Jaber is a National Board Certified teacher and focuses most of her research on engaging all students in equity work and advocating for Arab and Muslim students. Among other projects, she has worked on national and international equity-centered projects with Google and the National Board Association. Sawsan is a Pulitzer Teacher Fellow and a state TeachPlus Policy Fellow. She has been featured in several conferences and podcasts, and written several blogs, journals, and newsletter publications with the hopes to continue working with educators to empower students to work towards global equity and justice. She has published several scholarly works and a chapter in the book *Navigating Precarity in Educational Contexts: Reflection, Pedagogy, and Activism for Change* and a chapter in the book *The Intersections of Critical Pedagogy, Critical Literacy, and Social Justice: Toward Empowerment, Equity, and Education for Liberation*. She is co-writing part 2 of the book *Street Data* with author Shane Safir. Sawsan has several other publications. However, her favorite work is being an activist scholar and co-conspirator for justice alongside her students. Sawsan brings the perspective of being the daughter of refugees from Deir Yasin, Palestine.

Erin Kim (she/her) (One Heart Collective) is a high school senior attending in California who loves to be involved with ethnic Asian American Studies. She hopes to learn more about the history and story of her Asian American identity. She also wishes to achieve gathering more people who are interested in Asian American identities to share the exciting experience.

Esther June Kim is an assistant professor in curriculum and instruction and affiliate faculty of Asian Pacific Islander Studies at William & Mary. Her research focuses on how racial and religious identities (or different *origin stories*) might shape student understandings and embodiments of citizenship. She also explores how religious and racial narratives are taught (or not) primarily in secondary classrooms. Currently, her work includes collaborations with undergraduate students adapting archival research on Asian American histories to resources for K-12 students and educators. Esther is a former high school humanities and history teacher who taught in both South Korea and California.

Jung Kim is professor of literacy at Lewis University and co-chair of the Department of Education. A 1.5-generation Korean American, she has also worked as a high school English teacher and literacy coach. Jung has published on hip-hop in the curriculum, Asian American identity, and teaching with graphic novels. She is also serving her second 4-year term as an elected member of her local school board.

Paul Joo Hyun Koh is a Korean-Immigrant-American scholar focused on centering the experiences of racially marginalized communities, especially on the experiences of the Asian American/AAPI community. His research interests include cultivating transformational spaces; developing counternarratives and counterstories to racialized contexts; engaging in collectivist leadership actions; and forming cross-racial coalitions in pursuit of racial, social, and economic justice. For over 20 years, Paul worked as a history teacher, an assistant principal, a principal, principal supervisor, and assistant superintendent in the Bay Area and Wake County (NC). He is proud of his heritage, experiences as a learner at UC Davis, UC Berkeley's Principal Leadership Institute, and East Carolina University's International EdD program. As an assistant professor at Towson University, Paul is looking forward to continuing the journey in our struggle to enact racial, social, and economic justice.

Justin Le (he/him) (One Heart Collective) is a high school junior in Southern California who is passionate about Ethnic Studies and community solidarity.

Karina Li (she/her) (One Heart Collective) is a high school senior in California who is passionate about bringing Asian American Studies to fellow students in her community. She is driven to promote social change by educating youth and increasing awareness of social issues facing the AAPI community. She utilizes photography to help students represent themselves and share their stories.

Kirsten Mawyer is an associate professor of secondary science in the School of Teacher Education. As a Kanaka ʻŌiwi scholar her research focuses on teacher preparation with an emphasis on culturally sustaining and revitalizing approaches to critical and culturally ambitious science teaching and learning.

Edwin Mayorga is an associate professor of educational studies and Latin American/Latino Studies at Swarthmore College and a founder/co-researcher of the Education in Our Barrios Project in Philadelphia, PA and New York City.

Mohit Mehta is a PhD candidate in curriculum and instruction and the assistant director for the Center for Asian American Studies, the only academic program for Asian American Studies at a public university in the U.S. South. He was a former public school teacher of 7 years and has taught in India, Guatemala, Nicaragua, and Palestine.

Indira Moparthi is a 12th grader in high school in Austin, Texas who is interested in social and education advocacy and was one of the activists to bring Asian American Studies to her Texas high school.

Richard Mui is a teacher and teacher leader in the social studies department at Canton High School (Michigan) in the Plymouth Canton Educational Park. He attended the University of Michigan in Ann Arbor where he received his BA in history. Richard continued his education at Wayne State University where he earned a Masters of Arts in teaching. Since college, Richard has worked with numerous community organizations in many different capacities. Currently, Richard serves on the Association of Chinese Americans' board where he chairs the Public Affairs committee. He currently teaches AP U.S. History and an Asian American Pacific Islander History, Issues, and Culture elective course, the first APA elective offered in Michigan.

Freddy Netto (he/they) (One Heart Collective) is a university undergraduate senior at Chapman University pursuing a BA in history. He aims to become a secondary-level educator who can implement critical pedagogy, inspired by his educators, peers, community, and upbringing.

Bic Ngo (she/her) (One Heart Collective) is a high school senior in California who is interested and willing to learn about Asian American Studies, seeking to strengthen her identity as an Asian American. Her purpose steers her into joining an after-school program that empowers students to capture defining moments of their lives through the use of photography.

Amy Nguyen (she/her) (One Heart Collective) is a second-year fashion merchandising student with a substantial passion for sustainability and the transformative power Ethnic Studies carries to our past, present, and future.

Annie Nguyen is an English educator in Austin, Texas who has been teaching students from freshmen to seniors for the past 9 years. Driven by her beloved community, she is now proudly piloting the first Asian American Studies high school course in Texas.

Jennifer Nguyen (she/her) (One Heart Collective) is a high-school senior in Southern California who is involved within her Vietnamese community and passionate about the future of Ethnic Studies. She hopes to shine greater light within the impact of ethnicities and cultures within the medical field.

Karoline Nguyen (she/her) (One Heart Collective) is a high school sophomore in Southern California who is passionate about Ethnic Studies and Asian American Studies. She seeks to raise awareness of issues within her community through contemporary art and photography.

'Alohilani Okamura is an assistant professor of languages, culture and practice in the School of Teacher Education. She taught in the Hawai'i Department of Education for 25 years in mainstream education, Hawaiian-focused charter schools, and Hawaiian immersion. Her research examines culture-based education, multicultural/multilingual education, and place-based education.

Justin Parnjan (One Heart Collective) is an Asian American high school student based in Minnesota, active in youth social justice groups proactively creating change within education in a changing world. He centers himself in community-based and collective change, while balancing both education and relaxation each day. Passionate leadership leads to his desire to pursue law to help serve underserved communities in today's society.

LoRayne Reza (she/ella) (One Heart Collective), a high school educator with both a BA in elementary education and MA in language and literacy from ASU, was exposed to Chicano/a literature and critical pedagogy in her early undergrad classes, which taught her the fundamentals of her teaching philosophy—lead with the heart. She continues to do so 22 years into her teaching career as she advocates for, supports, and guides her students and their families.

Noreen Naseem Rodríguez is an assistant professor of elementary education and educational justice at Michigan State University. She is co-author of *Social Studies for a Better World: An Anti-Oppressive Approach for Elementary Educators* with Katy Swalwell and *Teaching Asian America in Elementary Classrooms* with Sohyun An and Esther Kim. Her current research, funded by the Spencer Foundation, focuses on the implementation of Asian American history mandates and the teaching of Asian American Studies across the United States in K-12 classrooms. Before becoming a teacher educator, Noreen was a bilingual elementary teacher in Austin, Texas for 9 years.

Norman Sales is an educational specialist who facilitates and coordinates the Hawaii Department of Education's Na Kumu Alaka'i – Teacher Leader Academy. Norman coaches teacher leaders to address student learning needs by intentionally collaborating within a community of educators. Norman developed his passion for multilingualism and empowering teacher leaders after a decade of teaching English language arts and coaching teachers at Farrington High School in Kalihi on Oahu. In 2019, he was one of the advisers of the multilingual poets who published the award-winning anthology *Voice: Poetry by the Youth of Kalihi*.

Lawrence Teng is a doctoral student in the STEM Education Program at the University of Texas at Austin. Before graduate school, he taught high school mathematics in Oakland, California and Taipei, Taiwan, where he grappled with the power of education to be empowering on the local level yet still connected to larger social inequities. Now, his research interests focus on how mathematics education can engender social justice. He would like his work to help build movements from the local level of students, teachers, and communities towards social realities defined by love and fullness of humanity.

Dr. Allyson Tintiangco-Cubales is a distinguished professor in the College of Ethnic Studies at San Francisco State University. Since 2000, she's been teaching Asian American Studies focusing on Filipina/x/o (American) Studies and also courses on Ethnic Studies, women studies, arts, and pedagogy. She is also interim chair of secondary education and an affiliated faculty member in the educational leadership. She is currently the director of curriculum for UCLA's Foundations and Futures: Asian American and Pacific Islander Multimedia Textbook. In 2024, she was honored with the Wang Family Award, one of the most prestigious honors faculty can receive in the California State University (CSU) system for her teaching, service, and scholarship. Also, in 2024, she became an American Educational Research Association Fellow. She was also featured in this year's Asian Women Are Strong event. And just yesterday, she received the announcement that she is being honored with the Association of Asian American Studies Mentorship award. She has mentored hundreds of critical undergraduate, master's, and doctoral students who are now teaching and working in schools, colleges, and community organizations across the nation. Prior to her position at SFSU, she did her undergraduate work at UC Berkeley in Ethnic Studies and received her Ph.D. from UCLA in education. In 2001, she founded Pin@y Educational Partnerships (PEP), a "barangay" that provides Ethnic Studies courses and curriculum, develops radical educators, and creates resources for Filipina/x/o communities and similarly marginalized people. She has worked with many educators, schools, and school districts throughout the nation to co-develop curriculum and frameworks that center pedagogies rooted in Ethnic Studies, social justice, wellness, artivism, praxis, solidarity, and humanization. She is also the co-founder and director of Community Responsive Education (CRE), a national firm that supports the development of responsive, equitable, and justice-driven educators. Dr. Tintiangco-Cubales is also a producer for *Larry the Musical* and the Art of Work Film, both premiering in 2024. She is the author of many books, articles, and essays focused on the applications of critical pedagogy, the Ethnic Studies curriculum, Motherscholarship, and Pinayism. She has also served as an editor and author for several anthologies and journals such as *At 40: Asian American Studies*, the *Journal of Asian American Studies, Asian American and Pacific Islander Nexus,* and co-editor for the *Sage Encyclopedia of Filipina/x/o American Studies.* Allyson is a loving partner to Val Tintiangco-Cubales, a phenomenal teacher and leader, and the mother of Mahalaya, a prolific dancer and artist.

Cheralen A. Valdez is a doctoral student in the education department at the University of California, Santa Cruz. She received her BA in child and adolescent development with a minor in Asian American Studies from San Francisco State University and her MA in educational leadership from San Jose State University. Her academic journey and experience teaching preschool for over a decade has inspired and informed her research interests focused on early childhood education and the intersections of Ethnic Studies and higher education in relation to teacher preparation.

Kai Yamamoto (she/her) (One Heart Collective) graduated from Millikan High School in Long Beach and is currently attending UC Berkeley. She is planning on majoring in political science with a minor in AAPI Studies. She hopes to make a difference in her community by joining the Asian American Association and Berkeley Model United Nations club. Kai aims to work for the United Nations in her professional career; an effort to bring the world together in difficult times.

Cathery Yeh (she/her) is an assistant professor of curriculum and instruction and a core faculty at the Center for Asian American Studies at the University of Texas at Austin. As a community-based researcher, her scholarship centers on creating change in education systems through collective leadership of educators, youth, families, and the community served. Prior to her role at the university, Cathery was a dual language classroom teacher and visited over 300 student homes while family and community members came into the classroom to co-teach mathematics. Cathery Yeh is the co-author of *Reimagining the Mathematics Classroom, Catalyzing Change in Early Childhood and Elementary Schools, and Upper Elementary Mathematics Lessons to Explore, Understand, and Respond to Social Injustice* and currently serves on the board of directors for the National Council of Teachers of Mathematics. Her favorite place is the classroom, learning with teachers, students, and families.

Index